Trends and Issues in Global Tourism

For further volumes:
http://www.springer.com/series/8406

Roland Conrady • Martin Buck

Editors

Trends and Issues
in Global Tourism 2010

In Collaboration with Pia Viehl

 Springer

Editors

Professor Dr. Roland Conrady
University of Applied Sciences
Erenburger Str. 19
67549 Worms
Germany
conrady@fh-worms.de

Dr. Martin Buck
Messe Berlin GmbH
Messedamm 22
14055 Berlin
Germany
buck@messe-berlin.de

ISSN 1868-0127   e-ISSN 1868-0135
ISBN 978-3-642-10828-0   e-ISBN 978-3-642-10829-7
DOI 10.1007/978-3-642-10829-7
Springer Heidelberg Dordrecht London New York

Cover design: WMXDesign GmbH, Heidelberg, Germany

Printed on acid-free paper

Springer is part of Springer Science+Business Media (www.springer.com)

Preface and Overview

As in previous years, the 2009 ITB Berlin Convention addressed the most important issues affecting the structure of the global tourism and travel industry in a series of lectures and panel discussions. This compilation unites the highlights of the convention in articles prepared by renowned professionals and scientists from the industry. Readers may benefit from this comprehensive vision of the developments that are shaping the structure of the global tourism industry today and in the future. This book is indispensable for tourism and travel professionals, as well as for academics and students analysing current global tourism and travel trends.

The first chapter describes the status quo in the tourism and travel industry.

The World Travel Monitor represents the world's largest and most important travel survey. It conducts interviews in over 50 countries worldwide. Dennis Pyka and Rolf Freitag provide an insight into data on European and German travel behaviour and travel trends that are dominating the market.

The economic importance of the business travel market segment tends to be underestimated. Gerd Otto-Rieke sheds light on this market segment using up-to-date figures, with a particular focus on the market slump brought about by the economic crisis. Otto-Rieke offers a perspective on business travel by outlining the cornerstones of a comprehensive business travel management strategy.

The second chapter deals with the challenges currently faced by the travel and tourism industry: the financial and economic crisis, oil prices and energy supply, climate change and CO_2 emissions, digital information and communication technology, and corporate social responsibility (CSR).

In September 2008, the global economy was heavily affected by the financial crisis. The slump in economic activity was synchronous (all markets affected simultaneously), sudden (within a few days) and dramatic (the most severe slump since the end of the Second World War). As expected, the tourism industry was not spared by the effects of the crisis.

Martin Buck details the onset of the financial and economic crisis, deals with the duration of the crisis and problems in measuring its effects, outlines the effects of the crisis on the tourism industry, and concludes by commenting on the adaptation measures taken by tourism providers.

Harald Pechlaner and Jörg Frehse investigate the effects of the capital market crisis on investment in the hotel market, which plays a central role in the global tourism industry. They discuss critically to what extent speculation in the hotel property market played a part in causing the financial crisis. An outlook for the hotel market rounds off the article.

Norbert Walter starts by giving a detailed analysis of the causes and effects of the financial crisis. He then discusses the effects of fluctuating oil prices on society's mobility. Historic highs in oil prices in 2008 showed a significant impact on the structure of the global travel and tourism industry. Norbert Walter concludes with a description of the key challenges for the global travel and tourism industry.

Today's society faces, like no generation before, two main energy-related threats: first, to guarantee secure and affordable energy supply and, second, to reduce and abolish environmental and climate damage caused by energy consumption. Claudia Kemfert predicts world energy demand, its constitution, and the challenges of energy supply. She goes on to describe the implications of energy consumption and transport processes for the climate. She sketches the basic outlines for a sustainable mobility future.

The transcript from the Round Table at the 2009 ITB Berlin Convention illustrates the position of the World Tourism Organisation on climate change by means of the introductory speech by Geoffrey Lipman, Assistant Secretary-General of the UNWTO.

Wolfgang Strasdas depicts the relationship between tourism and climate change. He then describes the functional principle of "carbon management". Four case studies taken from air travel, the hotel industry, the travel industry and tourist destinations show how well successful carbon management can work.

Joachim Hunold describes the challenges faced by the airline industry. He places particular emphasis on the financial and economic crisis and on air pollution due to CO_2 emissions. He outlines how a "four-pillar strategy" would make global air travel more environmentally friendly.

On December 30th, 2008, Air New Zealand completed the world's first commercial aviation test flight powered by the sustainable second-generation biofuel jatropha. Edward Sims describes the challenges in the use of aviation fuels and the measures taken by Air New Zealand which give us a glimpse into the future of fuel use in air travel.

For more than a decade, digital information and communication technology has been driving structural changes in the global tourism industry. In this time, a generation of "digital natives" has emerged, for whom, in contrast to "digital immigrants", the use of digital technology is matter of course. Urs Gasser and Miriam Simun analyse the generation of digital natives, offering advice to travel operators on how to organise their marketing efforts in order to be able to reach their target audience efficiently and effectively, now and in the future.

The fact that corporate social responsibility (CSR) has recently gained in importance in all industries gives rise to the third chapter. Decision makers from the political and economic spheres show the various aspects of the multifaceted concept of CSR in a number of articles and make recommendations for planning CSR activities in the tourism industry.

Aiko Bode defines the concept of CSR and describes the challenges for travel companies in implementing CSR measures, with a particular focus on certification methods.

Wolfgang Adlwarth analyses the market segment made up of tourists who place particular importance on CSR. On the basis of extensive empirical data from 20,000 respondents, he investigates the size of the market segment, as well as demands for travel offers and current travel behaviour. Of particular relevance to travel operators is the extent to which tourists are prepared to pay higher prices for travel conforming to CSR guidelines. The empirical results provide pointers for companies on how to design CSR strategies and measures.

Erika Harms describes the history of the development of sustainable tourism, the role played by the United Nations in promoting sustainable tourism, and concrete examples of successful sustainable tourism. Erika Harms establishes that sustainable tourism is a "need to have", not just a "nice to have".

Klaus Betz argues that CSR is still new territory for many travel operators. He advocates daring to look beyond the "horizon of tourism" and considering best practice examples from other industries. He illustrates success stories from other industries, which offer a guide for the tourism industry and an incentive to reinforce CSR measures.

The Ruhr Area is a European metropolitan area with an important industrial history which has shown a remarkable transformation into a modern economic structure with a diverse cultural range. After being awarded the title of European Capital of Culture in 2010, awareness of the Ruhr Area was raised among international tourists. Fritz Pleitgen illustrates the importance of "barrier-free" tourism, using up-to-date figures relevant to this frequently underestimated market segment. Concrete examples show how "social inclusion" can be practised.

The number of indigenous people is estimated at more than 370 million worldwide. The cultural heritage of indigenous peoples ("the wisdom of old ways") must be preserved – and not just in order to use it in the future for its tourist attraction potential. It is now widely recognised that tourism can play an important role. Using examples from Canada, the United States, Bali and the South Pacific, Imtiaz Muqbil demonstrates how cultural heritage can be preserved and existential problems of indigenous people can be resolved with the help of tourism.

Igde Pitana delves deeper into the example of Bali, Indonesia, to show how the preservation of a rich cultural identity in an economic and social system which is, to a high degree, dependent on tourism can succeed.

The fourth chapter deals with issues in product and communication policies. As in other industries, effective marketing strategies are of high importance for the competitiveness of companies in the global tourism industry.

Felizitas Romeiß-Stracke investigates changing values in modern societies: they are changing from hedonic fun societies to meaning societies. Understanding this change is necessary in order to be able to continue to offer marketable tourism products.

Using the examples of the tourist destinations South Africa and Costa Rica, Auliana Poon describes the performance, constraints and success factors of destination management. The best practice examples can serve as a guide for other tourist destinations.

In the wake of economic and tourism booms, megaresorts spring up everywhere. Klaus Lengefeld describes the prominent megaresorts, while looking into the sustainability of such resorts.

In the hospitality industry, various shared ownership business models are gaining in importance for the long term. Philip Bacon describes the new business models, dealing with the branded residences in greater detail. He also outlines the effects of the financial and economic crisis on branded residences.

Albrecht Steinecke looks at culture as a tourist attraction. A specially conducted empirical study deals with the following questions: How important is culture when considering a person's reason for holiday travel? How important are visits to cultural attractions? What does it mean to tourists to visit cultural attractions? What do tourists remember most about a visit to a cultural attraction? What is the potential demand for (self-)organised cultural and educational travel? What do tourists expect from organised cultural travel?

Understanding the modern media world is essential for an effective communication policy for companies. Norbert Bolz provides deep insights into the functional mechanisms of classic and digital media.

Negotiating in buying and selling tourist services plays a central role in the profitability of tourism companies. Michael Schneider illustrates how negotiation processes work for the business and leisure travel market segments and which methods can be used to achieve negotiation aims.

The fifth chapter contains outlooks on the future of various market segments in the tourism industry.

Futurologist Rohit Talwar gives an overview of the future of travel. He paints a picture of travel offers and buyers, which provides inspiration for planning entrepreneurial activities.

Irene Feige predicts travel behaviour in the year 2025. Using the scenario technique, she describes a vivid picture of road, rail and air travel of the future.

The future of air travel in general is predicted by Candan Karlitekin. Richard Aboulafia's contribution is dedicated to the particular aspect of the delivery of commercial aircraft in the next ten years. Historic highs in orders for aircraft and upcoming deliveries of aircraft are currently met by a notably low demand for air travel. Aboulafia describes the effects of this disparity. He focuses particularly on the market positions of the two major aircraft manufacturers: Airbus and Boeing.

Digital information and telecommunication technology will remain driving forces behind processes of change in the tourism industry. Carroll Rheem shows how mobile applications, the Semantic Web, customisation, new payment methods, Social Media and Metasearch will change travel processes.

This work could not have been achieved without the remarkable dedication on behalf of the authors, who for the most part have taken on executive positions in the tourism economy. Special thanks go to Pia Viehl from the Faculty of Tourism and Travel, University of Applied Sciences, Worms. She once again tirelessly dedicated herself with extraordinary commitment, remarkable skill and well-founded expert knowledge to ensure timely publication of the work. In the process, she never lost sight of our high quality standards and was thereby instrumental in the success of the work. Without her contribution, this work would not be in your hands now.

Our thanks also go to the team of highly competent and reliable translators from the Mainz/Germersheim University led by Hans-Joachim Bopst, including Colleen Chapman, Si-A Choi, Winfried Kern, Simone Riga, Ron Walker and Katie Wallace.

Frankfurt/Berlin, November 2009   *Roland Conrady*
University of Applied Sciences Worms

Martin Buck
Messe Berlin

Contents

Corporate Social Responsibility

Product and Communication Strategy in the Tourism, Travel and Hospitality Industry

Culture – Tourism – Media **197**

Norbert Bolz

Companies and Airlines: Negotiation Positions –
Negotiation Options **205**

Michael Schneider

Forecasting the Future of Tourism and Travel

Scanning the Horizon **237**

Rohit Talwar

The Future of Mobility – Scenarios for the Year 2025 269

Irene Feige

Future of Global Aviation 279

Candan Karlıtekin

Commercial Jetliners – History and Forecast...................................283

Richard Aboulafia

What's Next for European Online Travel?..299

Carroll Rheem

Authors

Aboulafia, Richard
  Vice President Analysis
  Teal Group Corporation
  3900 University Drive
  Suite 220
  Fairfax, VA 22030, USA
  raboulafia@tealgroup.com

Adlwarth, Dr. Wolfgang
  Executive Director
  GfK Panel Services Deutschland
  Nordwestring 101
  90319 Nürnberg, Germany
  wolfgang.adlwarth@gfk.com

Bacon, Philip
  Managing Director
  HVS
  c/ Velázquez 80 6 Izq.
  28001 Madrid, Spain
  pbacon@hvs.com

Betz, Klaus
  Spokesman
  Institute for Tourism and Development
  Ortsstraße 97
  71720 Oberstenfeld, Germany
  klarobetz@conkret.de

Bode, Aiko
  Global Head CSR and Sustainability
  TÜV Rheinland Holding AG
  Julius-Vosseler-Straße 42
  22527 Hamburg, Germany
  aiko.bode@de.tuv.com

Bolz, Prof. Dr. Norbert
  TU Berlin
  School I: Humanities
  Straße des 17. Juni 135
  10623 Berlin, Germany
  norbert.bolz@tu-berlin.de

Buck, Dr. Martin
  Director
  Messe Berlin GmbH
  Competence Centre Travel & Logistics
  Messedamm 22
  14055 Berlin, Germany
  buck@messe-berlin.de

Conrady, Prof. Dr. Roland
  University of Applied Sciences Worms
  Department of Tourism and Travel
  Erenburger Str. 19
  67549 Worms, Germany
  conrady@fh-worms.de

Feige, Dr. Irene
  Economist
  Institute for Mobility Research
  A Research Establishment of BMW Group
  Kurfürstendamm 31
  10719 Berlin, Germany
  irene.feige@ifmo.de

Frehse, Dr. Jörg
  Managing Partner
  Frehse Hotel Corporate Finance GmbH & Co. KG
  Nikolaistraße 15
  80802 Munich, Germany
  joerg.frehse@frehsehotels.de

Freitag, Rolf
  CEO
  IPK International
  Gottfried-Keller-Straße 20
  81245 Munich, Germany
  freitag@ipkinternational.com

Gasser, Dr. Urs
    Executive Director
    Harvard University
    Berkman Center for Internet & Society
    23 Everett Street
    Cambridge, MA 02138, USA
    ugasser@cyber.law.harvard.edu

Harms, Erika
    Executive Director of Sustainable Development
    United Nations Foundation
    1800 Massachussets Avenue
    Washington, DC 20036, USA
    eharms@unfoundation.org

Hunold, Joachim
    CEO
    Air Berlin PLC&Co.
    Luftverkehrs KG
    Saatwinkler Damm 42-43
    13627 Berlin, Germany
    aweber@airberlin.com

Karlıtekin, Dr. Candan
    Chairman of the Board
    Chairman of the Executive Committee
    Turkish Airlines General Management Building
    Ataturk Airport, Yesilkoy
    34149 Istanbul, Turkey

Kemfert, Prof. Dr. Claudia
    German Institute for Economic Research (DIW Berlin)
    Department Energy, Transportation, Environment
    Mohrenstraße 58
    10117 Berlin, Germany

Lengefeld, Klaus
    Sector Project "Tourism and Sustainable Development"
    gtz – Deutsche Gesellschaft für technische Zusammenarbeit
    Dag-Hammarskjöld-Weg 1-5
    65760 Eschborn, Germany
    Klaus.Lengefeld@gtz.de

Lipman, Geoffrey
   Assistant Secretary-General
   World Tourism Organization (UNWTO)
   Calle Capitán Haya, 42
   28020 Madrid, Spain

Muqbil, Imtiaz
   Executive Editor
   Travel Impact Newswire
   24 Soi Chidlom
   Bangkok 10330, Thailand
   imtiaz@travel-impact-newswire.com

Otto-Rieke, Gerd
   Akademie Neue Medien
   Am Schnepfenweg 52
   80995 Munich, Germany
   akademie@mobilitymanager.de

Pechlaner, Prof. Dr. Harald
   Catholic University Eichstätt-Ingolstadt
   Department of Tourism
   Pater-Philipp-Jeningen Platz 2
   85072 Eichstätt, Germany
   harald.pechlaner@ku-eichstaett.de

Pitana, Prof. Dr. Igde
   Professor of Tourism
   Udayana University, Bali
   Director of International Promotion
   Ministry of Culture and Tourism, Republic of Indonesia
   Jalan Merdeka Barat 17
   Jakarta 10110, Indonesia
   igdepitana@gmail.com.

Pleitgen, Dr. h.c. Fritz
   Chairman
   Ruhr.2010 GmbH
   Brunnenstraße 8
   45128 Essen, Germany
   geschaeftsfuehrung@ruhr 2010.de

Poon, Dr. Auliana
Managing Director
Tourism Intelligence International
An der Wolfskuhle 48
33619 Bielefeld, Germany
apoon@tourism-intelligence.com

Pyka, Dennis
Head of World Travel Monitor
IPK International
Gottfried-Keller-Straße 20
81245 Munich, Germany
pyka@ipkinternational.com

Rheem, Carroll
PhoCusWright Inc.
1 Route 37 East, Suite 200,
Sherman, CT 06784-1430, USA
CRheem@phocuswright.com

Romeiß-Stracke, Prof. Dr. Felizitas
TU Munich
Nederlinger Straße 30a
80638 Munich, Germany
felizitas-rs@web.de

Schneider, Michael
Director International Sales
AirPlus International
Dornhofstraße 38
63263 Neu Isenburg, Germany
mischneider@airplus.com

Sims, Edward
Group General Manager, International Airline
Air New Zealand
185 Fanshawe Street
Auckland, New Zealand

Simun, Miriam
Harvard University
Berkman Center for Internet & Society
23 Everett Street
Cambridge, MA 02138, USA

Steinecke, Prof. Dr. Albrecht
University of Paderborn
Faculty of Arts and Humanities
Warburger Straße 100
33098 Paderborn, Germany
albrecht.steinecke@uni-paderborn.de

Strasdas, Prof. Dr. Wolfgang
University of Applied Sciences Eberswalde
Friedrich-Ebert-Straße 28
16225 Eberswalde, Germany
wstrasdas@fh-eberswalde.de

Talwar, Rohit
CEO
Fast Future
19 Lyndale Avenue
NW2 2QB
London, United Kingdom
rohit@fastfuture.com

Walter, Prof. Dr. Norbert
Chief Economist
Deutsche Bank AG
DB Research
Theodor-Heuss-Allee 70
60486 Frankfurt am Main, Germany
norbert.walter@db.com

Status Quo in the Tourism and Travel Industry

Overview of World Tourism 2009

Dennis Pyka and Rolf Freitag

1 Introduction

This *Report* is primarily based on the 2008 results of IPK International's World Travel Monitor® – the continuous tourism monitoring system, which was set up in 1988. IPK now undertakes more than half a million representative interviews a year in 56 of the world's major outbound travel markets – 34 in Europe and 22 in the rest of the world – representing an estimated 90% of world outbound travel.

The interviews – more than 5 million of which have now been conducted since 1988 – are designed to be comparable from one year and from one market to another, and to yield information on market volumes and sales turnover, destinations, travel behaviour, motivation and satisfaction, travellers and target groups, recent tourism trends, and short- to medium-term forecasts.

The following report focuses on European trends 2009.

2 European Travel Trends in 2009

2.1 Overview of Main Trends in 2009

In 2008, according to IPK's European Travel Monitor®, European adults aged 15 years and over made 422 million trips abroad. This represented an increase of 3% compared to 2007, but was followed by a 7% decrease in the first eight months of 2009.

Of the 422 million trips made in 2008, 294 million (70%) were for holidays, representing an increase of 6%. With a decrease of 6%, 63 million (15%) trips were visits to friends and/or relations (VFR) and travel for other leisure purposes, and 64 million (15%) for business, which corresponds to an increase of 2%. The trend is now expected to reverse in the last few months of 2009 due to the economic slowdown. As expected in the first eight months of 2009, the business trip volume decreased by 7% and the holiday trip volume declined by 8%. The VFR trips continued their negative trend, with a decline of 3%.

Holiday travel decreased by 8% from January through August – almost the same rate as in the same period of 2008 the holiday travel increased. Most of the

R. Conrady and M. Buck (eds.), *Trends and Issues in Global Tourism 2010*,
Trends and Issues in Global Tourism, DOI 10.1007/978-3-642-10829-7_1,
© Springer-Verlag Berlin Heidelberg 2010

Table 1. European outbound travel, 2008-09

	2008	% change 2007/08	% change Jan-Aug 2009/08[b]
Trips[a] (mn)	422	3	−7
Short trips (1-3 nights long)	108	7	3
Long trips (4+ nights)	314	2	−10
Holiday	294	6	−8
VFR and other leisure	63	−6	−3
Business	64	2	−7
Overnights (mn)	3,943	1	−12
Average length of stay (nights)	9.3	−2	−5
Spending (€ bn)	379.7	0	−15
Spending per trip (€)	883	−3	−9
Spending per night (€)	96	−1	−4

[a] Trips made by adults aged 15 years and over

[b] Based on trends in the first eight months of 2009 from the leading 12 source markets, which account for 65% of European outbound trip volume

Source: IPK International's European Travel Monitor®

decrease was concentrated in the first part of the year. Holiday travel was down 10% in the first four months, but decline slowed to only 5% in May to August, according to the European Travel Monitor®.

In contrast to business and holiday travel, VFR and other leisure trips (undertaken mainly for educational, medical and/or religious purposes) only declined moderate by 3% from January through August.

It should be noted that the estimates for the first eight months of 2009 are based on trends in 12 leading European markets, which, according to IPK International, account for roughly 65% of total **European outbound trip volume**.

Sun & beach travel, which dominates the outbound holiday market in Europe, also had to document a decline of 3% in the first eight months of this year, after three years of growth. There were impressive double-digit decreases for touring, countryside and mountain holiday, and a modest drop in demand for city holidays. **Only snow and winter sport holidays showed an increase in the first eight months of 2009.**

The total European overnight volume on trips abroad, which reached 3.9 billion in 2008 and dropped by 12% in the first eight months of 2009 – the average length of stay decreased 5% to 8.8 nights. Nevertheless, according to the European Travel

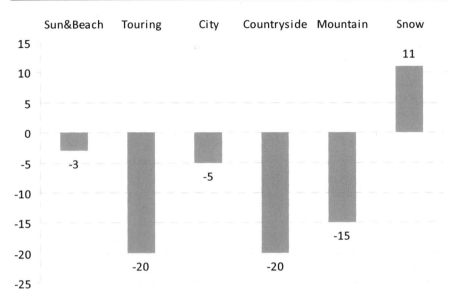

Fig. 1. Trends in European holiday travel by main type of holiday, January through August 2009 (% change on same period in 2008)

Note: the types of holiday are shown, left to right, in order of their importance

Source: IPK International's European Travel Monitor®

Monitor®, there is an 3% increase in short trips (of 1-3 nights) in the first eight months of the year but in contrast a 10% decrease in long trips (of 4 nights or more).

Total spending on travel decreased by 15% in the first eight months of the year, spending per trip declined 9% and spending per night 4%.

2.2 Leading Markets

The decrease in recent months seems to have spread across almost all European source markets, although there are of course big differences in the overall growth ranking in the first eight months of 2009. Great Britain was the market with the highest decline, closely followed by Russia and Sweden. Only Austria showed a modest increase of 2%.

According to the European Travel Monitor®, Europe's two largest sources of foreign tourists, Germany and the UK (which together account for about 35% of total European outbound trips) recorded an intense decline in the first eight months of 2009, and the third largest, France, actually shrank by 3%. These trends are broadly confirmed by the arrivals and overnight statistics filed by European Travel Commission (ETC) members on TourMIS.

The growing sense of economic unease had an increasing impact on the outbound performance of almost all markets. The intense decline in the UK market was blamed on a certain saturation in demand for secondary short breaks using

Table 2. Performance of selected European outbound travel markets, January through August 2009

Market	% change in trips
Great Britain	−15
Russia	−12
Sweden	−10
Spain	−9
Norway	−8
Germany	−5
Belgium	−4
Italy	−4
Finland	−3
France	−3
Denmark	0
Austria	+2

Source: IPK International's European Travel Monitor®

low-cost carriers, the gathering crises in the housing and financial markets, the weakening pound and some well-publicised failures of tour operators and airlines.

It is also clear that destinations in the **Eurozone** suffered from the strong euro, which diverted some of those Europeans who did decide to travel to cheaper Non-Euro destinations.

2.3   Leading Destinations for Europeans

The notion that relative exchange rates (in particular, in the first half of 2009, a strong euro, a weak US dollar and a weakening UK pound) had powerful effects on the choice of destination is partially confirmed by the ranking shown below. No **Eurozone** destinations are listed among the few growing destinations, but several destinations in Northern, Central and Southwestern Europe with strong currencies, did worse than average, with arrivals declining by more than −7%.

Turkey, Tunisia or Croatia and this year even Sweden, Great Britain and Korea as an Asian example (all due to a weak local currency) were very price-competitive, which undoubtedly held or even boosted demand for these countries.

2.4   Transport

So far in 2009, just travel by car showed an increase by 2% from January through August. The long-established trend for air travel to expand faster has come to an end and even documents a decrease of 8%. This is due in large part to the increase in airfares (including any fuel surcharges) caused by high international oil prices, but it

Table 3. Performance of selected destinations in the European market, January through August 2009 (% change on same period in 2008)

> –10%				
Finland	Spain	Malta	Romania	Cyprus
Czech Republic	Slovakia	Baltic	Poland	South Africa
Kenya	USA	Brazil	Mexico	Chile
China	Japan			
–5 to –10%				
Denmark	Norway	Ireland	Belgium	France
Germany	Switzerland	Portugal	Greece	Hungary
Russia	Canada	Thailand	India	
–1 to –4%				
Great Britain	Netherlands	Austria	Italy	Bulgaria
Croatia	Egypt	Tunisia	Dominican Rep.	Cuba
Even positive performance (+1% and more)				
Sweden	Turkey	Morocco	Korea	

Source: IPK International's European Travel Monitor®

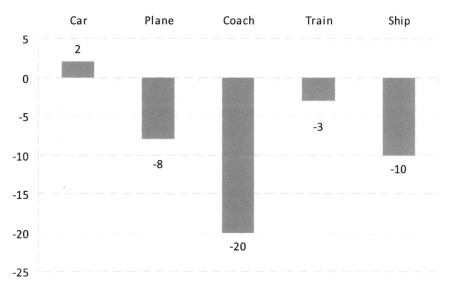

Fig. 2. Trends in European outbound travel by means of transport, January through August 2009 (% change on same period in 2008)

Source: IPK International's European Travel Monitor®

also appears to be related to a growing awareness of the hassles and delays involved in travelling by air. Another factor was the retrenchment of low-cost airlines from routes on which they had expanded over-enthusiastically during the boom.

There was a decline in the market share of low-fare flights. Trips using low-fare flights (39% of all trips by air) declined by 5%, while those on so-called 'traditional' airlines (61% of total flights) even decreased by 10%. However, as IPK points out, it **is becoming** increasingly difficult to draw a meaningful distinction between low-fare and traditional flights.

Also trips by train showed a modest decrease of 3%, whereas travel by coach and ship / ferry documented double-digit decreases by 20% and 10%.

2.5   Travel Distribution

Europeans who use the internet to help with their travel arrangements outnumber those who do not. Indeed, the share of internet users increased from 55% in

Table 4. European online travel trends, January through August 2008-09 (% of trips)

	Jan-Aug 2008	Jan-Aug 2009
Online booking	41	45
Online 'looking'	14	14
All internet users	55	59
Non-internet users	45	41

Source: IPK International's European Travel Monitor®

Table 5. Information sources used by European outbound travellers, January through August 2009

Source	% share[a]
Internet	59
Travel agency	29
Friends/relatives	17
Travel guide	9
Travel brochure	7
Newspaper	2
Tourist office	4
TV	1
Others	3
No information	18

[a] Multiple responses possible

Source: IPK International's European Travel Monitor®

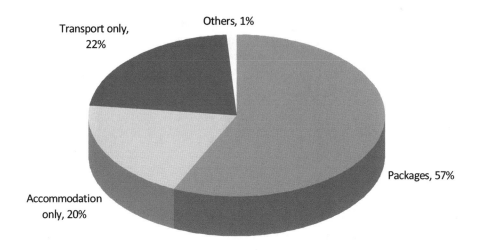

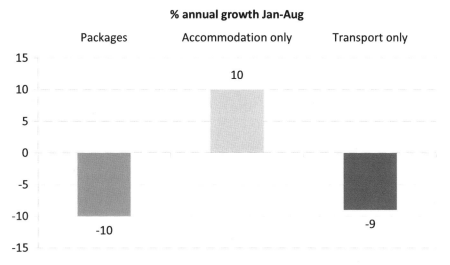

Fig. 3. Breakdown of European pre-bookings, January through August 2009

Source: IPK International's European Travel Monitor®

January-August 2008 to 59% in January-August 2009. And the use of the internet for online booking continues to rise faster than its use for simply 'looking' – gathering information prior to booking a trip. The share of online bookings (for at least part of a trip) has risen from 19% of total trips abroad in 2003 to 45% this year.

More than half of all European travellers now use the internet as information source for their trips, while the importance of the travel trade as a source of information continues to slide. But a notable development in this year's responses to this question in the European Travel Monitor® questionnaire is a twelve percentage point increase in those saying they pay attention to friends and relatives – to 17%.

The growing ease of direct bookings through the internet is working to undermine the role of the retail travel trade, but at the same time the rise in dynamic packaging offered directly by tour operators to clients booking online is working in the opposite direction. While nearly 45% of all bookings are made at least partly online, 23% involve travel agents, 110% are booked direct with hotels and 6% direct with transport companies. Just over a quarter of all European outbound trips do not involve any advance bookings at all.

The share of trips involving full packages declined in the first eight months of this year – by 10%, compared with a 10% increase in the number of 'accommodation only' bookings and a 9% decline in 'transport only' bookings. These full packages include online self-tailored packages, primarily as dynamic packages.

Among the full packages, there was a 6% decrease in accommodation plus flight bookings, a 5% decrease in accommodation plus train bookings, a remarkable 24% decrease in accommodation plus coach bookings, and a 10% decrease in accommodation plus other bookings. The 'others' might include travel insurance, car rentals, ferries, cruises and excursions.

Among transport-only pre-bookings, coach bookings declined by 15% and flight bookings by 11%, but train and 'other' (presumably mainly ferry and cruise) bookings both increased by 15% and 7%.

3   Looking Beyond the Short Term

Given the events of the last few months and the generally gloomy economic outlook, the prospects for travel and tourism in the short term – at least to the end of 2009 – are not very positive. There are no quick or easy fixes to the current crisis, which was many years in the making, and the situation is almost certain to get worse before it gets better.

Meanwhile, opinions on 2010 are mixed. There is no doubt that one of the main driving factors of the recovery will be the global economy, but other influences could also prove critical. But, given the rapidly changing situation, not to mention conflicting indicators and uncertainty about specific influences, the picture is very clouded, which makes it is almost impossible to predict with any assured degree of accuracy when that recovery might take place.

In response to questions posed by IPK International in autumn 2009 in the context of the European Travel Monitor about Europeans' travel intentions over the next 12 months, the following answers were given by people who travelled in the first eight months of 2009. Some 27% of respondents said that they would definitely travel in 2010, and maybe more often than in the last 12 months; 41% said yes, they would travel as often as in the last 12 months; 21% said yes, but maybe less often; and 11% said they would rather not travel. Respondents in Norway and Finland were more positive about their intentions, while those in Russia, France or Germany were more negative.

What's Hot in Business Travel Management?

Gerd Otto-Rieke

When the ITB Berlin Business Travel Days 2009 took place in March, the global crisis had left its first clearly visible footprints. Business travel, so far seen as a rock in even turmoil waters, had dropped sharply. Many corporations had introduced a down-scaling of mobility; even a de facto stop of all travel was observed in some cases. As the "VDR Business Travel Report Germany 2009" states, some 86,000 German companies reported that the recession had by then impacted their travel management. Of those enterprises that have implemented restrictive business travel measures as a reaction to economic developments, two out of three had reduced travel volume. One in three companies was reacting by cutting down on events.

On the other hand, in two out of three small to medium-sized enterprises (SMEs) the financial crisis has had few consequences for business travel until then, VDR – The Business Travel Association of Germany found out. The bigger the company, the more pronounced the impact and the more extensive the packages of measures. In the public sector only 11% of organizations were affected, which can be attributed in part to their activities and travel patterns (more domestic travel, fewer overnight stays).

The situation was and is at the time of writing this article far more dramatic, however, in companies with intensive business travel, for example VDR members. According to a survey, over 80% had felt the impact of the crisis by mid-February. This share was 60% in the months before. Over 90% of travel managers asked predicted a decline of business travel spending for the running year. About 70% thought the meltdown will be 10% or more. 44% expected a slump of 20% or more. 72% said that travel authorization had been toughened. 46% reported revised travel policies. Over 60% predicted normalization no sooner than in a year. More than 20% thought, this will take longer – or the old level will not be reached at all again.

Over 70% of German cities registered a decrease in incoming domestic business travel in the early summer of 2009, according to Deutscher Tourismusverband e.V. (DTV). For incoming international business travel, 60% of German cities reported a drop.

In public perception, the financial crisis began to take hold in Germany in the fourth quarter of 2008. But already in the third quarter 19% of the affected busi-

R. Conrady and M. Buck (eds.), *Trends and Issues in Global Tourism 2010*,
Trends and Issues in Global Tourism, DOI 10.1007/978-3-642-10829-7_2,
© Springer-Verlag Berlin Heidelberg 2010

nesses had begun to introduce control measures. This previously unknown finding supports the thesis that business travel is an early indicator for the state of the overall economy.

The economic crisis and subsequent job cuts mean declining travel volume for all suppliers. Airlines and airports are likely to be the biggest losers in the crisis, at least in the short term – 37% of German businesses anticipated decreasing demand for air travel in the current year. The forecast doesn't look much better for hotels (33%) and rental cars (29%). The railways likewise have to count on some losses (26%), but 11% of organizations at least have plans for more rail travel in 2009 – in keeping with the demands of corporate social responsibility. Travel in the public sector was not affected to the same extent; one in three of the organizations surveyed believed that travel volume will remain the same.

As soon as the first signs of an economic upswing are felt, business travel is hoped to pick up again. But it is probable, VDR warns, that a boost in demand cannot, and will not, help all areas of business travel to resume their former significance in proportion and in synchrony with the economic upturn. One can expect instead to see partial distortions of the market, leading some to lose their market and negotiating positions (both on the supplier and customer side), as well as structural adjustments. The business travel association comes up with these examples and scenarios:

- Companies whose airline ticket demand has dropped drastically can expect fewer turnover bonuses, or none at all. Frequent flyers' statuses will be downgraded and they will need some time to get back their privileges (lounge use, preferred check-in and boarding, etc.).

- Businesses that neglect to book regular room contingents for major events (such as fairs), might possibly be placed on waiting lists and forced to make new plans, as capacities will in some cases have been blocked in the meantime by other customers.

- The government car-wrecking scheme ("cash for clunkers") has had drastic effects on the residual value of used cars, upsetting the calculations of car hire and leasing businesses. Some market players are already insolvent, and others are completely revising their business concepts. Car model policies and conditions are being redefined, with mobility managers' CSR approaches increasingly playing a role.

- Service-oriented suppliers, such as travel management companies or travel agencies, will utilize the phase of short-time work even more than in the past to become leaner. Personnel will in future be deployed more productively. This goes along with a general trend toward minimizing the range and depth of basic products offered. In order to compensate for these pared-down services, customer relation management will take on increasing importance.

- Airlines risk their claim to time slots at airports ("Grandfather Rights") if they do not use these slots at least 80% – which is what is happening now. For the summer 2009 schedules, the European Parliament had passed a directive that temporarily suspends the principle of "expiry if not used". The future of these "hereditary rights" is open, however. The slump might have the effect of opening up historical chances to competitors, leading to shifts in air traffic choices, especially at secondary airports.

- An increasingly critical view will be taken of long business trips to remote destinations. The demand for regional services and products, for example for meetings and events, will rise sharply.

- In times of travel restrictions, people will take more frequently advantage of the versatile possibilities offered by modern telecommunications. Their high quality, further waves of innovations, the low price of hardware and network use, the affinity of the younger generation for technology and a habituation effect will lead to a fraction of business trips being replaced for good by virtual alternatives ("intelligent travel avoidance"). This is even more the case as CSR becomes obligatory and tangible dangers increase (there is no risk of terrorist attacks or medical infection at a web conference) and might even be reinforced by the increasingly relevant argument of the "duty of care".

Intelligent travel avoidance is increasingly part of the standard repertoire of mobility management. Two out of three businesses already now make use of video, web and/or teleconferences as an alternative to business trips. Virtual meetings also top the priority list when it comes to demonstrating corporate social responsibility in business travel. There's no question that telecommunications have become a major rival to travel. And with the trend pointing toward the mobile office, things are likely to stay that way.

So what can companies do in those areas where they have control over? Considerable synergy reserves still lay dormant, VDR claims. This is because those in charge tend to rely on organizational traditions rather than looking for strategic opportunities. Travel expense accounting tops the list of common travel management tasks with 42%. Other important mobility-relevant cost factors are taken into consideration much more rarely, for example event management (28%), fleet management (16%), travel insurance (13%) or mobile communications (11%). VDR's view is, what belongs together should grow together.

As is so often the case, small to medium-sized enterprises have the most homework to do when it comes to recognizing significant savings potential. Although travel expense accounting is typically part of the domain of those in charge of business travel, as stated above, this routine operational task is still carried out "by hand" in a surprising number of companies. A dramatic 85% of businesses with 10 to 250 employees choose to do without the (inexpensive) software available for this assignment.

The area of business travel has taken on substantially greater significance for businesses lately. Some 48,000 persons are involved today in Germany in organizational tasks having to do in a broader sense with business travel (2004: 31,200 persons). The topic of travel management has penetrated through to the management level in two thirds of Germany's businesses. Today management is examining more closely than it did five years ago the purpose and necessity of business trips and the expenses involved. Particularly in the crisis year 2009, corporate boards are taking advantage of the savings potential offered by travel management.

But in two-thirds of companies today, business travel, although ostensibly a top management priority, is still not part of any discernible strategic plan. And the concept of a "Travel Management Competence Center" has not been able to gain any appreciable ground in the past five years. This is unfortunate, because crises are the best time to call in the specialists.

Two out of three businesses in Germany work with a travel agency. However, the use of such services has gone down overall during the last five years. Online offerings have gained market share in this sector, with standard services increasingly found and booked on the Internet. As travel volume rises, so does the potential for saving costs. While half of small to medium-sized enterprises do without the services of a travel management company, 84% of businesses with over 1,500 employees do take advantage of such services.

Consider also this, VDR says: Business partners that have come to be held dear can be an expensive luxury. Travel experts are astounded at how the "corner travel agency" is still the partner of choice for German businesses. Without casting doubt on the expertise of independents, businesses are surely more likely to find state-of-the-art access to cost-saving technologies and value-added networks at the larger travel management companies. A (first-time?) request for proposals from various travel management companies could lead to an undreamt-of boost in efficiency.

Do difficult times blindfold corporations in respect of their resolutions made during better days? Do they now ignore Corporate Social Responsibility (CSR) – which refers to the principles and concepts that form the basis for companies to voluntarily integrate social aspects and environmental concerns in their activities and in their relationships with others? Three quarters of German organizations do not incorporate CSR approaches into their business travel, VDR found out. But, in absolute figures, around 45,000 companies actively take into consideration CSR in their business trips, and almost half of companies with over 1,500 employees do so (46%). In 58% of companies which pursue CSR, these concerns also have an influence on travel management tasks.

Suppliers of transport services are particularly likely to feel the competitive impact of CSR. The choice of mode of transportation is directly influenced in two-thirds of companies, but this goes even deeper: When companies are preparing to choose the right partner or services in the transport field, the principles of sustainability are important to about one in four of them.

In larger companies business trips are avoided more frequently and replaced by virtual meetings than in medium-sized businesses. One in five organizations with over 500 employees takes part in a program for climate compensation.

Among the beneficiaries of this trend are suppliers of products and services for virtual meetings. Two out of three companies with more than 500 employees cited virtual meetings as an alternative, whereby their frequency in the private sector is significantly higher (66%) than in the public sector (38%). In 42% of the businesses that pursue CSR approaches, they also have an effect on bids for tender and a concrete influence on decisions in the business travel area. This is even more the case in companies with 500-1500 employees (53%).

There is still a lot to be done in the traffic sector to reduce CO_2 emissions, Anja Hänel, Project Manager Transport Club Germany (VCD), said at ITB Berlin Business Travel Days 2009. This is difficult because it is necessary to change the behavior of people and this cannot be done by end-of-pipe technologies as used in the industry sector, she added. But the goal is clear: A reduction of another 26 million metric tons is necessary to avoid the worst damages. What catches the eye when looking at the modal split is the fact that the means of transport used the most in relation with business travel is the car. Studies reveal that travelling by plane, even though it is very often criticized, is not the main problem.

What are the most important points when it comes to environmentally friendly travelling? One reason for environmentally friendly travelling is "to be fit for the future". This implies that you need to be prepared for the changes to come, which may for example include car taxes in relation to CO_2 emissions or low emission zones. Furthermore, air traffic will become part of the emissions trade in 2012, so there are a lot of things you need to factor in as these will make your business travelling and your fleet a lot more expensive, VCD urges.

"Positive effects" is another motive for environmentally friendly travelling, and CSR strategies play a vital role for all kinds of companies in this context. Siemens is a perfect example for the positive effects the reorganization of the company fleet can have in the press, Ms. Hänel said. Even SMEs are currently making some effort in the field of CSR. CSR does of course not only comprise the environment and environmentally friendly travelling. But rather, mobility is a way to increase your credibility as it is connected to changing your behavior and cannot simply be bought but has to be lived. "Green washing" has a rather negative effect here, she warned.

Travel management has a lot of potential concerning improvement, efficiency and cost cutting. There are many possibilities for you to reduce your travelling costs when you know about your requirements and the necessary means of transport. This is also a significant plus when negotiating with travel agencies, Ms. Hänel advised.

Current studies about environmental awareness in Germany show that many people do care about the environment and almost 50% feel threatened by the climate change. Your employees are also a part of these 50%, she reminded the Berlin audience. The decision to accept a certain job is related to many different criteria. Among these is the fact that you do not only like your job but that your are also convinced of the quality of your company, that you can tell your friends about it and the sense that you are actively involved in protecting the environment. Employers can make this possible for their staff by including environmental aspects in travel management.

The following points need to be considered, according to VCD, when companies wish to develop and follow an overall strategy:

- Are there any unnecessary travels? A common alternative to travelling is the video conference. However, video conferences are often technically complex and not suitable for every company. By now there are also low-level possibilities to enter this field especially in the area of web conferences and last but not least there is still the good old telephone. By having a look at the guidelines, employees can find out which trips they should and can substitute by virtual conferences. Every trip they can substitute does definitely save costs and CO_2 emissions and in most cases gives some additional life quality to employees.

- Combine your trips. This is basically very easy, but the devil is in the details. What about the organization of travel management? Is it possible to know today that several employees will take part in the same meeting? In order to combine trips companies will have to integrate all their divisions and departments into travel management. By this all the different destinations of the employees are known which creates some room for interaction.

- Choosing the right means of transport. When it comes to business travel it is of course important to be flexible. It is vital for travel management to show the advantages of alternatives. The company "Infras" for example paid attention to the fact that its new business site was well connected to public transport and trains. They also coordinate time and place of an event with the timetables of public means of transport. An easy place to start the improvement of travel management is fleet management. This means buying fuel efficient cars and showing employees how to save fuel. Also car sharing should be considered. For short distances it makes sense to use bicycles.

- When it comes to means of transport companies should also take railway services into account as they are often better than their reputation, especially considering costs and delay.

Giving advice to a large audience at ITB Berlin Business Travel Days 2009, Lutz I. Stammnitz, President Procurement, Mobility and Logistics of Siemens AG, stated that the travel manager has never been so important than today. He nowadays should be a variation of the cost manager, the responsible person for mobility, logistic, work place environment, marketing communication and event management, he added. Siemens has its own spend manager who compares supply and demand to achieve the best price for the company.

One of the first things he changed concerning business travel management at Siemens was the way visa are acquisitioned. That topic is underestimated, Jochen

Mesenberg from CIBT Visum Centrale, agreed. Difficulties are becoming bigger. In a lot of cases, tourist visa instead of business visa are issued, what may lead to serious problems with the authorities. Visa acquisition is a stepchild of business travel management, as time is very important and visas are often organized too late, Christoph Wolf, Director Law of International Trade, Trade Facilitation of Association of German Chambers of Industry and Commerce, assents. Furthermore it has to be stressed that a visa is just the request for entry and not an entry permit.

A final advice at ITB Berlin Business Travel Days 2009 came from Michael Schneider of AirPlus. A good contract considers the interests of both parties, he said. What does a travel manager need to know about the negotiating range of his key account manager to achieve economic, effective and sustainable compromises? So before you go into a negotiation you should be aware that both sides already have several ideas about the topic, he said. The first aim of the salesman is influence on the buyer in the form of concession of the other. This influence can also be used by the buyer, while the buyer has different aims such as quality assurance, cost cutting, efficiency, problem solving and security of supply. It can be said that airlines are in any kind of crisis all the time and use this for negotiations, Mr. Schneider revealed. During the negotiations a lot of psychology can be found on both sides. The complexity between the objective targets, the preparation and the implementation has to be solved during the negotiation. A preparation like the multidimensional SWOT analysis doesn't take too long to prepare and conveys a feeling about the tenor of the buyer.

Actual Challenges in the Tourism and Travel Industry

Crisis? Which Crisis?

Some Remarks on Perceiving, Handling and Forecasting Economic Crisis in the Travel Industry

Martin Buck

When the global economic crisis revealed itself dramatically in September 2008 as Lehman brothers went broke, it took not very long before its effects became notorious in the travel industry as well. These consequences were widely discussed at the ITB convention in Berlin in March 2009 and they will certainly drive many panels and presentations at the ITB convention in March 2010 since the crisis is not over yet. Or is it? And if not: How long will it last?

The eventual thoughts might contribute to understand more clearly where the travel industry is actually standing when we talk about the crisis and where it is heading for in terms of recoverage and innovation. The following questions will help us to gain a better understanding:

- How does one describe the crisis, which indicators and benchmarks are being used to define it?

- How long will it last?

- How does it reflect on the travel industry?

- How do travel industry players react?

- What should the travel industry expect?

1   What Is the Crisis?

Crisis is something the travel industry tended to believe to have gotten used to over the past years. From a commercial perspective, crisis can be seen as an unexpected and massive shortfall of demand. 9/11, the Tsunami, SARS and several others caused such an effect to a varying extent but the contraction of demand always was more or less short and shallow.

Compared to the crisis we are now going through, something that has been rated as the most serious financial crisis since the Great Depression which con-

R. Conrady and M. Buck (eds.), *Trends and Issues in Global Tourism 2010*,
Trends and Issues in Global Tourism, DOI 10.1007/978-3-642-10829-7_3,
© Springer-Verlag Berlin Heidelberg 2010

tributed to the failure of key businesses, massive destruction in consumers and investors wealth, substantial financial commitments by governments and a dramatic decline of economic activity (cf. Wikipedia, 28.09.2009). As became evident particularly starting September 2008 and during the first half of 2009, the global financial crisis can be characterized by a set of phenomena taking place within a very short time span, among them dramatic stock market declines by more than 40%, numerous bank and insurance companies either going bankrupt or being bailed out by governments – Lehman, AIG, Hypo Real Estate, Northern Rock, Kaupthing, just to name a few, collapsing housing and real estate markets like in the US, the UK and Spain, dramatically falling investment and consumer spending, strongly shrinking export markets, shortage of bank loans ("credit crunch"), massive government interventions to boost demand, e. g. "Abwrackprämie" in Germany or "cash for clunkers" in the US (cf. Economicshelp.org, October 2008).

When we summarize what the media reported about the financial crisis since September 2008, crisis might be defined as a situation in which many unexpected things happen in a very short period of time, have a deeply negative and vital impact on many people and on most if not all key economic indicators and seem to be connected in a complex, difficult to explain if not inexplicable way.

But this crisis not only started unexpected – which indicates that the overwhelming majority of professional forecasters simply failed to do what they are supposed to do – namely to forecast. This crisis – and this has been so far its most specific feature – remains highly uncertain. No one really seems to know how long it will take and there is no unambiguous explanation available whether a certain pattern of development is to be anticipated.

Key economic indicators do not show a consistent trend yet. What they show is frequently contradictory (e. g. fast recovering share prices versus a constantly low or even further shrinking of bank loan allocation to enterprises). The retrospective scientific description of the crisis and the analysis of its reasons seem to be working in a way – at least answers are generated. However there is no economic model available that facilitates a credible picture how the near future will actually look like.

Attempts to explain the economic crisis by analyzing what has happened, why and what will happen are sometimes contradictory and belief, emotions and the so called "common sense" seem to have more or less substituted scientific explanations that are transparent, calculable, comprehensible and describe reality in a way that is useful and valid to mankind.

Explanations what triggered the crisis are manifold. From too cheap money causing eventually bursting bubbles (housing, dot.com) over fundamental deficiencies in regulating the banking system to insufficient financial cushions of banks to absorb large loan defaults, inhibiting their lending activities, thus slowing economic activity are the most common answers to the "why" question. Economists like Samir Amin (cf. Amir, S.: Die Zukunft des Weltsystems. Herausforderungen der Globalisierung, Hamburg 2002) or John Bellamy Foster (cf. Foster, J.B.; Magdoff, F.: The great financial crisis: Causes and consequences, New York 2009) believe that the "real" reason for the crisis lies in the constant decrease of

GDP growth rates in the Western countries since the early 1970s which is due to increasing market saturation.

We propose as a hypothesis that this will lead to a sustained downturn of western travel activity in the long run since an empirically proven correlation seems to exist between the course of GDP development and the one of travel activity. Another contributing factor is the demographic development in Western European countries which might lead to shrinking populations.

2   How Long Will the Crisis Last?

The question whether the crisis is over "now" (this article was written in November 2009) cannot be answered clearly and unambiguously. The development of a number of key economic indicators seems to confirm this optimistic assumption, e. g. the positive direction of manufacturing indicators like the indexes for new orders, production and employment. Surveys show that the manufacturing sectors of China, Taiwan, South Korea and India had begun to grow by April 2009, but the United States did not follow suit until August. In Europe, France is reporting moderate growth whereas Britain and Germany are stagnating and Spain, Ireland and Italy remain on a very low level. Employment continues to lag in most countries outside China. The US, Japan, Britain and the eurozone are estimated to suffer a total of monthly job losses of about 500,000 (cf. Norris, F.: In recovery, emerging markets lead, International Herald Tribune, October 17-18, p. 14).

Although the Dow Jones has reached more than 10,000 points in the second week of October 2009, the US economy finds itself in a dismal state of historic proportions. The unemployment rate is at 9.8 percent, state governments are tetering near bankruptcy and lending to businesses and consumers are dramatically down (cf. IHT, October 17-18, p. 6).

Summarizing the above it has to be stated that most indicators confirm an ongoing crisis in the traditional economic powerhouses like the US, the eurozone, the UK and Japan that happen to be at the same time of the crisis in the traditional powerhouses of travel activity as well. The emerging markets seem to be doing significantly better.

Without any doubt and as widely discussed unemployment is an evident and one of the most important indicators of the state of economic development. Is the extent of unemployment therefore also related to travel volume and intensity? This assumption seems to be extremely near lying when it comes to leisure travel. Why should somebody being threatened by unemployment or already laid off go on a vacation? Although this question sounds rhetorical at first glance, it actually leads to interesting empirical findings. Taking into account the development of the unemployment rate in Germany on one hand and the development of the German leisure travel demand on the other over the past decade, it seems to be confirmed that the latter is very "inelastic". Although the number of jobless fluctuated not insignificantly between 1998 and 2007, German leisure travel demand remained more or less stable.

3   How Does the Crisis Reflect on the Travel Industry?

What does all this mean for the travel industry? As mentioned before it seems to be plausible to assume that there is a correlation between GDP growth and travel activity, the latter being measured by number of trips or number of travellers. Both dimensions seem to be connected by a time lag.

Compared to 2007, GDP went down in 2008 in the US by minus 0.7%, in Germany by minus 7.1%, in Britain by minus 5.3%. It went up in China by 8.9% and in India by 6.1% (cf. New York Times Global Edition, October 26, 2009, p. 19). Currently the time lag also generates an information lag because it will take a significant while before the respective data of travel activity will be provided to UNWTO by the national statistics agencies, get processed and analyzed by UNWTO and presented by the latter to the relevant audience.

However what has already become evident at the – so to say "micro economic" level – of specific travel industry sectors is that selected indicators like load factors of airlines, occupancy rates of hotels, guest numbers and revenues of tour operators as well as incoming numbers to popular leisure destinations have more or less suffered in the first three quarters of 2009. All this leads to a number of assumptions.

The emerging economies – particularly China and India – have so far been more resilient to crisis and are recovering faster than traditional big economies. But due to their absolute GDP sizes, China and India cannot compensate for the losses of the US, the eurozone, UK and Japan who so far still generate the paramount share of the global travel market – not to mention that China and India are still lagging dramatically behind when it comes to individual travel intensity and spending.

Driven by the economic crisis, the demand for travel products is decreasing, but this takes place in differentiated ways. Whereas so far the corporate and the Mice travel business shrank very fast and strongly, the leisure travel business went down only comparatively moderate. Premium travel products like airline business class seats and five star or five star plus hotel rooms lost a lot of demand, on the other hand "budget" travel products like low cost carrier seats and two or three star hotel rooms are thriving.

4   How Do Travel Industry Players React?

The German travel market as one of the strongest in global comparison is rather anticipating a further deteriorating business. Based on the assumption of growing unemployment which so far never has had a significant empirical influence on leisure travel demand (see above), the forecasts of airlines and big tour operators for the coming winter season are pessimistic. There seems to remain a certain hope for late bookings which are incentivized by short term price reductions. The big tour operators are nevertheless planning to remove capacities from the market to a significant extent. Although the monthly reduction of air traffic passenger volumes has slowed down and load factors above eighty percent could be maintained, yields per August 2009 were laying twenty percent below in year to year comparison. All the above is based on current statements by Lufthansa, IATA, TUI and Thomas Cook (cf. dpa, 13.10.2009).

Kuoni, the fourth biggest tour operator in Europe, adapts to the crisis that temporarily lead to demand reductions for leisure travel packages of up to twenty percent (cf. FAZ, 29.9.2009, p. 24) by a tough cost savings program combined with a FIT focused premium product range. The most adequate strategy for tour operators seems to be represented by the following features:

- Minimizing fixed assets and reducing fixed costs to less than twenty percent of the total cost volume. "Disintegration": getting rid of own hotels and own aircraft

- Centralizing sourcing processes, increasing pressure on vendors by bundling purchasing power

- Concentration on high volume sales markets, eliminating involvement in markets that lack critical mass

- Sales focus on high yield premium products

- Acquisition of profitable niche products, buying specialized tour operators that have established products and stable niche market share.

In general, niche markets seem to gain relevance. A niche market is not inevitably so much of a new market since total travel demand in mature markets like the German one is rather stagnating regarding the total market volume. The focus is more on customizing the right product for a strongly differentiated set of individual needs. Tour operators who offer expensive study group tours to long haul destinations to the target group of well educated people at an age of 50 plus establish a good example for such a niche strategy. Another example are tour operators who concentrate on offering a wide variety of all inclusive packages at sun and beach destinations targeting particularly young families with kids. A last example are "youth travel" operators that target student travellers that look for a "work in travel" package abroad enabling them to improve their language skills and acquire foreign work experience at the same time.

5   What Should the Travel Industry Expect?

As shown above, economic forecasting is a very hairy business in general which has lost most of its credibility. Attempts to find out about specific types of future demand like that for travel products should therefore not be based – at least not entirely – on projections of the general economic development measured e.g. in terms of GDP. Expectations about where the travel market is headed for or how successful travel products must look like in the future, should not be deductive at all but try to build on bottom-up observations on the needs and the behaviour of a specific target group –the more specific the better. It will most probably always remain uncertain how the demand for a particular product develops until one offers it in the market, bearing the entrepreneurial risk by taking the investment cost in advance and hoping for profitable demand picking up eventually and as soon as possible. When demand is going down dramatically as it is typical for the crisis, corporate players have to try their best to adjust their product capacities to market needs which is difficult especially for hotels and airlines because their inventories are rather rigid than flexible and lack the capability of "breathing" or "being inflatable". The longer the crisis goes on one other vital question certainly is of growing relevance: will demand as being known from before the crisis will ever return or have customer needs changed in a way that only new products can satisfy them? The appropriate corporate answer to this challenge can only be a systematic handling of the trial and error process, providing a steady stream of new products that are being tried out by the customer who either likes or hates them. The permanent absence of crisis accompanied by permanent growth over many years with the same set of products certainly creates a culture of complacency which makes it difficult if not impossible to stay "innovative". Should this capability then be required "by surprise" because a crisis has made the corporate behavioural set that worked perfectly alright for many years obsolete, the vital question is whether the "right stuff" is available in the company or not. One thing that seems to be proven right by the current crisis is expressed by a quotation of Willy Brandt, former German chancellor and holder of the Nobel peace prize: "If you want to forecast the future you have to shape it."

Financial Crisis and Tourism

Harald Pechlaner and Jörg Frehse

Tourism has been heavily affected by the property and financial crisis. According to the World Tourism Organisation, UNWTO, the number of travel movements fell by a further 8 percent between January and April 2009 alone compared to the same period in the previous year (UNTWO 2009a). Tourist numbers are continuing to drop almost everywhere in the world. Consumers paralysed by fear of the crisis are persistently staying at home.

In addition, more and more companies are tightening their travel cost guidelines. Employees travelling on official business are barely allowed to book business class or even first class tickets any more, regardless of their hierarchy level. Car rental firms are also noticing companies' restraint with regard to business trips. When it comes to rail travel, many travel managers are instructing their business travellers to journey second class from now on. In the hotel industry, the high quality segment has been hit particularly hard by the property and financial crisis, by up to 20 percent of its turnover. Again, the reason for this is the absence of many business travellers, who traditionally tend to favour up scale accommodation.

But is it not more so the case that players on the global tourism market at present are being styled as victims of a real estate and financial crisis, in the development of which institutions and individuals from the tourism industry may have played some part? Are certain tourism organisations not victims of their own strategies? After all, they did steadily increase prices up until mid-2008 and they allowed themselves to be heavily supported by not only investment banks but also opportunity and private equity funds by means of global capital flows. During the real estate private equity boom, for example, a huge proportion of global capital stocks with the highest possible leverage of up to as high as 95% was invested in the asset class "tourism and leisure property" (Härle/Haller 2008).

The internal rate of return on equity of over 25%, that at first frequently resulted from this and in the meantime have fallen into disrepute, have certainly contributed to the fact that the preoccupation with institutions and initiatives, which are actually to be assigned to the international real estate industry, are now the topic of economic and social debate, not just in the industry, but over the entire spectrum.

However, as long as business was booming for all of the acting institutions and individuals on the market, these impressively high equity returns evoked fantasies of almost limitless increases in value and a wave of speculation, particularly as the

R. Conrady and M. Buck (eds.), *Trends and Issues in Global Tourism 2010*,
Trends and Issues in Global Tourism, DOI 10.1007/978-3-642-10829-7_4,
© Springer-Verlag Berlin Heidelberg 2010

gained increases in value until the resale (exit) of the property alone could virtually repay bank loans (Holzmann/Frehse 2008). Investors and financiers, even on the supposedly unremittingly growing tourist markets, appeared fatefully, up until the property bubble burst, to be able to forego the main function of capital resources – that is, to provide a cushion against possible losses.

The irritation over such procedures and ways of thinking, which has now unfortunately set in too late, seems all the more astonishing as the financial sector has, for some time, been using the theory of efficient capital markets in solving decision problems in uncertain circumstances (Rottke/Holzmann 2003). The core of this theory – which results from a variety of economic studies, including more recent studies – indicates that the only possibility of generating excess returns over the total market is to take on a higher risk, thereby exposing oneself to a proportionately increased risk of loss (Fama 1991; Schredelseker 2002; Drobetz 2007; Kunz 2007).

This paper focuses on the discrepancy between theory and practice and highlights, using in particular the hotel industry as an example of a key player in international tourism (Schräder 2000), the fact that – as with the acquisition of the Hilton hotel empire by US financial investor Blackstone – investments in tourist property portfolios were highly speculative activities and, thus, in a way particularly responsible for the current impacts of the property and financial crisis on tourism.

Corresponding conclusions, academically substantiated on the basis of selected practical developments, are presented below. Following this introductory chapter, the received earnings and risk positions up to the onset of the property and financial crisis will firstly be highlighted as a subject of the theory of efficient capital markets and aligned with the distinctive features of the tourism and leisure property, the hotel, as a operatored facility par excellence.

In the second chapter, selected conditions and interdependencies of the subprime crisis for tourism are then outlined, before a review of facts, figures and legacies of speculation is subsequently given, again using the hotel sector as an example. The fourth section concludes the paper with a brief outlook.

1   Investment in Tourism as a Subject of the Theory of Efficient Capital Markets

At its core, the theory of efficient capital markets states that prices of assets always completely reflects all existing relevant information. Due to this, there is also ultimately no possibility for property investors to develop strategies which systematically lead to an excess return over the total market. The only way to develop strategies which systematically lead to the generation of higher returns than the total market, also for tourism and leisure property, is, according to the theory, to take on a higher risk – represented as Beta Φ in financial theory – and thereby expose oneself to a disproportionately increased risk of loss (Rottke/Holzmann 2003).

While these theoretic assumptions are unreservedly held to be adequate on the stock market, even in business practice, the authority and application of the theory of efficient capital markets clearly showed itself to be "surmountable" for the institutions and individuals acting on the non-transparent continental European hotel investment markets, judging by their market behaviour.

Hotel properties, in particular, display a wide range of distinctive features in this regard: Hotels are transferred ready to use, feature a pre-opening phase and achieve stable results, as a rule, only after a warm-up period of two to four years. Furthermore, there is always an operation aspect as well as a property aspect to hotels (Elze 1995). The success – and therefore also the value – of a hotel is also very much dependent on the competency of the operator. In this regard, tourism and leisure properties are fundamentally different to commercial, residential and industrial properties, whose value generally results exclusively from the level of rent which can be attained. These rents are largely, and with regard to their level, independent of the commercial success of the tenant (Schröder/Forstnig/Widmann 2005).

Conversely, attractive potential for future increases in value in the case of hotel properties is based primarily on the success of the operator, as the value of a hotel is derived primarily from the surplus revenue associated with its management. This can be compared to the way in which the owner of a racehorse profits financially from the skills of "his" jockey. Worldwide, an estimated 98 percent of all hotels not managed by their owner are operated within the framework of a relevant management contract (Baurmann 2000), which regulates the running of the hotel by the hotel operator for account of the owner.

Consequently, in the case of hotels operated according to management contracts, the investor feels the full impact of negative as well as positive business developments and if an improvement in profitability is anticipated due to a change of management or equivalent Performance and Asset Management by the owner, the subsequently improved operation results are fully incorporated into the value assessment of the hotel property (Frehse 2004). In this respect, entrepreneurial chances, but also risks, for hotel investors or owners are by far the greatest in the case of hotel management contracts, and it is possible for hotel investors to achieve the value increase ("upside") necessary to generate their high equity returns primarily with such a contract model. Table 1 provides a simplified illustration of this.

Table 1. Relevant cash flow with hotel management contracts

	Gross Operating Profit
./.	FF&E-Reserve
./.	Management Fees
./.	Property taxes, insurance and other non-operational administrative costs
=	Relevant Cash Flow Management Contract

Source: Schröder/Forstnig/Widmann 2005, p. 98

Furthermore, there was no relevant market for tourism and leisure properties up until the middle of this decade due to the traditionally low transaction volume, particularly in continental Europe. This characteristic, in combination with the introduction of the Euro, reinforced the assumption of financial investors, particularly US investors, that the prices for such properties did not always reflect all available relevant information, but rather offered wide-ranging investment opportunities, which promised fewer risks or higher returns than the market price would suggest.

Thus, promising investment opportunities present themselves, particularly for those market players who recognise this type of potential sooner than the rest of the market due to better information, can make quick decisions because of flat hierarchies and flexible structures, and have access to the necessary material, human and particularly financial resources (Rottke/Holzmann 2003).

These types of opportunities, in turn, make up the core business activity of real estate opportunity and private equity funds, which are differentiated from conventional funds by their high expected return on equity. This differentiation is also clear by means of the classification of property investment strategies into the categories "core", "core plus/value added" and "opportunistic", demonstrated in Figure 1, which is prevalent in the USA.

As early as in the mid-nineties, this risk/return spectrum posed the question, in theory and in practice, of whether it is even possible to achieve internal rate of returns of 25 percent. In the past, however, even international rating agencies supported the myth that high debt ratios in investing were safe. For many market players, this is the premise which allowed financial investors to tap the global capital markets on an unprecedented scale for the funding of property portfolios and to disperse the risks resulting from this all over the world up until the onset of the crisis (Burghof/Prothmann 2008).

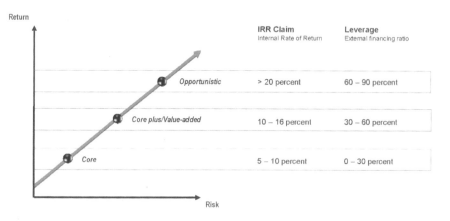

Fig. 1. Risk/return spectrum of property investment strategies

Source: based on Rottke/Holzmann 2003

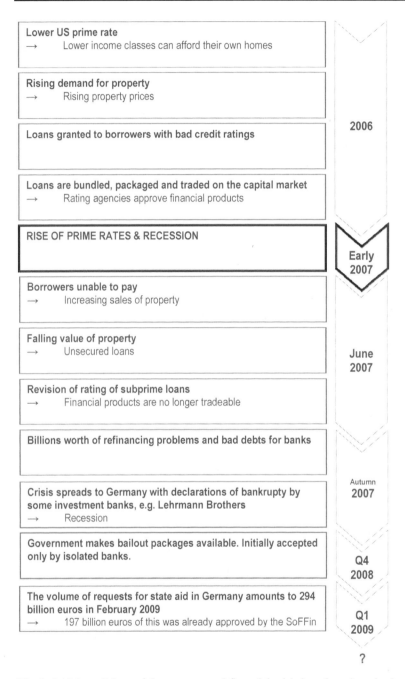

Fig. 2. Initial conditions of the property and financial crisis based on the subprime crisis in the USA

Source: Jones Lang LaSalle Hotels 2008b

2   Conditions and Interdependencies of the Subprime Crisis for Tourism

Many compare the property and financial crisis, which is also currently afflicting tourism, to the world economic crisis of 1929 in its scale and dangers. The dynamisation of the crisis is particularly surprising. Because of the aforementioned wide dispersion of the risks, all of the relevant countries and markets are simultaneously affected, for the first time since the depression of 1929.

The cause of the crisis, based on the US property market and the weak credit borrowers segment (subprime segment) has, at this stage, been exhaustively discussed in both economic and tourism literature. Against this background, a summary of the development of the property and financial crisis is included in this paper only within the framework of the following recapitulatory diagram in Figure 2.

Two main factors made a crucial contribution to the fact that the above-displayed interdependencies, as well as individual interdependencies initially limited to specific regions and countries, would lead to a global crisis which now shows a significant impact on tourism:

The first factor has long been known and applies to a fundamental, financial theoretical construct: Both investment banks and opportunity and private equity funds attempt to capitalise on the leverage effect by increasing the debt ratio, because excess returns can be generated under certain conditions (especially through the attainment of an early resale/exit) only on the correspondingly low volume of equity. In this respect, the impressively high returns on equity effectively earned by companies like Blackstone, Whitehall, Colony Capital or Fortress, and then initially also in the tourism industry, in the years before the onset of the crisis can, to a large extent, be traced primarily back to the high leverage.

To this end, loopholes in the state equity regulation of credit institutes were consequently exploited and "levered" on a hitherto unprecedented scale i.e. with only an extremely small equity ratio put down (Härle/Haller 2008), as Table 1 illustrates using selected hotel portfolio sales of international hotel chains.

Secondly, financial instruments have been developed since the mid-nineties to pass credit risks from the banks' accounts on to the global financial markets. For this, a large number of outstanding debts were bundled and securities were issued in several tranches on the thus-created pool. This so-called Asset Backed Securities (ABS) were given the seal of approval by internationally recognised rating agencies and could then be sold worldwide as an alternative investment form with a risk-opportunity profile which seemed very attractive.

The way in which the risk from these tranches should be dispersed was even the topic of various economic studies with the aim that, despite the risk transfer, it would continue to be possible to allocate credits in a prudent manner and to adequately monitor credits which had already been allocated. Unfortunately, these abstract considerations did not seem to interest the designers of these types of financial products, or the rating agencies who evaluated them, at least as long as equity returns of over 25 percent could actually be generated, against the warning signs of the theory of efficient capital markets.

Table 2. Selected hotel portfolio sales of international hotel chains

Portfolio	Country	Purchaser	Seller
Holiday Inn Portfolio (73 Hotels)	United Kingdom	LRG Acquisition Limited	InterContinental
Accor Portfolio (76 Hotels)	France, Belgium	Foncière des Murs	Accor
Crowne Plaza & Holiday Inn Portfolio (24 Hotels)	Continental Europe	Westbridge Hospitality Fund	InterContinental
Marriott Portfolio (46 Hotels)	United Kingdom	Royal Bank of Scotland	Marriott
InterContinental Portfolio (7 Hotels)	Continental Europe	Morgan Stanley	InterContinental
Accor Portfolio (30 Hotels)	United Kingdom	Land Securities	Accor
Scandic Portfolio (132 Hotels)	Scandinavia	EQT Partners AB	Hilton
Mac-Donald Hotel Portfolio (24 Hotels)	United Kingdom	Moorfield Group	Mac-Donald Hotels
Hilton Portfolio (10 Hotels)	Continental Europe	Morgan Stanley	Hilton
Accor Portfolio (91 Hotels)	Germany, Netherlands	Moor Park Capital	Accor

Source: authors' illustration

3   Facts, Figures and Legacies of Speculation in Tourism

These high returns which were effectively achieved in the beginning certainly contributed to the fact that real estate private equity and opportunity funds, in particular, became increasingly active on the European property market from approximately 1997 and recorded enormous influxes of funds, as Figure 3 explains.

Declining returns in the USA, the accustomisation to EU jurisdictions and taxation laws and reasonable room rates as compared to international standards were also important factors in bringing the financial investors to Europe. In addition, cross-border transactions were significantly easier and more transparent after the introduction of the Euro (Frehse 2004).

With regard to the European hotel investment market, it is very clear, in retrospect that the – initially primarily Anglo-American – opportunity and private equity funds did not reckon with consistently low occupancy and room rates. In addition, according to the acting staff members, many of these hotels did not fully exploit their economic potential. Simultaneously, European tourism companies were still experiencing a shortage of own capital and outside capital, so that institutions

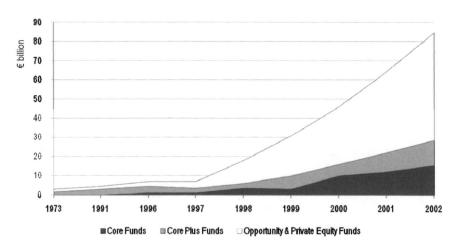

Fig. 3. Growth of unlisted property funds in Europe

Source: based on Rottke/Holzmann 2003

from the hotel real estate private equity and opportunity funds sector, in particular, saw wide-ranging opportunities to also invest in Europe – under the banner of "Recovery" – in a tourist property category with which they had long been familiar in terms of their domestic markets.

International hotel chains, in particular, responded accordingly to this trend in their role as hotel property owners. While a large proportion of hotels had been purchased by hotel chains up to just a few years previously, in order to also secure the hotel business alongside the rising value of property, almost all international hotel companies separated management and ownership of hotel properties during the investment boom. Operating instead of owning was the order of the day in the European hotel industry (Pütz-Willems 2003). On the one hand, property sales for international hotel chains were almost forced, because of the extreme amounts of capital which streamed into the European market, as described above; on the other hand, hotel companies as sellers had the big advantage that returns were low and prices were, consequently, astronomically high.

As a consequence, hotel companies also engaged in price rigging and persistently sold large hotel portfolios, focusing at the same time on closing long-term management contracts as growth options, whereby they no longer considered themselves obliged to point out either the operational or the investment overall risk. After all, the urge for expansion among large international providers was heavily restricted time and again precisely by direct investments and fixed-lease contracts with comprehensive security deposits and guarantees, especially in continental Europe, which was traditionally more security-orientated.

Furthermore, listed hotel companies, in particular, are still facing the dilemma of having to fully balance previously received contingent liabilities from fixed-lease contracts, due to the international accounting standards which are also appli-

cable in Europe for the foreseeable future. Through their aggressive selling activities, hotel companies revised their balance sheets, on the one hand, and liberated
an abundance of resources for their ambitious growth strategies, on the other hand.
They were also called on to do this by analysts, who consider the value of hotel
companies to no longer be in the property business, but rather in the operational
business (Härle 2007, p. 13).

As Figure 4 documents, the European markets for hotel investment also boomed
correspondingly, before they heavily plunged due to the crisis in 2008; in 2009 the
market is continuing its downward slide. Even in comparison to the same quarter
last year, which was already very weak, single asset transactions fell by a further 72
percent and portfolio transactions by a further 90 percent. Experts in the industry
predict that the market level for the total year 2009 will not reach a level higher than
that of 2002 – not even if the performance in the hotels improves again.

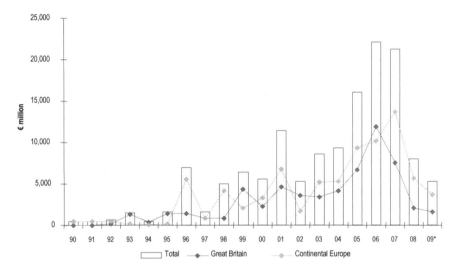

Fig. 4. Hotel transaction volumes in Europe from 1990 (in millions of Euro)

Source: Jones Lang LaSalle Hotels 2008a

However, there is no question of an emerging improvement in performance in view
of the sharp decline in demand which was evident at the outset and is currently still
continuing. Correspondingly, both hotel developers and hotel operators are trying to
postpone or completely back out of new construction projects to a hitherto unprecedented degree. The granting of loans, which has now become a problem, and the
continuingly uncertain economic outlook is further dampening spirits.

An analysis of articles and commentaries recently published in the tourism
trade press shows a basic increasing tendency to forget that, in the short term, it is
more likely to come to a further intensification of competition with fewer and
fewer travellers than to a recovery. After all, those projects which were signed in

the times of the economic boom and which are currently under construction are highly likely to open, even with the risk that they will no longer be able to avail of external finance.

During the boom times, however, the willingness of market players to take higher risks for equity returns of over 25 percent also rose, as we know. As this went well for at least a certain time, new investors continuously entered the market, which consequently led to an increase in demand also for new hotel projects. The legacies of the speculation and of such a herd instinct are now visible to their full extent, as Figure 6 makes clear using selected tourist destinations. Because of such undesirable developments, a market recovery will doubtless not materialise until 2012 and 2013. However, this may only last until the next speculation and project wave.

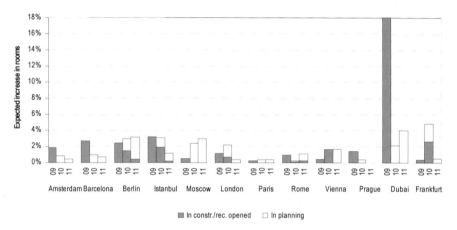

Fig. 5. Effects of the recent investment boom on growth in supply

Source: Jones Lang LaSalle Hotels 2008a

4   Outlook

It is clear that the property and financial crisis has grave consequences for tourism. Some hotels also reported massive slumps, for which, in retrospect, the hotel concerns themselves have been shown to be partly responsible. They willingly created more and more new brands, in order to sell property equipped with a brand name which was as "strong" as possible at massively inflated prices.

Irrespective of this, the past offers a reason for hope in the midst of the crisis. International tourism has namely always succeeded thus far in withstanding the various crises, as Figure 7 documents using the example of the two key hotel markets in Europe, London and Paris. The UNTWO is also maintaining the expectation that tourism will, in the long run, hold its ground as one of the main driving forces of the world economy (UNWTO 2009b). Furthermore, according to certain results of a recent study by the respected consulting firm Deloitte, which deals with current developments and prospects of European tourism, the outlook is not altogether negative (Deloitte 2009).

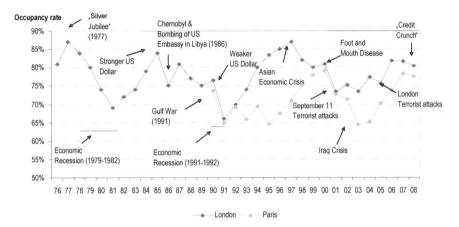

Fig. 6. Effects of selected crises on the London and Paris hotel markets

Source: Jones Lang LaSalle Hotels 2008a

However, the property and financial crisis also offers cause to critically scrutinise opinions and preconceptions which are prevalent in the economic sciences about the efficiency of a globalised capital and financial market as the crisis makes clear, above all, the actual value of a large variety of institutions within a financial system, as well as the co-existence of very diverse financial systems in a healthy competitive environment. System errors in certain forms would then no longer be able to spread with such momentum. In addition, the regions less badly affected could support the institutions and brands which had been hit by the crisis and, ultimately, the existence of valid alternative forms would allow for creative exploration of possible solutions for a crisis.

Accordingly, it would be important, particularly in a globalised world, for institutions and individuals to retain their differences and to act according to different criteria, in pursuit of different aims. Particularly for the global players among the tourist organisations, which influence a variety of cultures, there is huge potential in this regard to strategically consider and develop regional differences and characteristics. Judging by the actual activities, however, the question arises as to whether international hotel concerns would even be able to, let alone want to, achieve a "retrogression" of the brand standards which are, for the most part, already uniformly implemented worldwide. Whether tourism, with its inherently high degree of internationalisation, will find the appropriate balance in the controversial field of globalisation and regionalisation in order to develop competitive products, remains to be seen. This is all quite apart from the fact that the property and financial crisis as an economic crisis could also gain social relevance and therefore lead to not yet discussed consequences.

References

Baurmann, J. (2000): Vertragsmodelle der Hotellerie, in: Top Hotel, Nr. 3, p. 2-12.

Burghof, H.-P./Prothmann, F. (2008): Bankenkrise: Ursachen und Maßnahmen, in: Wirtschaftsdienst, Nr. 11, p. 703-707.

Deloitte (2009): Hospitality Vision – European Performance Review, London.

Drobetz, W. (2007): Empirische Finanzmarktforschung – Renditen, Markteffizienz und Ereignisstudien, http://www.unibas.ch/cofi/teaching/courses/ss2005/m-cofi2/material/Effizienz_Eventstudies.pdf, 16.10.2007.

Elze, C.R. (1995): Die Wertermittlung von Hotelimmobilien. Immobilien & Finanzierung, in: Der langfristige Kredit, Issue 3, 46. Jg., p. 14-16.

Fama, E.F. (1991): Efficient Capital Markets II, in: The Journal of Finance, Issue 5, 46. Jg., p. 1575-1617.

Frehse, J. (2004): Die Wertermittlung von Hotelimmobilien bei Markttransaktionen, in: Tourismus Journal, Issue 4, 8. Jg., p. 449-474.

Härle, Ch. (2007): Die neue Generation von Eigentümern verfolgt eine andere Strategie, in: Cost & Logis, Kolleg 2007, 30. January 2007.

Härle, Ch./Haller, T. (2007): Veränderte Rahmenbedingungen auf den europäischen Hotelinvestmentmärkten, in: Frehse, J./Weiermair, K. (Ed.): Hotel Real Estate Management, Berlin, p. 191-205.

Holzmann, Ch./Frehse, J. (2007): Exitstrategien bei Hotelimmobilien: Verkauf en gros und en détail, in: Frehse, J./Weiermair, K. (Ed.): Hotel Real Estate Management, Berlin, p. 133-146.

Jones Lang LaSalle Hotels (2008a): Wie wird sich der Hotelinvestmentmarkt 2009 entwickeln? München, London.

Jones Lang LaSalle Hotels (2008b): Die Finanzkrise und ihre Auswirkungen auf den Hotel- und Hotelinvestmentmarkt, München, London.

Kunz, M.R. (2007): Effizienz der Finanzmärkte, http://www.unibas.ch/cofi/teaching/courses/ws2005-06/afm/material/AFM13_Markteffizienz.pdf, 17.10.2007.

Pütz-Willems, M. (2004) Institutionelle Investoren interessieren sich vor allem für starke Marken und professionelle Betreiber, in: Handelsblatt, 09. Mai 2004, p. 37.

Rottke, N./Holzmann, Ch. (2003): Wertschöpfungsstrategien von Opportunity Funds, in: Immobilien Manager, Issue 12, p. 28-30.

Schräder, A. (2000): Netzeffekte in Transport und Tourismus, Bern et al. 2000.

Schredelseker, K. (2002): Grundlagen der Finanzwirtschaft, München, Wien, p. 405-479.

Schröder, M./Forstnig, J./Widmann, M. (2005), Bewertung von Hotels und Hotelimmobilien, München.

UNWTO (2009a): World Tourism Barometer, June Edition.

UNWTO (2009b): Touristenströme in einer unsicheren Zeit, VII Nationales Tourismusforum.

Oil Price and Holiday Mobility: Will We Still Be Able to Afford Vacation in the Future?

Norbert Walter

This article is a postscript of an introductory speech of Prof. Dr. Norbert Walter to a panel discussion on ITB Berlin Convention 2009. It contains some remarkable references on the relationship between tourism trends and the financial crisis.

I will start by explaining the origins of the world wide recession and move on to its effects on energy prices. Afterwards, I will discuss the implications for tourism.

A long economic upswing lies behind us. There were excesses, especially in expenditures for certain kinds of assets – in particular in real estate. When you tell this tale in Germany, you have a hard time making people understand it, because Germany did not notice the exaggerations going on in other countries. To put it bluntly: between 1995 and 2005 housing prices doubled in the US; in France they went up 2.5 times, in Spain and England 3.5 times and in Ireland even 4.5 times while they did not change in Germany. Where these real estate prices increased, people felt richer and richer and banks judged them to be ever more creditworthy.

Cheap money was put at many people's disposal even if they did not have a reasonable income. The countless types of mortgage loans made it possible for people in the countries mentioned above to even finance furniture, a vacation or a car on top of their house. The result was a widespread boom. This overlapped with an upward trend in many, in fact nearly all, newly industrialising countries (NICs), with the trend further reinforcing the global boom. The Central and Eastern European countries caught up further in the process of European integration. Asia became the world's most dynamic economic area with hard-working and ambitious people who integrated into the world economy. Latin American countries – being rich in commodities – continued to improve their managerial training. All these economic areas grew significantly. During this process, the demand for commodities was growing ever more strongly – not only for energy but also for metals and agricultural commodities.

Worldwide, the rate of inflation increased and in 2007 the central banks raised their interest rates to combat inflation. This abruptly corrected the exaggerations taking place and the rising interest rates made the refinancing of car loans for example suddenly more expensive. Then the refinancing market dried up.

R. Conrady and M. Buck (eds.), *Trends and Issues in Global Tourism 2010*,
Trends and Issues in Global Tourism, DOI 10.1007/978-3-642-10829-7_5,
© Springer-Verlag Berlin Heidelberg 2010

Participants in capital markets became uncertain; some people were not able to continue paying their installments and had to sell their houses which they had used as collateral: foreclosures started to mount. After that, housing prices began to trend downward. This process started in the US where it was called the subprime crisis. The subprime crisis did not remain a problem exclusively for American financial institutions. Since these institutions had bundled and securitised mortgage loans and sold them internationally, everyone who had bought these securitisations sustained losses – both to less-known institutions in Dresden and Duesseldorf as well as to better-known ones in Zurich. The write downs for these securities was eating into their equity and banks got into difficulties. During this phase of the financial crisis it became more and more difficult to finance large projects by leveraging – especially for big companies planning their restructuring, such as the Schaeffler Group.

The process continued without big eruptions due to ready capital injection from private institutions and sovereign wealth funds until summer 2008 when something happened that had been unthinkable before in the United States: the bankruptcy of Lehman Brothers. Since then, the world has not been the same. Letting a bank of such systemic importance as Lehman Brothers go bankrupt affected the world like a tsunami. Many contracts were and still are under threat and a large number of financial institutions were led to the point where their equity was used up and they could no longer obtain any capital in the private market. Even the world's richest people, like Warren Buffet, and government funds of countries that had become very rich now refused to provide their support. At that point, governments started to help out while at the same time more systemically important banks were on the brink of collapse. The crisis widened and impacted upon the real economy. The first consequences were seen in the automotive sector – at least, this is where we first noticed them in the statistics. Automotive suppliers were affected and immediately afterwards producers of plastic components suffered. Less obviously, but by no means less significantly, demand for everything linked to logistics collapsed simultaneously. As early as in fall 2008, we saw a particularly dramatic downward trend in freight – especially sea but also air and railway freight. Later the crisis spread comparatively fast to the core of the manufacturing industry – the mechanical engineering sector.

In this situation, rescue programmes became necessary, not only for financial institutions, but also for businesses in other sectors and the economy as a whole, i.e. programmes to stimulate the economy. Many countries took the required steps, first and foremost the US even though the country was in the middle of presidential elections. Other countries and their governments, including Germany, were much more hesitant. In many cases, they believed that they were not affected. Obviously, they did not think about the fact that they are an integral part of the world economy and would be affected indirectly, even if they had not made any mistakes domestically.

The government programmes to stimulate the economy were made by people who did not believe in Keynes. Therefore, the programmes in Washington, Berlin,

London and Paris are not very appropriate for anti-cyclical purposes but a mixture of everything. On the one hand, they are not thought big enough and are rarely focused on a quick boost in demand in order to compensate for the current lack of demand. Moreover, all countries worked independently in order to save themselves instead of getting together to develop a common policy and pursue it in unison. These individual actions have a weaker effect than joint action, because of so called leakages. The support is rarely comprehensive, broad instead it is only of benefit to selected sectors. These distortive government incentives have to be criticised. On the other hand, one cannot help but observe that populations, especially in Europe, view every economic stimulation programme with great scepticism. Why is that the case? Because it means more governmental expenses and higher debt, i.e. an increased burden in the future; and that at a time when we have just learned how dramatically high the level of debt already is and how severely public debt already burdens a shrinking population with interest and redemption payments. All these factors have delayed the process of implementing anticyclical measures.

Where are we now? We are in March 2009, in the deepest recession any of us have ever experienced. The crash is steep and broad. Not all countries are affected in the same way; in fact they are all affected quite differently. The only common denominator is the similarity of the final dramatic effect on the (gross) national product. In the US, the downward trend mainly affects the real estate industry, the construction industry, the financial sector and now also private consumption. The trend is practically the same in England. But the pattern is completely different in a country such as Germany: we neither experienced a property boom nor a consumption binge. Therefore, in Germany there are no dramatic declines in these sectors, but being the world's leading exporter brings other problems in times like these. We, some 80 million inhabitants, export more than the 120 million Japanese, the 300 million Americans or the 1,300 million Chinese – therefore, we are disproportionately affected by a collapsing global economy. The declines in the automotive sector and in mechanical engineering are very dramatic. This is the reason why our level of production is exceptionally low, too. The impact of the crisis on unemployment is certainly much more pronounced in other countries, such as the US, because there the recession has lasted longer, but also in Spain where the crisis affects the construction industry, which is much more labour-intensive than the manufacturing industry. In Germany, we have achieved a greater degree of flexibility in the employment of the labour force. For now, we are able to absorb the decline in demand with flexible methods like reducing working hours, such as the reduction of working-time accounts, and by setting up very generous arrangements for short-time working. Therefore, we have not been forced to axe a considerable number of employees yet. In Spain, the unemployment rate is almost 20%. In Germany, the unemployment rate is just beginning to rise. Over the last couple of months, unemployment in the US has been increasing by 600,000 per month. This shows how severe the crisis is.

The crisis certainly affects the tourism industry as well. As always in this industry, the effects kick in with a time lag. It is not surprising that tourism expenditures lag behind the economy, especially in a country like Germany where people plan nothing in such detail as their vacation. In Germany, it takes almost a year before the economic situation is completely mirrored in tourist spending. This has always been the case and it will not be very different this time around.

The last winter was very snow-rich and therefore exceedingly successful. The crisis, which has already been running since summer 2008 has begun to leave its mark in the second quarter of 2009. People will be more careful with their spending because they fear unemployment. Until now, income development and mass incomes have not changed unfavourably yet. And in 2009, in contrast to 2008, disposable income will not be eaten up by price increases. In 2009, the price level will be just as high as in the year before. We have clearly achieved noticeable savings already, especially because of the gasoline price, which has been declining since July 2008, and also the price of heating oil. Over the course of the year gas will become cheaper for consumers, as will electricity in 2010. In other words: budget strains will ease because of the development of energy prices and we will have no dramatic decline in disposable mass incomes. Unemployment is just starting to rise – this is going to accelerate in the second half of the year. And again, because of the lower inflation rate, a smaller part of the rising incomes is going to be used for expenditures that help the oil sheikhs and more will be left over for entertainment. This could potentially mean more funds for the tourism budget. In my judgment, the changes in expenditures for summer tourism will basically be related to a more careful attitude by the consumers towards expenses during their vacation. All those who are concerned about the possibility of losing their job or about their current short-time work turning into unemployment will probably be more careful than they are at present. But I believe that this will not yet lead to a dramatic downturn. Concerning tourism expenditures, I expect the drastic downward changes in the winter season 2009/2010 and the complete effect of the current crisis to become apparent during the summer vacation of 2010. I would be surprised if it were any different!

Let us switch to the topic we wanted to talk about initially and to the question: What will happen to energy prices? How will this affect the various areas of tourism? First of all, I have to admit that I am not able to give you an oil price forecast. I can tell you what I said in June 2008 for you to decide how good or bad a forecaster I am. In June 2008, when the oil price was 150 dollars per barrel I said: "The oil price will rise to 200 dollars per barrel – as Goldman Sachs presumed at this time – but only after it will have fallen under 100 dollars per barrel during the coming recession." And what I meant was that the lower turning point of the oil price would be about 70 dollars per barrel in 2009. These were my expectations in June 2008. We all know this was a very good proposition in terms of the trend. At that time, people looked critically at my ungrounded optimism for a reduction of the oil price. Today, they laugh about my hesitation because I was obviously way off the mark since the oil price was not at 70 but at 35 dollars per barrel when it was hitting bottom. And it seems as though the severity of the recession has bestowed on us a similarly low price level for the future because we know: the last winter was very cold across the whole of the northern hemisphere and it cost us quite a lot of gas, coal and oil. In other words, we had a rather difficult season but despite this difficult time the prices of oil and gas did not continue to rise but settled at this low level.

We basically have to make a forecast about how the prices will change. We also have to take something else into account and I think this has not yet been sufficiently considered by many people: many oil and gas providers have higher production costs than the revenue they receive at the current market price. And because I am talking in front of many businessmen I do not have to tell you: if a producer thinks he can continue producing in a time when he covers only about ¾ or 2/3 of his costs by selling his products, he soon will be bankrupt and will not be producing anymore. And when these types of producers withdraw from the market, there is only one obvious outcome: the oil price will rise – even if the economy stays as bad as it is at the moment.

It is realistic to assume that the current low oil prices are a temporary phenomenon – even with an ongoing poor economy. If the economy does not stay depressed, there will not only be adjustments in supply processes but there will also be price increases resulting from rising demand. At least, that is the analytical message. Let us get to the question of probability now. If everything goes well, which means if the rescue packages work, if the important countries of the world develop a more cooperative way of thinking instead of making economic policies only for themselves, then we will be safe from protectionism. But if ministers of finance or heads of government save GM, Opel or the Schaeffler Group, they will not be very happy if producers in other countries are supported by these rescue plans. They will emphasise the fact that tax payers money should only be used to save jobs in their own countries. Therefore, countries and governments making this kind of rescue plan for companies and sectors will develop protectionist tendencies. If protectionist tendencies are developed, something nobody in this room has ever experienced could happen: namely the same thing that happened in the early 1930s. At that time, there was a great intensification of protectionism and in the end also a brutal and global depression – with (gross) national product declining by a quarter, and up to one third in some countries. This is a risk which cannot be denied!

The only chance to avoid this risk is the leadership of the Obama government – there is nobody else to guide us. We Germans have Angela Merkel. But after winning the parliamentary elections, she will first have to constitute a new government. This will take some time. Therefore, it is possible that we will have to rely on Obama alone when it comes to the question of an international cooperative attitude. But in the US they have also quite a few protectionist members in Congress. You might remember Obama's economic stimulus package – with large programmes for the infrastructure – to which Congress added: "If we are constructing bridges in the US, we should use American steel exclusively."

Fortunately, the international community noticed this and pointed it out to Obama. And Obama deleted this passage from the programme. I hope international vigilance will continue to exist. I also hope that other regions of the world – such as Africa, Asia or Europe – will take an equally internationally oriented attitude. This should be an attitude that understands economic issues and interdependencies between countries and then turns into corresponding action. If that is the case, the economy – after a deep downswing in production and demand this year – could possibly be stabilised with the help of low interest rates, cheap commodities and economic stimulus packages towards the end of this year. But still there will be – and I am thinking again about you and your industry, tourism – a rising unemployment rate because the labour market is a lagging indicator. And since unemployment is rising and therefore mass income will shrink, uncertainty and the propensity to save will stay high. Expenditures that are not absolutely necessary will possibly be postponed or even cancelled completely. This risk exists not only for the purchase of cars or furniture but also for vacation trips.

In my judgment, the oil price will be higher than today a year from now and commodity prices will start rising as well mainly because of the relatively high demand for these products from relatively better performing emerging countries. I imagine the new president of the US will not just talk about environmental awareness but will also take steps in accordance with this awareness. A corresponding policy will probably include support for renewable energies and thus a relative or even absolute burden on fossil energies. Besides the increase in producer prices for oil and gas, there will also be an increase in costs due to environmental policies burdening these using fossil fuels. It is also possible that an environmentally oriented policy will initiate regulations favouring fuel-efficient cars over less efficient ones. There is thus some indication that not only energy prices but also regulatory measures will result in growing mobility costs. I think there will either be a gasoline tax in the US or certificates for CO_2 emissions imposing costs on those who cause them. Unfortunately, debate on the subject is dominated more by ideological considerations rather than ecological or economic ones. If we decided to use the possibilities to save CO_2 and energy in stationary settings, i.e. energy efficient buildings in particular we could avoid CO_2 at much lower costs than for example when aiming at cars or planes. It is quite easy to achieve enormous progress by using better insulation for houses or more efficient furnaces in our basements instead of seeking to retrieve the highest level of efficiency from combustion engines. The same would be true if we were prepared to replace old power stations by new ones. The increases in efficiency gained by such steps would reduce the use of fossil fuels and thus CO_2 emissions enormously. If we moved on conceptually to implement rigorously the principle of cogeneration of heat and electricity, we would take a huge step in energy efficiency. We would use the accumulated waste heat directly wherever we produced heat locally. I hope that all industries will take efforts to recognise and implement the possibilities to conserve energy and to protect the environment. These offer the most promising potential for ecological and economic achievements at the same time.

What will happen when energy prices rise again? Mobility will become more expensive. When mobility becomes more expensive and households remain on a tight budget, people will consider how to combine their aim to go on vacation with lower energy consumption and fewer emissions. In this context, there will probably be a new orientation concerning holiday patterns. If all people were the same, a long trip by plane for just one or two days on a weekend would not be a realistic holiday solution anymore in a world where mobility is constantly becoming more expensive. Bookings of long-distance flights for just a short holiday would decline drastically, under the condition that people taking such trips would have to incur financial penalties. However, it is not the average working-class family with three children that makes these trips but the rich who just want to play golf or go to the theatre. If their income does not change, these people will continue to make such trips. But will that be the case? Will the income of the rich remain undiminished in the future? For investment bankers the situation will be different in the next three years. If you are a Porsche dealer or a tour operator for trips like the ones mentioned above, you should consider reducing your workforce. But there are also several groups of people who will not be affected. When you are an insolvency administrator you do not need to worry. We should not generalise the effects of rising prices but differentiate their effects. In an overall view, however there will certainly be less short trips over long distances, and certainly fewer business trips, certainly in business and first class.

In summer 2008, a lot of factors indicated that for budget airlines 2009 would be the hardest year ever. But things turned out rather differently. According to current predictions taking into account an oil price which will remain low for another two years, budget airlines will stay in the market because their costs will remain low and more and more people will have to consider prices before booking. Demand for these flights is likely to increase and people will accept disadvantages such as no meals or closer seating. Due to the low oil prices the adjustments in the airline industry will not come about as expected. On the contrary: budget airlines will increase competition. Corporate policy on business trips will develop to the disadvantage of traditional airlines and will continue to do so as long as the recession lasts.

What conclusions can be drawn from these insights? People with an average income and large families will shift their means of transport in favour of the car. In the future, simpler accommodation will be given priority, including camping trips. Five and six-star hotels in Dubai will be difficult to fill in the summer of 2010. When mobility becomes more expensive, the aspect of distance is added and becomes more important the farther away the destination is. The question is whether to take a longer vacation when you make a longer trip. The answer to this question is not easily found. Obviously, the yearning for faraway places will remain. Due to rising mobility costs people will change their holiday patterns. Instead of travelling to Bali twice in two years, they will fly there only once in two years for three or four weeks and spend their vacation locally the following year, for example in the Harz Mountains.

These are the trends for the years to come. In households with lower or average incomes, the car will experience a comeback and camping trips will become more important. Likewise, there will still be rich people representing a segment which also has to be served. Energy and mobility costs alone will not change consumer behaviour. There will be another trend in forthcoming years: the retirement of the children of the baby boom years. A lot depends on their behaviour as pensioners. They will be very significant in numbers and therefore they will shape the holiday patterns and mobility use of the future.

Energy Demand Forecasts and Climate Policy Agenda

A Sustainable Energy Mix Needs to Be Clean, Clever and Competitive

Claudia Kemfert

Summary

Today's society faces as no generation before two main energy related threats: first, to guarantee secure and affordable energy supply and second, to reduce and abolish environmental and climate harms caused by energy consumption. Over 80 percent of today's primary energy consumption is coming from non-renewable fossil fuels, as coal, oil and gas. If we do not change our behaviour, futures share of fossil fuel resources remains as high as today. As the major oil and gas reserves are located in few areas of the world, importing countries would become more vulnerable to supply disruptions and energy price shocks. Furthermore, fossil fuel consumption causes CO_2 and greenhouse gas emissions and therefore climate change. As the International Energy Agency said in its recent report, the future energy mix should not be under-invested, vulnerable and dirty but *clean, clever* and *competitive*.

Secure, reliable and affordable energy resources are fundamental to sustained economic development. The threat of disruptive climate change, the erosion of energy security and the world's growing demand for energy all pose major challenges for energy decision makers. To meet these challenges and transform our energy system, a better use of existing technologies will be required along with significant scientific innovation to spur the adoption of new energy technologies. Therefore, urgent action is needed to rapidly advance available energy efficiency and low-carbon technologies and practices. Basic science and energy research funding has been declining in the public and private sectors for the past several years. Additional funding is critically needed to develop a sustainable energy future. Research priorities encompass inter alia photovoltaics, carbon capture and sequestration (CCS), biofuels and hydrogen generation, storage and use.

R. Conrady and M. Buck (eds.), *Trends and Issues in Global Tourism 2010*,
Trends and Issues in Global Tourism, DOI 10.1007/978-3-642-10829-7_6,
© Springer-Verlag Berlin Heidelberg 2010

1   The Challenge

Increasing energy prices especially for oil and gas and recent geopolitical events, like the situation in Iran or the "Russian-Ukrainian gas conflict" have reminded us of the essential role affordable energy plays in economic growth and human development, and of the vulnerability of the global energy system to supply disruptions. Securing energy supplies is once again at the top of the international policy agenda. Yet the current pattern of energy supply carries the threat of severe and irreversible environmental damage – including changes in global climate (Kemfert, 2007). Reconciling the goals of energy security and environmental protection requires strong and coordinated government action and public support. As a consequence, the decoupling of energy use and economic growth, a diversification of energy supply and the mitigation of climate change causing emissions is more urgent than ever.

Nowadays the major share of primary energy demand is coming from fossil fuels, oil, gas and coal. The main suppliers of oil are the OPEC region, Russia and the USA. If the oil demand will continue to grow as fast as in the last decades, the demand for oil will be higher than the supply in 15 years from now (depletion point). Although the oil price would also rise with increasing demand, and other oil reserves as oil shale or tar sands would be financially attractive to exploit further, oil still remains the scarcest fossil resource on earth, followed by gas. The world's largest gas reserves are in Russia, followed by Qatar and Iran. The supply of coal is more widely spread in many countries of the world, the coal reserves will last over 200 years.

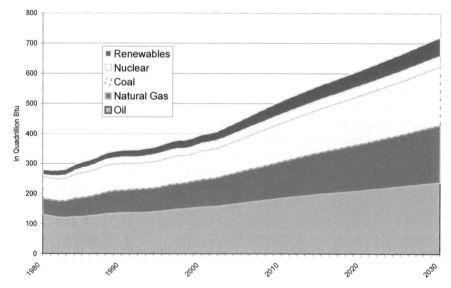

Fig. 1. World energy use by fuel type, 1980-2030, in quadrillion BTU

Source: IEA 2006

Energy forecasts demonstrate that the share of fossil fuel supply would remain high if no policy to reach a sustainable energy future takes place (IEA 2008). As major OECD countries have successfully decoupled their energy consumption from economic growth primarily by increased energy efficiency, developing countries continue to grow fast. The enormous economic and fuel consumption growth in developing countries, especially China followed by India, leads to higher energy supply scarcity and energy prices, but also to higher CO_2 emissions. If no sustainable policy would take place, global energy-related carbon-dioxide (CO_2) emissions would increase by 55% between 2004 and 2030, developing countries accounting for over three-quarters of the increase in global CO_2 emissions.

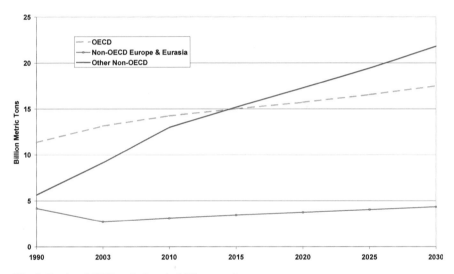

Fig. 2. Regional CO2 emissions in billion metric tons

Source: IEA 2006

Because of the high economic and energy growth, OECD and developing Asian countries become increasingly dependent on imports as their indigenous production fails to keep pace with demand. By 2030, the OECD as a whole will import two-thirds of its oil needs, compared with 56% today. Much of the additional imports come from the Middle East, along vulnerable maritime routes. The concentration of oil production in a small group of countries with large reserves – notably Middle East OPEC members and Russia – will increase their market dominance and their ability to impose higher prices. An increasing share of gas demand is also expected to be met by imports, via pipeline or in the form of liquefied natural gas from increasingly distant suppliers.

Meeting the world's growing hunger for energy requires massive investment in energy-supply infrastructure. The International Energy Agency (IEA) estimates cumulative investments of around 20 trillion USD (2005) within the next 25 years. However, if these investments would not be made, a secure energy supply could not be guaranteed anymore.

The largest share of CO_2 emissions is caused by fossil-fuel combustion for energy production and transportation. Methane is also produced by the energy (gas exploration) sector as well as by agriculture. In order to reduce emissions, fossil fuels need to be replaced by CO_2-free energy technologies, energy efficiency needs to be improved considerably, and more sustainable energy and agricultural production procedures need to become standard. As energy security, competitiveness and the effect on climate cannot and should not be separated, future policy options should combine all aspects. Europe as the first nation in the world has taken the lead in combining concrete targets for energy and climate policy (European Commission, 2007). Europe intends to cut emissions by 20% by 2020 compared with the 1990 level and to increase the share of renewable energy by 20% in the same time period. However, Europe intends to reduce even 30% of its emissions if other nations are willing to accept climate policy commitments. It is important that Europe demonstrates the willingness and ability to cut emissions drastically. The Kyoto protocol needs to be fulfilled, the emissions trading scheme needs to be improved and a fair burden sharing needs to be implemented. Europe can convince other nations to agree on any kind of climate commitments only if Europe is willing to reduce 30% by 2020.

2 A Sustainable Energy Future

A sustainable energy future must be CO_2 free, environmental friendly and secure. A future energy system cannot only rely on one energy source, but must be as broad as possible. Energy security means also that energy imports are reduced and diversified from many different supply countries and that domestic energy sources should have a major contribution. Many domestic energy sources are not sustainable as coal emits climate harming carbon dioxide emissions and nuclear energy causes high environmental risks. Conventional nuclear energy can therefore only be a technology that bridges the gap between the fossil fuel and carbon free technology area. Four main pillars contribute to a sustainable energy future:

1. Energy efficiency. Economic growth and energy consumption growth needs to be decoupled. Many developed nations as Europe and Japan have been quite successful in this; others can improve (e.g. USA) or need to start soon (e.g. China, India). Global energy consumption and emissions can be reduced by 24% until 2050 only by energy efficiency measures.

2. Increase of share of renewable energy for electricity production, as alternative to fuel and for heating. For electricity production, renewable energy can increase from 5 to 16% globally; the share of biofuels can also be in-

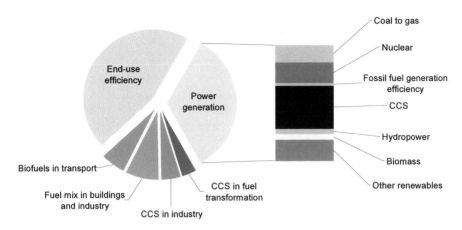

Fig. 3. Emission reduction by technology area ACT (Accelerated Technology) map scenario (IEA 2006)

creased drastically, up to 10% globally (IEA, 2006). Especially the aviation sector urgently needs alternative fuels.[1]

3. Carbon Capture and Sequestration. Coal power plants can be made more environmental friendly ("CO2 low power plant") by capturing and storing the CO2 emissions. However, both environmental and financial risks are not enough explored yet. If the technology will be available in the future, production costs can be doubled (IPCC, 2005; IEA, 2005).

4. CO2 free, save and affordable mobility technology. A sustainable mobility concept is urgently needed – i.e. more intensive usage of public transport, increase of share of biofuels as well as innovative emission free mobility technology. Whether or not hydrogen, fuel cells or electro engines might be the next technology solution engineers have to find out. Economically, all technology solutions will be market relevant with economies of scale and high oil and fossil fuel prices.

The main aim is to make future's energy system sustainable by on the one hand increasing energy efficiency and on the other hand establishing innovative, carbon free and environmental friendly technologies. In 100 years, the share of renewable energy can increase up to 80%. In between these areas, the carbon capture and storage technology can play a dominant role.

Climate protection offers huge market potentials. Climate protection is the way out of the economic crisis. Especially fast growing countries will implement new energy technologies, like sustainable mobility, energy efficient technologies and low carbon technologies.

---

[1] Air New Zealand tested biofuel blend of 50:50 jatropha and Jet A1 fuel was used to power one Boeing 747-400's, see http://www.airnewzealand.com/aboutus/biofuel-test/biofuel-test-flight.htm, 24.04.2009.

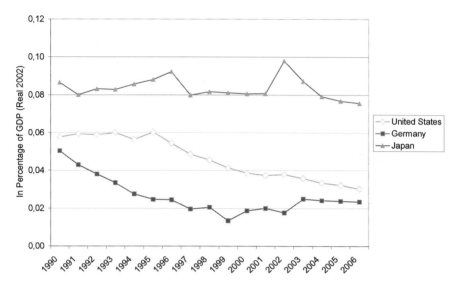

Fig. 4. Public R&D expenditures for energy research

* USA: without defense

Source: AAAS: Department of Energy R&D, 2006

3   A Sustainable Mobility Future

Transport is a key activity and a crucial component of economic development and human welfare. Because economies grow all over the world, transportation activities grow rapidly as well. Transport largely relies on a single fossil resource, petroleum that supplies 95% of the total energy used by world transport. The transport energy use amounts up to 26% of total world energy use (IEA, 2008). Today, transport is responsible for approximately 25% of world energy-related greenhouse gas (GHG) emissions. The largest share, i.e. about three quarters, comes from road vehicles. Road transport currently accounts for 74% of total transport CO_2 emissions. Over the past decade, transport's GHG emissions have increased at a faster rate than any other energy using sector.

It can be expected that transport activity will continue to increase in the future as economic growth fuels transport demand and the availability of transport drives development. The majority of the world's population still does not have access to personal vehicles and many do not have access to any form of motorized transport. But, this situation is rapidly changing. We observe that freight transport has been growing even more rapidly than passenger transport in the past years and is expected to continue to grow in the future. Urban freight is moved predominantly by truck, while international freight is dominated by ocean shipping. The modal distribution of intercity freight varies greatly across regions in the world.

Transport activity is expected to increase strongly over the next decades. Unless there is a major shift away from current patterns of energy use, world transport energy use is projected to increase at a rate of about 2% per year and it can be expected that the highest rates of growth will come from the emerging economies. Total transport energy use and carbon emissions are projected to be about 80% higher than current levels by 2030.

First and foremost, an improvement of energy efficiency offers a tremendous opportunity for transport GHG mitigation by 2030. Biofuels can have the potential to replace a substantial part but not all petroleum use by transport. Studies estimate that biofuels' share of transport fuel could increase to about 10% in 2030 (IEA, 2004). In addition to alternative fuels more advanced sustainable mobility concepts need to be elaborated and implemented. Public transport systems needs to be widely provided as well as their related infrastructure and promoting non-motorised transport. In order to increase the share of public transportation system, large investments in infrastructure are necessary. This offers great economic opportunities for innovative emerging economies.

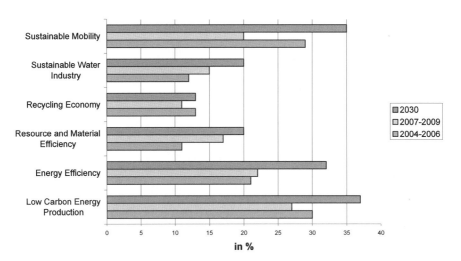

Fig. 5. Emerging climate markets – profit growth potentials, in %

Source: Roland Berger

While transport demand certainly responds to price signals, the demand for vehicles, vehicle travel and fuel use are significantly price inelastic. The concept of an open, international emission trading system for the air transport sector could bring the relevant price signals. Since currently available mitigation options will probably not be enough to prevent growth in transport's emissions, technology research and development is essential in order to create the potential for future, significant reductions in transport GHG emissions. This is especially relevant for hydrogen fuel cell, advanced biofuel conversion and improved batteries for electric and hybrid vehicles.

The most pressing problems associated with this increasing transport activity which needs to be solved are traffic fatalities and injuries, congestion, air pollution and petroleum dependence. Especially fast growing economies of the developing world face these challenges. Mitigating greenhouse gas (GHG) emissions can take its place among these other transport priorities by emphasizing synergies and co-benefits.

The most important five options for sustainable development in the transport sector are: biofuels, energy efficiency, public transport, non-motorised transport and urban planning. Implementing these options would generally have positive social, environmental and economic side effects.

References

International Energy Agency (IEA) (2008): The World Energy Outlook 2008, Paris 2008.

IEA (2005): Reducing CO_2 Emissions, the potential of Coal, Paris 2005.

IEA (2006): Science for Today's Energy Challenges, Paris 2006.

IEA (2004): Energy Technologies for a Sustainable Future: Transport. International Energy Agency, Technology Brief, 40 pp.

IPCC (2005): Intergovernmental Panel on Climate Change: Special Report on Carbon Dioxid Capture and Storage, Cambridge University Press 2005.

Kemfert, C. (2007): The European Electricity and climate policy: Complement or substitute? In: *Environment and Planning / C* 25 (2007), 1, p. 115-130.

ITB Workshop: Carbon Management in Tourism

Introductory Statement of Geoffrey Lipman

Good morning ladies and gentlemen. The first good news is I have no slides. The second good news is that I am also moderating a session somewhere else at the same time. So I have to be as brief as possible. You'll all be happy about that. I wanted to do this nevertheless for two or three reasons: the first reason is – some of you may remember – that last year at ITB we actually organized with ITB a whole session on the climate change issue. And the bottom line of that session was a commitment of the WTO to work with ITB, to work with everybody in a continuing path that we have been embarking on since 2003 with the World Meteological Organization and latterly with the World Economic Forum. We call this the Davos Declaration Process and the whole point is that there aren't any leaders on this issue and it's a reality. It's an evolving reality but it is only evolving in one direction. If we don't fix the issue by 2050, our children won't have any issue to fix. And if we don't fix it in a way that commits to start now because as Nick Stirns said: The longer we wait the more it costs. But the reality is that the longer we wait the more difficult it is to fix. And that's why the meeting in Copenhagen at the end of year and the meeting before that for the private sector are so important to give us a new platform to move forward on this whole issue of climate neutrality which Carbon Management is a critical part of. It doesn't matter what the numbers are, at least at this stage, that come out at Copenhagen at the end of the year. What matters are some fundamentals. There is a system movement and the UN system as a whole is an important part of that in tourism now because the WTO has a seat at the table. The UN is leading or trying to lead a road map towards climate neutrality by 2050 to put a date out there. They have to fix something everybody rich and poor will some kind of deal which looks after the poor particularly and make sure that at to the extent possibly economy keeps tuning along in the right way. And we have to make sure that whatever is done it embraces everybody. There is nobody who is going to be out of this deal whether it 's a special interest whether it's airlines because of difficult situations everybody has to be in this deal.

Another point I want to mention – this is not my point but this is Achim Steiner's – is that it is not going to be a sort of systematic fix. It's going to happen everywhere at the same time in the same way. He has described it as a mosaic: a world made of a mosaic where some spots get greener as people move towards the right way of moving for them and for the world. And then eventually the whole lot

R. Conrady and M. Buck (eds.), *Trends and Issues in Global Tourism 2010*,
Trends and Issues in Global Tourism, DOI 10.1007/978-3-642-10829-7_7,
© Springer-Verlag Berlin Heidelberg 2010

becomes green. And what we have to have is a common commitment to all of this and this is my last point: it relates to the current situation, it relates to what we are doing at UNWTO. Of course we have an economic crisis – we have lots of crises: we have a resource crisis, we have a population crisis and we have 24 on 7 news which tell us that today's crisis is the biggest crisis. But the fact is that all these crises are inter-connected. And we have to keep getting a fix which is inter-connected and which moves along so that the long term and the short term are dealt with together. In WTO we announced at the beginning of ITB what we call a road map for recovery. It focuses on the economy but fundamentally also on two important points: Get tourism into the stimulus packages and the right tourism, smart tourism, intelligent tourism and most important: use tourism for the trans-formation to the green economy. That's a message, that's the message I want to leave you for today. I really apologize for having to run but the reason that I'm here is because I think that the grassroots movement which I have been a part of in the last 20 years, the green movement, the grassroots movements are vital to push-ing the establishment and bureaucracies in the right direction and I hope that the WTO is one of those bureaucracies which is one of the kinds that doesn't need to be pushed too much. Thank you very much.

Carbon Management in Tourism –
A Smart Strategy in Response to Climate Change

Wolfgang Strasdas

The ITB 2009 was dominated by the global financial and economic crisis. Compared to the ITB 2008, when global warming was a major issue, one could almost get the impression that climate change and resource conservation were problems of the past and no longer of interest. Unfortunately, climate change is not going away. In reality, the opposite is the case. Recent studies indicate that things have gotten worse than predicted by most scientists. The Arctic is warming up faster than anticipated, with the Greenland ice shield being of particular concern. As a consequence of this, sea levels are also rising faster. While the financial crisis may soon be over, the impacts of climate change will stay with humanity for the centuries to come (Stock 2009).

Thus, for tourism, climate change will remain a major challenge, with long-haul tourism and aviation, winter tourism and beach tourism in Southern latitudes being the most vulnerable segments of the industry. In addition, there is the prospect of rising oil prices once the present slump is over, of stricter emission regulations and a growing environmental awareness of tourists. In this context, carbon management is seen as a key strategy for tourism companies and organisations, not just to mitigate their own contribution to global warming, but also to adapt to the direct and indirect impacts of climate change in their own economic interest.

This article is largely the result of a panel discussion organised by Eberswalde University of Applied Sciences in the framework of the ITB 2009 Convention. It summarizes the presentations and discussion results of the panel as well as some background information, but does not pretend to provide an in-depth analysis of carbon management in tourism – a field that is still in an infant stage in the industry.

1 Background: The Interrelationship Between Tourism and Climate Change

Worldwide, tourism is responsible for about 5% of energy-related CO_2 emissions (UNWTO/ UNEP 2008). While this share may appear to be relatively small, it becomes more significant when comparing it with other sectors or countries. Roughly,

R. Conrady and M. Buck (eds.), *Trends and Issues in Global Tourism 2010*,
Trends and Issues in Global Tourism, DOI 10.1007/978-3-642-10829-7_8,
© Springer-Verlag Berlin Heidelberg 2010

tourism's share of CO_2 emissions equals the one of the chemical industry. If tourism were a country, it would range in 5th place after the USA, China, Russia and India and well ahead of major polluters such as Japan and Germany (WRI 2005). However, this amount is unevenly distributed among tourism subsystems and types of tourism. 75% of overall emissions are attributed to transportation, of which air transport accounts for 40% and automobile traffic for 32%. The share of accommodation is 21% (ibid.; see Figure 1). This means that emissions of aviation-dependent long-haul tourism are substantially higher per travel day. In Germany, for example, domestic tourism represents only 1.6% of national emissions (with a transportation share of 62%), while on intercontinental trips taken by Germans, their flights alone account for over 90% of the overall trip emissions (UBA/Öko-Institut 2002).

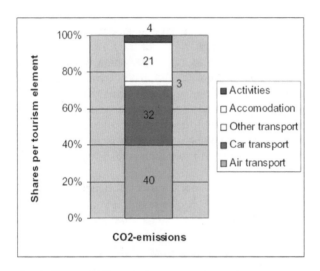

Fig. 1. Shares of CO_2 emissions per tourism sub-sector
Source: UNWTO/UNEP 2008

The issue is further aggravated by scientific evidence that non-CO_2 emissions from aircraft at high cruising altitudes increase the overall warming effect (or "radiative forcing") of aviation. However, due to the high complexity of the various factors involved, scientific knowledge of the exact interactions and impacts is still sketchy. It is now believed that the overall warming effect from aircraft may be twice as high as if CO_2 alone was taken into account. The Intergovernmental Panel on Climate Change (IPCC) in its 2007 report uses a factor of 2.7 because some studies suggest that radiative forcing from aircraft may be substantially higher due to the formation of cirrus clouds from contrails (see Strasdas 2007, a.o.).

On the individual consumer's level, a lifestyle of frequent flying and long-haul holidays "devastates" personal climate "footprints". A single roundtrip flight from Frankfurt to Sydney emits the same amount of greenhouse gases (GHG; calculated as CO_2 equivalents) as driving a middle-sized car over an annual distance of 12,000 km for six years (average for Germany; www.atmosfair.de).

Cruise tourism, still comparatively small, but one of the fastest growing industry segments, is another point of concern. Even though the energy consumption of cruise tourism is not well researched yet, it is estimated that the emissions of one passenger day equal about 500 km flown by aeroplane (Becken/Hay 2007).

Most national governments in the world have now accepted that global warming should be kept within a limit of +2°C, if unmanageable impacts and drastic consequences to humanity are to be avoided. This means that substantial reductions in GHG emissions need to be achieved, in particular by industrialised countries, but increasingly by emerging economies as well, decoupling their economic growth from a further increase of emissions. It is now widely believed that global emissions must decrease no later than 2020 and that industrialised countries need to reduce their emissions by 80% by 2050. Tourism, like all other industries, needs to play its part in this. However, business-as usual-scenarios for global tourism forecast an emission increase of about 250% (tripling of emissions for international tourism and domestic tourism in the developing world) by 2035, even with modest energy efficiency gains already taken into account (UNWTO/UNEP 2008). It is clear that such a development is totally unacceptable. If tourism is to continue to thrive as an economic activity, substantial savings in emissions need to be made.

Apart from any ethical considerations that these figures may prompt, tourism's energy intensity also poses a number of future risks to the industry itself, if substantial mitigation measures are not implemented. The most obvious one is costs. Prices for fossil-based fuel have soared in recent years and now represent a significant portion of operational costs for airlines and other transport companies, but also for hotels. It is, of course, difficult to forecast the development of prices of oil and oil products, but with a growing world economy and the progressing depletion of existing oil deposits, it seems likely that the trend will continue (Gössling 2009a).

In addition, impending climate protection regulation will further increase energy prices or impose absolute emission limits, especially for the automobile and aviation sectors. The European Union will start to implement an emissions trading scheme (ETS) for all aircraft arriving and departing from EU airports in 2012. This scheme will impose a cap of 97% (95% from 2013 on) of baseline emissions recorded from 2004-2006. Furthermore, there is now a widespread agreement that international aviation should become regulated under a post-Kyoto agreement, although it is not yet clear what exactly this would entail (Lyle 2009). However, the less the industry is willing to make emission savings voluntarily, the stricter regulations may be in the future.

A further factor is the growing public awareness of automobile traffic's and aviation's contribution to climate change in some of the world's major tourism source markets, especially in Western Europe, Australia, New Zealand and North America. Although this generally high level of awareness has not yet translated into significant changes of travel patterns, tourism's and aviation's reputation has already suffered, possibly due to the industry's apparent lack of action to combat global warming (Gössling 2009a).

2   Carbon Management: Principles and Strategies

"Carbon management" can be defined as a management system that aims to reduce a company's or organisation's GHG emissions as much as possible, ideally to zero. The use of the term "carbon" in this case is actually quite narrow in that in its strict meaning it would not include non-CO_2 emissions. However, as the discussion above has shown, it is imperative to include other GHG as well, especially for aviation. Therefore, the more correct term would be "greenhouse gas management". In the context of this article the term "carbon management" is preferred for its greater ease of use, but shall be understood in a more comprehensive way. The overall warming potential of emissions would then be measured in CO_2 equivalents (CO_2-e). The term is mostly applied to individual companies or agencies, but may also be used for larger operational units, such as industry associations or destination management organisations (DMOs), covering geographic areas at different scales.

As a systematic approach, carbon management is to be implemented through the following steps:

1. **Measure** and analyse emissions (Where and when do emissions occur? In which departments, by which products or activities? For which reasons?)

2. **Eliminate** or avoid emissions by foregoing energy-intensive products or activities (such as scenic flights or weekend trips by aeroplane)

3. **Reduce** energy consumption (by increasing energy efficiency of appliances, processes, etc.)

4. **Substitute** fossil energy sources with renewable energy sources (e.g. through fuel switch or alternative electricity providers)

5. **Offset** remaining emissions by investing into certified compensation projects elsewhere

6. **Communicate** carbon management to customers, employees, suppliers and other stakeholders.

Steps 2) to 4) are sometimes summarised as "de-carbonisation" (see UNEP 2008 a.o.). It is important to point out that these steps should precede the compensation of emissions, a strategy that is seen as valid by the author of this article, but is fraught with a number of shortcomings, including the risk of failure. However, in many cases, carbon offsetting can deliver immediate results improving a company's climate-related performance, whereas de-carbonisation may be a longer process.[1]

---

[1]   It is not possible in the limited framework of this article to further discuss the complexities of carbon offsetting. For more details, see Strasdas 2007.

Reducing GHG emissions to zero would be the ideal goal of carbon management. This is often referred to as "carbon-neutral" or "climate-neutral". "Climate neutrality" has recently become the aim of some tourism companies and destinations, and some businesses (especially hotels) have already achieved this ambition.[2] The term itself can be questioned in that it is close to impossible not to produce any GHG emissions unless a tourism organisation's entire operations can be fuelled by renewable energy sources. However, if de-carbonisation is combined with carbon offsetting, remaining emissions can credibly be *compensated* (not really "neutralised"; see discussion by Gössling 2009b) by using high-quality offset projects that follow key sustainability criteria such as additionality and permanence (Strasdas 2007).

Carbon management can be implemented by a combination of strategies or tools:

- **Techn(olog)ical** (e.g. combustion technology, insulation of pipes/buildings, heat recovery, renewable energies, automated systems in guest rooms)

- **Managerial** (optimising logistics or processes, staff management, customer information, traffic management, purchasing, etc.)

- **Modal shift** (shifting tourist mobility from more energy-intensive to less energy-intensive modes of transport, i.e. away from automobiles and aeroplanes to trains, busses and muscle-powered vehicles)

- **Behavioural** changes and development of corresponding travel **products** that are less energy-intensive (especially increased length of stay in exchange for fewer trips and preference of nearby destinations with less energy consumption per day of travel)

- Giving preference to domestic and nearby regional **source markets** over long-haul markets

- Applying principles of **social marketing** as a tool to instigate behavioural change and sell climate-friendly travel products

- Using **carbon labelling** as a communication and management tool

- On the **policy** level: use of different instruments such as **regulation** (emissions taxes, cap-and-trade systems, building regulations, emission standards for vehicles, etc.), financial **incentives** (e.g. for investments into energy efficiency and renewable energies) and more **investments** into climate-friendly public infrastructure (railways, bike paths, etc.).

(Peeters et al. 2009, Strasdas 2007)

---

[2] For an analysis of climate-neutral tourism products, companies and destinations in the German-speaking countries, see Rumpelt, S.: Master thesis in Sustainable Tourism Management, Eberswalde University of Applied Sciences (upcoming).

In light of the enormous emission reductions that need to be realised in order to stabilise global warming at manageable levels, a combination of measures will be necessary. Many tourism companies already implement technological and managerial emission reduction measures to increase energy efficiency because it is in their immediate interest (cost saving) to do so. But this usually serves to perpetuate the status quo or to work within the tourism system as we know it today. There are also technological limitations that have to be taken into account. This is particularly the case in the aviation sector where fuel efficiency gains have been outpaced by the quantitative growth of the industry. The only way to solve this problem technologically would be to switch to non-fossil fuels. While the use of renewable energy sources is on the rise in the accommodation sector (even though significant investment barriers due to high initial costs remain) and improved fuel efficiency may be expected in the automobile industry in the coming years, this prospect is still decades away in the aviation sector (ibid.). Therefore, structural changes in terms of travel behaviour, products offered and markets targeted are also needed. It is estimated that a combination of modal shift, increased length of stay and more frequent selection of nearby holiday destinations can achieve emission reductions of as much as 44% compared to the business-as-usual scenario (UNWTO/UNEP 2008).

However, in the absence of coherent international regulation, it is also clear that individual companies can influence stakeholders and structures around them only to a limited degree. Modal shift, for instance, only works for nearby or mid-range destinations and would require substantial investments into infrastructure, especially high-speed railways – something that has been neglected for decades outside of Western Europe and Japan. On the other hand, tourism companies (especially the larger ones with their enormous marketing budgets and bargaining powers) do have the power to influence their suppliers and customers to be more climate-friendly.

3   Carbon Management: Case Studies

In the panel discussion at the ITB 2009 Convention good-practice examples from four different tourism sub-sectors were presented:

- Aviation (Finn Air)
- Large-scale accommodation (Scandic Hotels)
- Tour Operators (Intrepid Travel, Australia)
- Destinations (Caribbean Community – CARICOM).

All three invited companies have implemented a comprehensive carbon management system and achieved more or less substantial GHG emission reductions.

They can therefore be regarded as "front runners" in their respective sub-sectors, although their selection was not based on a systematic benchmarking process, but rather on the organisers' intimate knowledge of climate change mitigation activities in the tourism industry. This is not to say that there are no other companies with similar commitment and achievements. In fact, several smaller tourism companies (often individual hotels and special-interest tour operators) are more advanced and have already achieved carbon-neutrality. However, it is recognized that carbon management is more of a challenge for international airlines, hotel chains and long-haul tour operators.

The example of CARICOM is even more complex because in this case an entire region, which in addition is almost exclusively dependent on air transport, strives to become climate-neutral. This is extremely ambitious on the one hand, but currently not more than a project on the other hand. Carbon management in the Caribbean is incipient at best.

Finally, it should be noted that the following case studies are not the result of an in-depth analysis, but rather based on the ITB presentations of the respective company representatives and additional information also provided by the companies themselves.

3.1   Finn Air[3]

Finn Air is a medium-sized airline that has 66 aircraft and transports about nine million passengers annually, with a strong focus on traffic between Europe and Asia. The company presents itself as cost-efficient and economically healthy compared to their competitors. It also sees itself as a "responsible world citizen", emphasizing quality and striving to become the "airline of choice for ... environmentally conscious travellers in intercontinental travel in the Northern Hemisphere".

Finn Air's environmental strategy is based on four pillars: technology, operations, economic measures and infrastructure. On the technological level, Finn Air has begun to renew its fleet. Its European fleet is less than five years old on average. For long-haul the company's old MD 11 aeroplanes are to be replaced by more fuel-efficient Airbus aircraft by 2010, with expected fuel efficiency gains of up to 30% per seat. The addition of winglets and slimmer seats further decreases fuel consumption. Operational reduction measures include frequent washing of engines to increase efficiency as well as reducing the weight of service elements and equipment onboard.

One of Finn Air's biggest environmental assets is the location of its hub in Helsinki. An uncongested airport reduces holding times and extended taxiing, thus lowering fuel consumption. The airport also facilitates a more fuel-efficient Continuous Descent Approach (CDA). Furthermore, Helsinki is on the most direct flight route from Europe to Eastern Asia. In addition, a stopover in the Finnish

---

[3]   The following statements are based on the ITB 2009 presentation by Kati Ihamäki, in charge of environmental management at Finn Air.

capital reduces the amount of fuel that the aircraft has to carry. It is expected that the creation of a Single European Sky will further decrease emissions.

Finn Air has an emissions calculator on its website, which is based on actual fuel consumption and load factor. Apart from CO_2, the airline's calculator also includes NO_x emissions, but does not offer its passengers the opportunity to offset their personal flight. Instead, the company has supported the introduction of the European ETS for aviation and is now actively engaged in a group of airlines, the Aviation Global Deal Group, that advocates the inclusion of all international aviation in the Kyoto Protocol with reduction targets ranging from 0-20% by 2020 and 50-80% by 2050 (Lyle 2009).

3.2   Scandic Hotels[4]

Scandic operates about 150 hotels and claims to be one of Europe's biggest hotel chains. The company has about 6,500 employees and an annual turnover of EUR 850 million. In 1994 Scandic Hotels created an environmental policy and pledged to contribute to a sustainable society, which it considers a prerequisite for successful business. Energy and carbon management are essential elements of the company's environmental strategy. Scandic plans to reduce GHG emissions by 25% by 2020 (compared to 1990 levels), even though business volume is expected to quadruple during the same period.

Energy savings already start with building design and construction as well as the purchase of furniture and appliances. For this purpose, Scandic has developed its own "Environmental refurbishment, equipment and construction standard". Measures to improve carbon efficiency on the operational level include automated energy control in guest rooms, the use of low-energy light bulbs, reduced food miles in hotel restaurants and fuel-efficient company vehicles. Switching to renewable energy sources is another cornerstone of the company.

Environmental certification is important for Scandic Hotels: 110 of its 150 properties are certified by either the Scandinavian "Nordic Swan" eco-label or by the "EU Flower" outside of Scandinavia. Both certification schemes require high environmental standards and include credible verification procedures.

In 1996 Scandic began to systematically measure, report and monitor key environmental performance indicators in all of its properties, including energy consumption and CO_2 emissions (overall and per guest night). The company claims to be the first hotel chain in the world to introduce and monitor the CO_2 indicator throughout its operations and to publish the results on its website. Scandic's aim is to become carbon-neutral by 2025 for its direct activities. However, the company's environmental engagement extends beyond immediate hotel operations to include their own business travel, staff commuting, suppliers and guest mobility.

---

[4]   If not indicated otherwise, the following statements are based on the ITB 2009 presentation by Stephan Stahl, Scandic's vice-president of sales, and information provided on Scandic Hotels' website, www.scandic.com.

According to Scandic's "Environmental Live Reports", energy consumption per guest night was close to 39.81 kWh in 2008, down from 52.87 kWh in 1996, a reduction of 25%. This is well below the Green Globe 21 benchmark of 133 kWh, and still below the *Energiekampagne Gastgewerbe*[5] benchmark of 40 kWh, but not as good as one of the most energy-efficient hotels in the world, the Best Western Hotel Victoria in Freiburg/Germany, a four-stars, privately owned city hotel with 63 rooms, which (according to its own website) consumes only 30 kWh per guest night on average, apart from being climate-neutral for its extensive use of renewable energies. Nevertheless, Scandic Hotels' results in terms of energy management are remarkable for a hotel chain which has to operate under different local circumstances, not all of which are conducive to environmental protection.

CO_2 emissions at Scandic have decreased even further than energy consumption: down from 4.5 kg per guest night in 1996 to 2.8 kg in 2008 – a reduction of 39%. However, the level of CO_2 emissions was already lower in 2000, sharply grew in 2001 and subsequently decreased only slightly. No explanation for this is given in the environmental report. A possible explanation may be that for Scandic's facilities in Sweden and Norway electricity is completely purchased from renewable sources. This is not yet possible in other countries that the company operates in.

3.3   Intrepid Travel[6]

Founded in 1989, Intrepid Travel of Australia has expanded from a small company to a mid-sized tour operator catering to about 80,000 customers nowadays. With offices in the United Kingdom and North America and several incoming representations in its major destinations Intrepid Travel is still an individually owned company. It offers small-group travel (average of 10 persons per group) with a focus on cultural "immersion" and nature-based activities. The average age of customers is 35 years.

Responsible travel and sustainability are among Intrepid's core values. Furthermore the company recognizes tourism's important contribution to global warming, particularly since most of Intrepid's trips are long-haul. Carbon management is a central part of this endeavour. The company employs a full-time responsible tourism manager since 2000 and a carbon-offset manager since 2007. Carbon management covers three levels of the company's operations: corporate operations, Intrepid's package tours (which usually do not include international flights), and flights taken by customers, some of which are sold by Intrepid Travel itself.

---

[5]   An online energy measurement and benchmarking tool for the hospitality sector provided for free by the German federal Agency of the Environment (*Umweltbundesamt*) and the German Hospitality Federation (*Dehoga*).

[6]   The following statements are based on the ITB 2008 presentation given by Nari Blackett, IntrepidTravel's European sales coordinator, and the ITB 2009 presentation by Robyn Nixon, Global sales and marketing manager of Intrepid Travel, as well as on Intrepid Travel's "Carbon offset media kit".

For all three operational levels, the company largely follows the carbon management steps outlined in the previous chapter: Measure – Avoid – Reduce – Offset – Communicate.

For internal operations electricity and other energy uses at the offices (heating/cooling, lighting, printing, computers, etc.) are systematically measured, along with business trips taken by staff. Energy audits are conducted on a regular basis. Mitigation strategies include energy efficiency measures in the offices, avoiding unnecessary business trips and switching to more environmentally friendly modes of transportation, if possible. Remaining emissions (1,200 t of CO_2-e in fiscal year 2007/08) are completely compensated by Intrepid's offset partner agencies, investing into verified renewable energy, energy efficiency and sequestration projects in Australia, India, China and Peru. However, corporate operations produce less than 1% of the company's overall emissions. Flights taken by Intrepid customers in 2006 produced an estimated 300,000 t of CO_2-e.

The second important field of operations are Intrepid's package trips on the destination level. Emissions are substantially reduced by using ground transport or even public transportation, whenever reasonably feasible. Intrepid also prefers simpler, locally run hotels which tend to use fans or natural ventilation instead of airconditioning (the source of over 50% of energy consumption in upscale hotels in the tropics[7]) as well as locally grown food, thus reducing "food miles". In 38 out of its 459 trips, Intrepid measures and then offsets all of the emissions thus produced. Offset costs are minimal at not more than AUD 1.50 per person/day. Intrepid Travel pre-purchases the corresponding amount o carbon credits and then incorporates them in the package prices of these so-called "offset trips" which are especially advertised in the company's catalogue.

The most important contribution to climate protection, reducing and offsetting flight emissions, has turned out to be difficult. Intrepid's average trip length is 14.08 days (2007), up from 13.32 days in 2006. 14 days is the minimum length of stay for long-haul trips in *forum anders reisen*'s code of conduct.[8] It is not known whether the company has intentionally attempted to increase length of stay in its packages. Its travel catalogue includes an 84-days "epic low-carbon adventure" from Singapore to St. Petersburg by ground transport only. Still, according to their own measurements, almost 97% of overall trip emissions accrue to transportation alone. In January 2007 Intrepid started to incorporate offset costs into all the flights departing from Australia and sold by the company itself. As a result sales dropped initially, but recovered in the course of the first year. In 2007, 18,700 tons of CO_2-e emissions were compensated. In 2008, this figure rose to 23,500 t. It is not clear whether non-CO_2 emissions of aircraft have been taken into account.

Intrepid Travel has pledged to become carbon-neutral by 2010 for its internal management and all trips and flights it sells. It is hoped that customers will in-

---

[7]   Becken/Hay 2007.

[8]   *Forum anders reisen* (www.forumandersreisen.de) is an association of special-interest German tour operators committed to sustainable tourism.

creasingly compensate flights not purchased through Intrepid. So far, Intrepid's exemplary carbon management policy has paid off. A survey conducted among customers in 2006 revealed that the company's efforts to reduce its environmental and climate footprint are highly appreciated by an overwhelming majority of travellers, many of whom showed a high level of awareness and a certain willingness to act in relation to climate change.

3.4   Caribbean Community (CARICOM)[9]

Several tourism destinations (including Costa Rica, Sri Lanka and the Maldives) have announced that they are planning to become carbon-neutral, usually as a reaction to concerns that in the future long-haul holidays may be shunned by climate-conscious vacationers, or that they might fall victim to international aviation regulations aiming to mitigate climate change. CARICOM has been of the first to react by pointing out the region's achievements in terms of sustainable tourism. In reality, however, while contributing less than 1% to the man-made greenhouse effect, the Caribbean may be one of the most energy-intensive tourism destinations in the world, in view of its almost complete reliance on flight as the mode of transportation and the important role of cruise tourism in the region. Apart from regulatory and reputational risks, the Caribbean is also believed to be particularly vulnerable to the direct impacts of climate change (storms, sea level rise, coral bleaching and higher incidence of tropical diseases). Climate change mitigation is therefore in the long-term interest of the region and can also be seen as a "smart" adaptation strategy to the impacts of global warming.

The ensuing CARIBSAVE Project aims to enhance the resilience of Caribbean economies and livelihoods towards climate change. Becoming the "world's first carbon-neutral tourism region" is one of the cornerstones of this strategy, using three destinations (Bahamas, Belize, Turks and Caicos) as the first model countries. Initially, it appeared that CARICOM intended to "jump" directly to the carbon-offsetting without paying much attention to the prior de-carbonisation steps. Furthermore, it is not yet clear how carbon-neutrality is to be achieved. This criticism also applies to most other destinations who have announced to become carbon-neutral.[10]

In order to remedy these inherent problems, a research project and feasibility study is being prepared which will look at the following options:

- Introduction of a carbon levy on flights to the Caribbean which will supposedly be paid into a Carbon Trust Fund to be administered by the Interamerican Development Bank

- Survey of acceptance of this levy by foreign tourists

---

[9] The following statements are based on the ITB 2009 presentation by Murray Simpson, Senior research associate at the Oxford University Centre for the Environment.

[10] For an in-depth, critical discussion on carbon-neutral destinations, see Gössling 2009b.

- Use of the Carbon Trust Fund to enhance adaptive capacities and speed up the introduction of climate friendly technologies. Energy costs are already high due to the need to import fossil fuels and limited economies of scale in small island states.

- Analysis of technologies that are appropriate for the specific needs of small islands

- Capacity building and creation of an auditing and certification system for carbon management in hotels and other destination-based facilities.

4   Conclusions

The case studies featured above show that substantial GHG emission reductions through systematic carbon management can be achieved, even within a prevailing socio-economic and political environment which does not directly reward voluntary mitigation efforts. It has also been demonstrated that several co-benefits of carbon management (cost savings, process optimisation, enhanced product quality, improved public image, catering to climate-conscious demand segments) are already tangible now. Finn Air and Scandic Hotels also cover more mainstream market segments, thus contributing to mainstreaming carbon management. All three companies portrayed here are economically highly successful, showing that climate protection and economic objectives do not necessarily contradict each other. In addition, early action and adaptation may improve preparedness to climate change risks that are looming on the horizon.

However, even more uncompromising action and more widespread dissemination of carbon management practice in the tourism industry are needed in order to avoid global warming levels with disastrous consequences. This can only be achieved by a worldwide regulatory framework which will create equal conditions for all players in the market place. At the same time climate protection policies would grant an advantage to smart early adapters – such as the ones presented at the 2009 ITB Convention.

References

Becken, S. & J. Hay (2007): Tourism and Climate Change – Risks and Opportunities. Channel View Publications, Clevedon

Gössling, S. (2009a): Carbon-smart Tourism – Reducing vulnerability, increasing profits. Presentation at the ITB 2009 Convention, March13, 2009

Gössling, S. (2009b): Carbon-neutral destinations: a conceptual analysis. Journal of Sustainable Tourism, Vol. 17, No. 1, January 2009, 17-37

Lyle, C. (2009): The control of aviation emissions reaches a critical juncture as Copenhagen draws near. www.airtransporteconomics.ca

Peeters, P., S. Gössling & B. Lane (2009): Moving towards Low-Carbon Tourism – New Opportunities for Destinations and Tour Operators. *In*: Gössling/Hall/Weaver 2009, 240-257

Stock, M. (2009): Tourism and Climate Change – A state-of-the-art overview. Lecture given at Eberswalde University of Applied Sciences, June 15, 2009

Strasdas, W. (2007): Voluntary Offsetting of Flight Emissions – An effective way to mitigate the environmental impacts of long-haul tourism? Publ. in German *in*: Egger, R. & T. Herdin (2007): Tourismus – Herausforderung Zukunft. Lit Verlag, Berlin/Wien

Umweltbundesamt (UBA)/Öko-Institut (2002): Umwelt und Tourismus – Daten, Fakten, Perspektiven. Erich Schmidt Verlag, Berlin

United Nations Environment Programme (UNEP) (2008): Climate Change Adaptation and Mitigation in the Tourism Sector – Frameworks, Tools and Practices. Paris

World Resources Institute (WRI) (2005): Navigating the Numbers – Greenhouse Gas Data and International Climate Policy. www.wri.org

World Tourism Organization (UNWTO) and United Nations Environment Programme (UNEP) (2008): Climate Change and Tourism – Responding to Global Challenges

ITB Business Travel Day: Where the Journey Is Taking Us – Major Challenges for Aviation in 2009

Keynote Speech of Joachim Hunold

Right from the start, the history of civil aviation has always faced challenges because of its very considerable dependence on external conditions over which it has little influence. The industry is particularly susceptible to strong political influence and to cross-influence from other economic sectors, whether in terms of the framework conditions associated with individual airports, or in terms of the increase in fuel prices, an increase that is partially driven by speculation.

If we look at recent growth forecasts for air traffic focusing on the time bar from 2007 to 2013, we can see that in 2007 the average expected growth was 3 to 4 per cent. The aviation experts, whether at Boeing, Airbus or ICAO, were all agreed in their analyses. Some of them even forecast growth of up to 4.9 per cent. However, these forecasts have changed rapidly over the past year. The key factor, to which I will return later, was the above-average increase in the price of fuel that directly confronted the aviation industry. The airlines had made different preparations for such an eventuality: Air Berlin had implemented a hedging policy to cover a large proportion of its fuel requirements, while many competitors handled the situation in other ways. Nevertheless, they all have one common element: the increase in the price of fuel resulted in a dramatic decline in passenger growth. This was further exacerbated by the global financial crisis that had been triggered by the financial sector. The figures published by the ADV (Association of German Civil Airports) clearly reflect the rapid decline in passenger growth from November of last year, which until then had looked rather healthy. And if we examine the current ADV forecasts for this year, we can see that the Association expects a 3 per cent decline.

However, airlines continue to be severely affected by the fact that the initial fuel crisis in which the aviation industry was suddenly caught up was then overtaken by the banking crisis. And this banking crisis has had major repercussions as far as aviation is concerned. A striking example illustrates just how near international civil aviation came to a collapse in the global economy. The US government had to rescue AIG, the world's largest insurance company (and consequently also the largest reinsurer for the global airline industry). If AIG had collapsed, airlines in particular would no longer have had any insurance cover. As a result, civil avia-

R. Conrady and M. Buck (eds.), *Trends and Issues in Global Tourism 2010*,
Trends and Issues in Global Tourism, DOI 10.1007/978-3-642-10829-7_9,
© Springer-Verlag Berlin Heidelberg 2010

tion found itself – very nearly – in a situation where insurance companies world-wide were simply unwilling to carry the risks, as was the case after the attacks of 9/11. At that time Air Berlin and other German airlines received government backing for their liability, without which they could not have obtained any insurance cover. If this had not been done, passenger aircraft all over the world would have been grounded. Air traffic as a whole would have been paralysed. But that situation, thank God, was averted.

And yet the financing situation for the airline industry has not undergone any major change. In fact, banks are continuing to withhold funds, despite the provision of government guarantees. Companies operating in a capital-intensive market, and this applies to the airline industry, are essentially dependent on banks. Today, unfortunately, it is extremely difficult to obtain any funding – unless a company has already made long-term financing arrangements. Naturally this also affects sectors such as aviation.

1   The Financial Crisis Was Followed by a Change in Travel Behaviour

If we again look at the changes affecting airports in Germany, we can see how quickly the economy adjusted in response to this, let us say, degressive behaviour – or what was practically an economic collapse. Of course this led to tumbling profits among IATA companies and to rapid changes, especially in the business travel segment. If we consider the analysis of a survey conducted by the VDR[1] among its members in October 08 and January 09, we can identify significant changes in travel behaviour, even in this short three-month period. While in October 2008 49 per cent answered "No" to the question "Has the financial crisis affected travel behaviour in your company?", that number had dropped to just 22 per cent in January 2009. This question alone is a clear indicator of the extent to which the economic crisis also influences or adversely affects air traffic.

Here are a few figures to give you an idea of how closely the aviation industry in Germany is tied in to the economic climate and the orders of magnitude involved: The aviation industry in Europe accounts for 4 per cent of the EU's GNP[2], which equates to 4 per cent of the total working population or around 8 million jobs, making a contribution of approx. 220 billion euros to GNP. If, in addition to these direct jobs or their GNP equivalent, we also consider the sectors or industries indirectly associated with the aviation industry, we obtain a total that corresponds to 11 per cent of GNP in the EU, or 12 per cent of the entire working population, i.e. 24 million jobs or 4000 jobs per million passengers.

---

[1]   Verband Deutsches Reisemanagement e.V. / Association of German Travel Management, N = 199.

[2]   Gross national product.

So overall we are talking about an economic output that accounts for around 820 billion euros of GNP.

As I mentioned earlier, the price of aviation fuel has an enormous effect on the airline industry. In particular it strongly influences the pricing of fares, because fuel costs today are already the most significant cost factor of an airline, even exceeding personnel costs. The longer the route, therefore, the higher the fare – on account of its dependence on the current price of fuel. At the same time we need to consider that price sensitivity decreases massively and disproportionately as fuel prices rise. In July 2008 we were facing a price level of 147 dollars a barrel. The airlines carried out various calculations in line with their cost structures in order to determine which capacity, at which fuel price, was still a feasible marketing option. The response of many airlines to the dramatic increase in fuel prices, and particularly in view of the forecast of further increases, was to hedge a greater portion of their fuel requirements.

2   Fuel Hedging at a Price

This forecasting in particular – and finding an appropriate response – is of course a vital aspect as far as our industry is concerned: What is my assessment of the market, how do I arrange hedging, if at all, or how can I obtain funding lines from banks. This affects every airline worldwide. The fuel price did drop again in December of last year, but since most airlines had hedged at a higher level, we will still be operating with a relatively high cost structure for some months to come – due to hedging fuel costs. Of course the situation varies from one airline to another. At present we anticipate that the fuel price will be relatively stable this year. However, we must also consider that global fuel resources are limited. Even if we are now experiencing a short period of recovery, it is still likely that this recovery will not be long-lived and that it will not be sustained.

The rapid and enormous increase in fuel prices and the subsequent economic crisis have hit the airline industry hard and have also resulted in a considerable number of airline insolvencies. It appears that more than 60 airlines worldwide, including major names in Europe, such as Futura or Sterling, have ceased trading since 2007.

Other airlines throughout the world have also reduced capacities. If we compare the winter of 2008/2009 with the winter of 2007/2008, then the flight capacity has decreased by 3.5 per cent, seating capacity by 1.9 per cent and the available seat miles by 1.1 per cent. As regards the planning position for the winter of 08/09 in Germany, the number of flights alone has decreased by around 6.5 per cent in comparison with the winter of 07/08. Of course these figures are subject to further monthly capacity planning adjustment and the strategies/reactions in light of the current global economic crisis are different for each individual airline.

I would now like to mention a few details regarding the policy that Air Berlin has adopted. Our business model differs a little from that employed by the majority of our competitors. We cannot claim that our business model is unique, but it is definitely one of Air Berlin's USPs that we provide services for a range of business areas. Air Berlin started off in tourism, then concentrated on scheduled services as a second pillar, which contributed greatly to our growth. Air Berlin has also implemented a strategic expansion of its scheduled operations, despite the cost trend and despite the reduction in capacities, primarily with regard to German domestic routes and the business travel segment. And this is also one of the key elements as far as our future planning or development is concerned: Will business travellers still be prepared to fly in future, or do we have to offer a certain price-performance ratio to retain business travellers – and ensure their loyalty?

If we look at the current economic situation and the analysis of how individual companies operating in the aviation industry are positioning themselves or competing in that market, then it is of course also important to look at the results and how they were achieved. When comparing the individual airlines' quarterly results, we can see that we have succeeded in taking up a good position in the market, an achievement that is due to Air Berlin reacting relatively quickly to the fuel crisis by reducing capacities and concentrating on profitable routes. As a consequence Air Berlin reported one of the best EBIT margins among international airlines for the 3rd quarter in 2008.

3   Sustainability in Aviation

When we talk about the framework conditions and the challenges facing aviation, then energy policy naturally plays an important part as well, as it will continue to exert great influence on aviation in the future. Of course there will be some lasting effects on demand in the aviation industry if airlines are to be burdened with the not inconsiderable additional costs under the emissions trading scheme. In this context we should not forget that aviation accounts for only 2 to 3 per cent of CO_2 emissions worldwide, and that aviation technology has also undergone constant development over the years, which means modern aircraft consume 70 per cent less fuel than around 40 years ago. I firmly believe that this is an enormous technological advance which the airline industry has achieved, and one that should not be played down. Let us compare, for instance, the CO_2 emissions of energy production and the CO_2 emissions of aircraft: a typical coal-fired power station generates around 20 million tons of CO_2 emissions per year. A single-aisle aircraft such as the Airbus A320 or the Boeing 737-800 produces 21,000 tons CO_2 per year. That is the equivalent of 2.5 tons of kerosene per hour. If we base our assumptions on standard scheduled flight operations, this equates to about 2700 block hours per year, which gives us a figure of 225 hours a month or 7.5 hours per day. At a conversion factor of 3.15 for kerosene consumption to CO_2 emissions, we find that a single lignite-fired power station emits as much CO_2 as 950 medium-range aircraft.

4   "Four-Pillar Strategy" for Reducing CO_2 Emissions

Aviation and environment, is that a contradiction? No. At Air Berlin we have developed a "four-pillar strategy" with the aim of reducing CO_2 emissions. First of all this involves operational measures with a fuel-saving programme based on technological progress, and in this respect we are dependent on the industry that develops new engine technologies. Then the infrastructure, especially at airports, is a key element, as is the Single European Sky, something that the industry has long demanded but that, for some considerable time now, has failed to be implemented.

And the Single European Sky should be introduced before politicians and the public start talking about emissions trading, because this measure delivers much more in terms of immediate and concrete CO_2 reductions than any possible emissions trading scheme restricted to the EU area. Furthermore, the latter solution also results in discrimination against European airlines, compared with competitors from non-EU countries.

Of course we do not want to deny that economic instruments are also important, and that they can be useful regulatory measures for reducing aircraft emissions. And then there is emissions trading. We are not arguing against such a scheme, provided that it does not result in distorting competition.

Air Berlin's aim for 2009 is to save around 32 tons in carbon trading this year. This corresponds to the CO_2 emissions of an Airbus A330 on 225 flights from Düsseldorf to New York. Air Berlin was a driving force behind persuading Boeing to fit winglets to their 737s. This led to a serious internal struggle at Boeing, which I was able to follow.

5   How Did the Wings Get Their Winglets?

Because all the executive jets have these little winglets, Air Berlin wanted to have some on its 737s as well. That is not a fairytale, it is fact. This led to an internal dispute among Boeing engineers who said that it was absolute nonsense. At least, that was the opinion of the established experts. But Boeing's Business Jet Unit came along and said they would check with their old engineers – and so they used a computer to generate a program that showed how winglets could in fact be fitted to the wings. Of course the established Boeing engineers resisted such a move. But even at that stage, we at Air Berlin felt it was important to insist on having the 737 with winglets. And then Air Berlin was the first airline that had winglets on its aircraft, simply because we had already foreseen the rise in fuel prices and the shortage in resources over the coming years.

This anecdote teaches us that it is sometimes necessary to exert a lot of pressure on the manufacturer to obtain innovations in the technical sector. That is why we still think about minor details at Air Berlin, so that we can reduce costs.

One of these minor details, for instance, is the electronic flight bag, also known as a paperless cockpit. In 2008 this meant a saving of 1150 tons in fuel for Air Berlin alone, and consequently we are also the first airline worldwide to operate a commercial 737 fleet without paper charts. The weight saved by this measure alone means that the aircraft uses less fuel, thereby reducing its CO_2 emissions as well. In terms of weight, our paperless cockpit will mean a saving of 6 million sheets or 28 tons in 2010. Then we turned our attention to the entire load carried by our aircraft. We stripped the aircraft down to its bare envelope and looked at what we really needed on board for a long-haul flight. After all, the tendency is always to carry much more on board than is strictly necessary to meet any passenger request. But here too we have a lot of experience regarding passenger behaviour, and this can help us to optimise the load. So we gradually put all routes to the test and finally managed to save up to 400 kg per aircraft. This again allowed us to reduce CO_2 emissions by 1.7 tons on a long-haul flight.

Another area where we can reduce fuel consumption and CO_2 emissions is the approach procedure. By implementing a continuous descent, we can achieve reductions of 37 per cent, although another major benefit is the noise reduction, which is of not inconsiderable significance when approaching an airport located near a city centre.

6   Minor Causes – Major Savings

The fuel policy of airlines will become increasingly important. After all, since resources are scarce, the price of fuel will rise again. Today no airline can avoid defining a fuel conservation programme to keep its cost structure down and to ensure the sustainability of its passenger stream in the aircraft. Of course these are small details that we have been working on at Air Berlin, but it is those very details, such as rethinking our loading concept and achieving savings of about 400 kg per long-range aircraft in 2008, that make a noticeable difference when it comes to the big picture. There is still some potential for improvement and the industry continues to achieve reductions, but of course it is more difficult to combat the framework conditions. That is why we have to rely on technological progress and investment in research programmes so that we can achieve still greater efficiencies. This is a key element in terms of the development of aviation for the future.

Let us now consider the Single European Sky (SES). It is absurd that in Europe we currently have more than 30 air traffic control centres, while in the US, if you are flying from New York to Los Angeles for instance, your flight will be handled by just one control centre, because the entire US airspace is monitored from a central location. We estimate that the SES will result in savings of around 4 billion euros per annum, as well as a 12 per cent annual saving in fuel, along with reduced CO_2 emissions. This shows that the aviation industry is also prepared to make a contribution in ecological terms. But in this respect we are subject to the framework conditions and there are political obstacles that we have to overcome. Consequently a unified airspace in Europe is a very significant development that we demand from politicians today.

Another important economic factor for the aviation industry is the emissions trading scheme, which will be introduced in 2012. In its current form the emissions trading scheme would place a burden of about 1 to 2.5 billion euros per year on the airline industry in Europe. That corresponds to a very high percentage, given the margins with which airlines currently operate. We are in favour of the emissions trading scheme – but it must be introduced as a global measure. It is also important in this context that, logically, the emissions trading scheme should not be applied until we have a Single European Sky.

ITB Aviation Day: Environmental Sustainability in Aviation – Bio Fuel Technologies at Air New Zealand

Keynote Speech of Edward Sims

Let me tell you one important point about your speaker today … I am a polluter.

I am the senior person accountable for a jet fleet that burns the equivalent of two swimming pools of Jet A-1 every hour of every day. When you know that this is your responsibility, you have the urgency and the authority to do something about it.

Air New Zealand has two primary spokespeople on the environment – myself and our Chief Pilot, Captain David Morgan. Between us, we manage most of the airline's emissions – and have the mandate to do something about it. Airlines appointing an 'Environmental Manager" have awareness without commitment – they know what they **need** to do but don't always have the ability to do it.

Things are different at Air New Zealand. I have flown from one of the world's most far-flung nations. I couldn't have made this journey by train or ship.

However, I'm acutely aware that for me to be here today, I've created a personal carbon footprint of 4.2 tonnes of CO_2 – a footprint calculated to cost €56 to offset. Managing my carbon footprint is important to me and the 2.5 million visitors to New Zealand every year. We can't afford our customers to think like the journalist who asked me recently "surely flying to NZ is like driving to a Greenpeace rally in a Hummer?"

How will we keep them coming in an era of heightened environmental concern is not a fad or an altruistic cause – it's a commercial imperative – for the carrier, for the country.

Seventy percent of New Zealand's native bird life, 100% of New Zealand's amphibians and reptiles as well as two bat species are unique and indigenous to our islands – the UK by contrast has around 5 or 6 endemic species.

New Zealand's unique species and its stunning natural environment are primary drivers for our international visitors, who drive an $18 billion tourism industry. Protection is as much a commercial as a compassionate consideration …

Let's look at Daisy the cow – both of her ends produce approximately 20% of New Zealand's emissions. The agriculture sector produces 48% of all New Zealand's emissions. In an economy as dependent on primary and agricultural ex-

R. Conrady and M. Buck (eds.), *Trends and Issues in Global Tourism 2010*,
Trends and Issues in Global Tourism, DOI 10.1007/978-3-642-10829-7_10,
© Springer-Verlag Berlin Heidelberg 2010

ports, the temptation for the airline is to hide behind relativity. It's too easy to say that air travel and air freight are economic necessities. Realistically it simply increases the obligation to do something.

This is OKA – an Air NZ 777-200. Its daily operation supports 10% of New Zealand's global economic activity and 10% of our national employment. Its back end produces less than 3% of global CO_2 emissions. What is important is NOT the relativity. It is what we as an industry or as a business are prepared to do about it.

Air New Zealand's aspiration is to be the world's most environmentally sustainable airline.

We are aggressively striving to minimise our environmental impact and at what can we do to assist environmental restoration. We also see it as a strategic marketing platform which defines our brand and fits with the protection of New Zealand's most important strategic asset – our 100% purity.

We are working toward products and services which reflect the policy of reduce, reuse and recycle. Our aircraft operations will be the most visible demonstration of this for customers. But throughout the business, behind the scenes, all sorts of other activities will be – and are now – taking place.

You're entitled to be sceptical. Every airline claims to take this seriously. Every airline has a carbon offset scheme on its website. Every airline is currently contributing to an $8.1 billion forecast industry-wide loss – leading to the question of whether we can currently afford to have a conscience.

Areas like bio-fuels, as alternatives to eroding fossil fuel supplies, seemed compelling with kerosene at $150 per barrel. Maybe less so at $40?

Without question, the bio-fuel industry is at an early stage of development and lacks the infrastructure built in developed countries to support traditional fuel supplies. BUT shouldn't we be as scared of the hold that fossil fuel providers will have over this industry in 2015, 2020 as we are about the current credit crisis?

And we have made solid progress towards our aspirational environmental goal over the past decade.

Since August 2004 we have implemented fuel saving initiatives that save in excess of 100,000 tonnes of CO_2 each year. Our target is to increase the annual CO_2 savings to a minimum 130,000 tonnes by December 2010. The savings implemented to date equate to 38.4 million litres of fuel annually.

Within the past four years alone, we have instigated more than 40 projects which have had or are having a positive environmental impact.

We are prepared to take some economic risks for the sake of progress to achieve our corporate goal and to show leadership internationally. We're also prepared to speak out on environmental issues and make sure our opinion counts. We constantly balance long term strategic positions like bio-fuels versus every day improvements – the removal of over 90kg of weight on every flight we operate, the more regular washing of engine turbines that reduced drag by 1%, taxiing a 747 on two engines not four. These process changes have already reduced consumption by 40,000 tonnes of fuel, saving $36 million over four years.

We recently announced that we are fitting performance-enhancing winglets onto our five Boeing 767-300ER aircraft, which is expected to save us more than NZ$7.5 million in fuel and 16,000 tonnes of CO_2 emissions annually.

Additionally, we are retrofitting zonal dryers across four of our jet fleets to reduce fuel burn and emissions. The dryers typically remove around 200kg of water from each aircraft, which reduces fuel consumption. As a result we expect to save 1.9 million litres of fuel a year across 42 aircraft.

We have many other green initiatives underway throughout our business. These include more efficient flight planning and tracking, continuous descent profiles, more effective use of engine power in all phases of flight and greater use of electric power when aircraft are parked at the airport. We are involved in a ground-breaking initiative at San Francisco Airport to increase the efficiency of air traffic. This saved in the first six months an estimated 48,000 litres of fuel and 120 tonnes of CO_2 emissions. This programme allows our 777 aircraft to make full use of interlinked onboard and ground technology to descend into the airport, with minimal direct Air Traffic Control intervention.

One of the most recent initiatives is to fly our aircraft at slightly lesser speeds, which adds very little to flight times, but maximises our fuel resources.

Our Aspire 1 flight was designed to demonstrate the potential for the commercial aviation industry to reduce carbon emissions by millions of tonnes annually. Operated under optimum flight planning conditions through the involvement of our partners Airways New Zealand, the FAA and Airservices Australia, the flight from Auckland to San Francisco had all practical operational restraints removed.

On 30 December in Auckland we completed the world's first commercial aviation test flight powered by the sustainable second-generation bio-fuel jatropha. More than a dozen key performance tests were undertaken during the two hour test flight, with a bio-fuel blend of 50:50 jatropha and Jet A1 fuel used to power one of the Air New Zealand Boeing 747-400's Rolls-Royce RB211 engines.

We are investigating a number of potential sources of bio-fuel including Jatropha. We have been non-negotiable about the three criteria any environmentally sustainable fuel must meet for the test flight programme – social, technical and commercial. Firstly, the fuel source must be environmentally sustainable and not compete with existing food resources or forest land. Secondly, the fuel must be a drop-in replacement for traditional jet fuel and technically be at least as good as the product used today. Finally, it should be cost competitive with existing fuel supplies and be readily available.

Concurrently, we are actively exploring the potential for algae to deliver against our three criteria. We may yet find that new alternative bio-fuel sources like algae could prove more commercially viable than the second generation sources we have tested to date.

From a fleet perspective, we will soon have one of the youngest, most environmentally friendly and technologically advanced long haul fleets in the world. Our new 787s will be 20 per cent more fuel efficient than comparable aircraft today and the 777-300ERs will be around 15 per cent more fuel efficient.

We are also the launch customer for the aerodynamic enhancement package on the fleet of eight Boeing 777-200 ER aircraft. These new aircraft offer significant environmental benefits through higher fuel efficiency and reduced carbon emissions.

Our fleet of Q300s and A320s are less than four years old and our ATR aircraft are one of the most fuel efficient and environmentally friendly in their size class.

Finally, let's remind ourselves that all airlines operate in a highly regulated environment. We firmly believe that sustainability will shortly be subject to at least the same scrutiny as our operation integrity and commercial competitive environment. We firmly believe that as Governments introduce Emission Trading Schemes and carbon taxes, these should be structured to reward and recognise innovation and effort, behind sustainability. If governments are keen on 'green taxes' they should target the gas guzzlers, the binge flyers – not the customer choosing to fly on carriers staking their reputation on green credentials.

Our tourism industry needs to focus on protecting our environment – not protecting individual economies. Thank you for letting me share the view from our seat.

Digital Lifestyle and Online Travel:
Looking at the Case of Digital Natives

Urs Gasser and Miriam Simun

The integration of digital technologies into daily life is transforming human behaviour and social practices. This change has come especially quickly to many
commercial activities. The travel industry has been especially transformed. Where
once the travel agent was the chief mediator between the customer and a multitude
of travel services, travel consumers are now enabled to interact with travel services directly from the comfort of their home. With the emergence of an Internet
travel market, travel information and services have become marked by fragmentation. Further, a multitude of user-created travel information and services now
augment and compete with traditional commercial enterprises. Digital Natives –
young people who can not imagine a life without Google, Youtube and Wikipedia
– are often found at the forefront of recent transformations in the travel experience
– and therefore, the travel industry.

1   Digital Natives: Some Characteristics

Who are these Digital Natives exactly? At the Digital Natives Project we define
this cohort as a particular population of young people roughly born around 1980,
with access to digital technologies and the skills to use these technologies.[1] The
project examines the ways in which this population uses digital technology and the
impacts of their use upon society, economy, education, and law. In the following
essay we extrapolate our findings in order to understand what the implications of
the new behaviours and attitudes we found among Digital Natives are for the
travel industry. In order to understand how the travel industry will transform, we
must first understand what sets the digitally fluent travel consumer apart from
those that have come before.

Digital Natives socialize, learn, and play online. Growing up daily immersed in
the use of digital technologies, new forms of behaviours are developing. Among
the most noticeable is the often momentous multi-tasking in which young people

---

[1]   See Palfrey, John and Urs Gasser (2008). *Born Digital*, pp. 1-15.

R. Conrady and M. Buck (eds.), *Trends and Issues in Global Tourism 2010*,
Trends and Issues in Global Tourism, DOI 10.1007/978-3-642-10829-7_11,
© Springer-Verlag Berlin Heidelberg 2010

engage. A 2005 study showed that nearly one-third of young people either talk on the phone, use instant-messaging, watch TV, listen to music, or surf the Web for fun "most of the time" that they are doing homework – and the trend is growing.[2] Digital Natives are accustomed to receiving input from a number of sources and media simultaneously. More multi-tasking does not always translate into higher levels of productivity – this largely depends on the type of task at hand – but nevertheless, young people are big multi-taskers and those trying to reach this demographic must keep this in mind when creating content for Digital Natives.

Besides such more obvious patterns of behaviour, the more fundamental, almost tectonic shift occurs as we move from the paper world to the digital world, the one into which these young people are born and grow up in. This essential change is about the relationship to information: how young people relate to information, how they use information, and how they communicate information to each other. The first part of this shift occurs in the ways in which young people search for information and assess quality, methods that differ from the traditional quality evaluations of generations before. Digital Natives turn first, and often only, to the Internet when searching for all kinds of information; they largely depend on peer-networks and other forms of non-traditional expertise as their first stop in their search; and they asses the quality of information often using unreliable cues such as design issues and name recognition.[3] Faced with a virtually endless amount of information available online, Digital Natives have acquired habits – some more successful than others – of coping with information overload and finding the information they need in new ways.

The second shift occurs in the ways Digital Natives receive information – no longer passive recipients, they are increasingly creators, editors and reviewers of information. They post content online, they review products and services, and they contribute to networked collaborative projects such as Wikipedia and Fanfiction sites. Empirical research shows a growing number of Internet users, especially young Internet users, creating and posting content online. Approximately 64 percent of online teens in the United States have created some sort of content on the Internet.[4] And the phenomenon is global: In Hungary, Denmark, Iceland, Finland, Norway,

---

[2]   Kaiser Family Foundation, News Release, "Media Multi-Tasking: Changing the Amount and Nature of Young People's Media Use," March 9, 2005, http://www.kff.org/entmedia/ entmedia030905nr.cfm. See Gasser, Urs and John Palfrey, "Mastering Multitasking," Educational Leadership 66 (2009):14-19.

[3]   For more in-depth discussion of the changes in information processing see Born Digital, pp 165-169; Agosto, Denise E. "A Model of Young People's Decision-Making in Using the Web," Library and Information Science Research 24 (2002): 311–341.

[4]   See Amanda Lenhart, Mary Madden, Alexandra Rankin Macgill and Aaron Smith, "Teens and Social Media," December 19, 2007, http://www.pewinternet.org/pdfs/PIP_ Teens_Social_Media_Final.pdf, p. i. For a 2004 survey, see Amanda Lenhart and Mary Madden, "Teen Content Creators and Consumers," http://www.pewinternet.org/pdfs/PIP_ Teens_Content_Creation.pdf, p. i. (finding that 57 percent of online teens have participated in one or more content-creating activities).

Germany, Poland, and Luxembourg, for instance, a majority of young people have posted messages to chat rooms, online newsgroups, or forums.[5] About half of all Korean Internet users have created websites or blogs. In China, blogs, bulletin boards, online communities, instant messaging, and the like are on the rise.[6] While there certainly exists a participation gap among young people in terms of their levels of creative engagement online,[7] research shows that the overall growing global trend is toward more creative participation online. Around the world, Digital Natives are no longer passive consumers but are engaged in participating in the information environment in active ways.

With growing levels of creativity and sharing occurring online, Digital Natives have developed a very different understanding of what constitutes private information versus public information.[8] Travel is just one example of information that previously was considered more private, whereas now Digital Natives are posting their current locations and planned trips in very public online forums and sharing this information with large audiences. This distributed network of sharing personal information changes not only the social aspects of life, but how this population interacts with various commercial enterprises. With a sophisticated and thorough peer information network at their fingertips, young people are often relying more on their peers than on service provides or traditional sources of industry review for information about travel. Further, decisions are now made within a context of a great deal of knowledge about others in ones network: where they are, what they are doing, and what they are saying about their experiences.

So what does this all mean for the travel industry? There is little empirical data available to find a precise answer to this question, but our general findings and additional anecdotal evidence suggest a number of trends and developments that the travel industry might want to consider. In order to understand how the habits of Digital Natives effect their travel experiences, it is useful to identify the three stages of a travel experience, and understand how digital practices shape each one of these stages: First is the preparation for travel, often a fairly extensive process of using digital media to prepare for a journey in a number of different ways. Next, the journey itself is now experienced in many ways with and through a digital connection. And finally, upon return, the travel in a practiced way once the traveler has already returned home.

---

[5] Organisation for Economic Co-operation and Development (OECD), Directorate for Science, Technology and Industry, Committee for Information, Computer and Communications Policy, Working Party on the Information Economy, "Participative Web: User-Created Content," Report DSTI/ICCP/IE(2006)7/FINAL, p. 5, n. 14, http://www.oecd.org/dataoecd/57/14/38393115.pdf.

[6] Ibid., p. 11 (with references); see also "Surveying the Scenesters: China in the Web 2.0 World," *Yahoo! News,* November 20, 2007, http://news.yahoo.com/s/adweek/20071120/ad_bpiaw/surveyingthescenesterschinaintheweb20world.

[7] See the work of our colleagues Henry Jenkins and Eszter Hargittai.

[8] See Born Digital, pp. 53-82.

2   Stage 1: Preparing for Take-Off – Researching and Connecting

The ways in which young people prepare for a trip, choose destinations, select providers and carriers, and how they think about and find out about different modes of transportation is very much based on their digital social and learning practices. As Digital Natives prepare to travel, they turn to the Internet for both tools and communities to aid them in their research of where to go and the best ways to get there. This is done through tools and communities that help them find flights, hotels, and destinations, as well as more indirectly making use of user-generated content in the form of blogs, comment posts, reviews, photos and videos to learn about different places and others' travel experiences.

Aggregation tools have become vital for planning a trip. As a consumer, travel information is experienced as very fragmented: there exist a vast number of web-sites of airline carriers, hotels, travel agencies, and trip organizers. This makes it quite difficult to find out who has the best offer for the type of travel a consumer desires. Aggregation sites become very important as they offer a metasearch function that allows customers to easily compare different service providers in price as well as other categories. Digital Natives consistently turn to the Internet as their first (and often last) source of information, and they are well versed in using online tools.

And yet, commercial services are not the only place to which Digital Natives turn as they prepare for travel. The importance of user created content is a growing factor. Young people are relying ever more on information they acquire through peer networks such as Facebook or MySpace. Photos, videos, travel blogs and forum messages that friends have posted online become an important source of information. Subsequently sites like Facebook, Photobucket and YouTube become indirect sources of information when researching a destination. Peer experience becomes vital, and Digital Natives incorporate what they have learned from user created content in their online networks as they consider their future travels.

Travel preparation for Digital Natives is not only about researching and planning the trip, but also very much about connecting with people. Young people are increasingly connecting with people at their travel destinations and creating friendships before they ever leave home. LonelyPlanet, a publisher of guidebooks for low-budget travellers, hosts the popular online "Thorn Tree Forum", with an entire section devoted to "Travel Companions: Hook up and head off ..."[9] Here young people from around the world post messages about their travel desires and plans, searching for others to join them. Another kind of pre-travel connection is offered on the popular website Couchsurfing.[10] This site enables users to create profiles and search for other users that live in their destination of choice. Once

---

[9]   See http://www.lonelyplanet.com/thorntree.

[10]   See http://www.couchsurfing.com.

they have connected, users may stay with them for a night or more, meet them once they arrive, or simply learn more about the place they plan to travel. While there do exist some privacy and safety concerns involved, this site provides extensive reputation systems for users.[11] Couchsurfing has become very popular among young people (73.3% of the sites users self-report to be ages 18-29), facilitating over 1.3 million "successful surfing experiences" since its inception in 2004.[12]

3   Stage 2: I Connect, Therefore I Am – Connecting and Documenting

Connection is a central aspect of what it means to be a Digital Native. They are "constantly connected" with their friends and with information, through a variety of media platforms. This connection does not end once they depart for a travel destination – for many digital immigrants, a vacation is a time to break away, to disconnect – not so for wired youth. As they connected with others in preparation for their trip, so too do they continue to connect digitally during their travels – with contacts they made in preparation, with their friends at home, with their unchanging digital life, and with new friends they make along the way.

This constant connection while on the go offers Digital Natives a different kind of travel experience – for in connecting digitally to their lives back home, they mentally and emotionally locate themselves at home, even while physically travelling to the furthest corners of the earth. Sherry Turkle writes about this phenomenon:

> "The director of a program that places American students in Greek universities complains that they are not 'experiencing Greece' because they spend too much time online, talking with their friends from home. I am sympathetic as she speaks, thinking of the hours I spend walking with my fifteen-year old daughter on a visit to Paris as she 'texts' her friends at home on her cell phone. I worry that she is missing an experience that I cherished in my youth, the experience of an undiluted Paris that came with the thrill of disconnection from where I was from. But she is happy and tells me that keeping in touch is 'comforting' and that beyond this, her text mails to home constitute a 'diary'. She can look back at her texts and remember her state of mind at different points of her trip ... A friend calls my daughter as we prepare for dinner at out Paris hotel and asks her to lunch in Boston She says, quite simply: 'Not possible, but how

---

[11] See "Couchsurfing – Safety." Available http://www.couchsurfing.org/safety.html. Accessed July 31, 2009.

[12] "Couchsurfing- Statistics." Available http://www.couchsurfing.org/statistics.html Accessed July 31, 2009.

about Friday.' When I grew up the idea of the 'global village' was an abstraction. My daughter lives it on her cell phone. Emotionally, socially, she has not left her life in Boston."[13]

While young people's reliance on constant connection with friends may, in some ways, not always create the best structure for experiencing travel to a new place, it is a growing reality. As they live more of their social lives online and mediated through digital technologies while at home, it becomes ever easier for them to continue these social practices undisturbed irregardless of their physical locations. This new trend is an important one to consider as we think about the future of travel.

And yet, digital technologies do not only offer the traveler an ability to stay connected to home. The availability of digital tools, the growing creative tendencies amongst youth, and their habits of capturing and sharing moments of their lives enables Digital Natives to document their trips as they experience them. Websites such as travelpod, travelblog, and trekearth are exclusively devoted to hosting travelers' writings and photos, and host hundreds of thousands of users' travel documentation.[14] The digital media available to young people today makes possible a documentation process that is fast, immediately available and interactive. This allows Digital Natives to experience their travels through the documentation and sharing of their thoughts, photos and videos with others around the world. Resultantly we see the rise of travel blogs, of travel photos on Facebook and Flickr, of travel status updates and calls for travel tips, of services that track individuals' location information and connect friends that may unknowingly be in the same place. What emerges is a global culture of sharing and information, an on-the-go fluctuating network of individuals sharing and connecting both digitally and in 'real space' intermittently and without much differentiation.

4 Stage 3: Return, Review, Remix – Evaluating, Editing and Connecting (Again)

The travel experience of a Digital Native is in many ways much more integrated into their daily lives than for older generations. Young people are constantly tuned into their social worlds through digital means – and just as this translates into their taking some of their home lives with them on their journeys, it also allows young travelers to continue parts of their travel experience upon their return home. The process of experiencing through documentation, through engagement and through connection does not cease because Digital Natives have physically finished their travels.

---

[13] Turkle, Sherry. "Always-On/Always-On-You: The Tethered Self." *Handbook of Mobile Communications and Social Change*, James Katz (ed.) Cambridge, MA: MIT Press.

[14] See http://www.travelpod.com; http://www.travelblog.org; http://www.trekearth.com.

Upon their return Digital Natives engage. They add their own voice to the very information sources they used to find information for their travels; they provide feedback and write reviews of services they used, places they visited, and people they stayed with. They take part in the global conversation that is occurring online as they comment on old friends', new friends' and other travellers' blogs or social networking sites, continuously referring to each other. The interactivity continues. Once at home they have the time to edit photos and videos they may have took on their trip, re-living their experiences through this process and sharing them with the world. The connections they forged while abroad do not cease to exist as Digital Natives remain in contact with these friends on through the same digital mediums that they use to keep in touch with their friends at home.

All of these forms of engagement share some thing in common: they are permanent. Words, images and videos shared in online spaces accumulate in connection to the Digital Native. An internet search for an individual may illuminate her or his travel experiences. In this way travel becomes a sort of marker of identity. Many applications on social networking sites capitalize of this idea of travel experience as identity, enabling users to indicate information such as what cities and countries they have visited, the people they have visited or with whom they have been travelling. Through such services Digital Natives broadcast their interests and experiences, and compare them with others in their networks.

Travel looks different for a Digital Native then for those of generations prior. Digital Natives experience travel as less of a disconnection from their daily lives and more as an expansion. They begin their journeys in advance of ever leaving their desk at home and they continue them after they have returned. They use different tools to plan their travel, they are highly connected while travelling, and they continue to be creative and interactive about their experiences and with people they have met while travelling once they are home. For the travel industry this presents new possibilities to engage with consumers: a plethora of digital mediums are available to connect, to interact and to reach out to Digital Natives. Certainly aggregation and syndication tools are important technologies to understand and make use of in reaching consumers. But also the creativity of Digital Natives, and their habits of sharing and voicing their opinions offers new ways to listen and learn about the business and about the travel experience of young customers, as well as a chance to anticipate the desires of this next generation of customers. For Digital Natives the traditional mode of travel has changed, it has become more relational, more collaborative, and to certain standards more virtual and also more responsive. The travel industry has access to their customers' experiences like never before, and understanding Digital Natives as actors in collaborative travel experiences rather than simply passive consumers of travel will enable the industry to serve their customers in much better ways.

Corporate Social Responsibility

Practical Aspects of Corporate Social Responsibility – Challenges and Solutions

Aiko Bode

1 Introduction

Over 200 million people earn their livelihood from working in the area of tourism. Thus the tourism industry has become a growing and meaningful business sector and increasingly sees itself confronted with stakeholder demands and allegations of wrong-doing. It is interesting to note that a business sector that has always been a front runner in addressing global or local impacts has only recently been finding its role in the CSR debate.

As in many other economically relevant endeavours, the global financial crisis of the year 2009 has its repercussions on the growth scenarios of the industry. As a result each company and entrepreneur in the sector will need to look for the short-term economic well-being if not their very survival. However, even in a moment of crisis, the topics stakeholders and aware clients wish the tourism industry to address will not simply vanish.

When tourism became more than the individual decision of travelling to a place, booking a hotel, lodge or "bed and breakfast" in order to find recreation, relaxation or the sensual experience of a different culture or environment, tourism started to strongly impact on a variety of ecological and social factors. Formerly remote and poor villages were turned into modern megatourism sites, be it through the development of new infrastructures such as hotels, harbours or airports, or through a transition into an entirely different place from what it originally was. It seems little has been done to consider the downside effects of such fast and one-sided developments: decent waste and wastewater removal was missing, food and beverages were imported from far away places and local communities, if at all, only served as a folkloristic or service environment. Tourism, it seems, for a long time only consumed the sites it was advertising, rather than considering them as the basis for a sustainable income generation.

Despite the fact that some organisations, governments and tour operators believe in an exploitative business model, awareness among clients and affected communities has shifted the expectations that are closely linked to a more responsible way of global interconnectedness.

R. Conrady and M. Buck (eds.), *Trends and Issues in Global Tourism 2010*,
Trends and Issues in Global Tourism, DOI 10.1007/978-3-642-10829-7_12,
© Springer-Verlag Berlin Heidelberg 2010

2   CSR Challenges

Today, Corporate Social Responsibility not only is a buzzword in many business and not-for-profit communities. It has become an agenda for excellence and quality as well as a brand and image matter. CSR incorporates two major principles: the principle of voluntarism beyond legal compliance and the principle of equal consideration of environmental, social and economic aspects. CSR covers philanthropic and to a much bigger degree business-related activities, linked to all core processes and products of a company. Therefore the challenge to address CSR in the tourism industry is to look at various points along the value chain. From planning to travelling, the actual "holiday experience" as well as the after-sale care once a tourist has come back home: all these steps require very particular attention to and the observance of environmental, social and economic factors.

To give some examples and point into possible directions of consideration, responsible industry representatives and travel bureaus may wish to ask the following questions when looking at their impact:

- How is our company/ product/ service communicated to the customer: are there hidden costs, negative environmental or social impacts and how much importance do we attribute to the identified challenges?

- How far is my reach? What is the scope of the delivered service (do we assist in travel planning? Do we inform clients and staff on CSR-relevant partners/services/concerns? Do we offer services before/during and after a holiday trip?)?

- What expectations do our advertisements or descriptions raise and how do we ensure their fulfilment?

- What means of transportation do we use or offer? How do we make sure that climate concerns and overall considerations of sustainability are taken into account?

- What is the emotional side of the holiday experience? Is there a fear/expectation of rioting near tourist sites or around tourist accommodation? Or do communities, social and societal embeddings play a role?

- What is our local impact on the workforce? Are fair salaries paid? Can seasonal workers sustain their lives and those of their families?

These questions do not claim to be comprehensive but they do point out various aspects when it comes to CSR-relevant considerations: if costs of travel are not transparent and hidden costs pop up late, customers and customer-advocacy groups will begin to blame industry members publicly; customer concerns and fair business practices are increasingly considered CSR-relevant aspects which need to be attended to.

Already in the planning and booking stage a company has a good opportunity to show that it is committed to sustainability and takes on social responsibility. Even the question at what time in the day a holiday trip begins (e.g. early morning or late night family tours) may impact on the image and brand name of a company.

At the destination, embedding the holiday experience into the local community, nature and socio-cultural environment is becoming increasingly important. It is more and more a standard operating procedure to run a risk assessment before investing or getting involved in business activities. While this might be a bit of a heavy burden when it comes to the tourist industry, it can be a competitive advantage in risk-prone developing country contexts. Ideally talks with the local government and representatives, the local stakeholders and advocacy groups, environmentalists and religious or cultural leading figures take place before an investment, construction or tourist site planning is done. This is to ensure that the endeavour a company plans to undertake is well understood by all parties and that all voices and viewpoints have been heard. Only under these circumstances a transparent systematic way of investments, revenues and revenue sharing can be negotiated and eventually publicised in order to allow concerned and affected groups to find out what their benefits are and what price they have agreed to pay. It should also be considered that revenues are shared appropriately among different ethnic groups to avoid conflicts.

Apart from that, local communities should benefit from a tourist operation: by producing goods such as food, equipments for hotels, busses, local recreation tools or providing services in direct relationship with a tourist operation. They might even profit indirectly from new infrastructures and technological transfers.

However, "green field planning" will not occur too often. More likely, established destinations and structures will need to be assessed and evaluated under social, environmental and economical considerations. Conflict situations often arise when natural resources are scarce or depleted (e.g., water, waste water), pollution increases (dumps, burning of solid wastes at night etc.) and access to land or cultural sites is denied (national parks; hotel or golf course surroundings). Also, if food stuff that could be produced locally, is imported from the origin countries of the tourists, little benefits are to be expected for local communities; in fact all too often the downside effects rest with the locals.

Other challenges reside in the national variations of standards if looking at the "star"-rating of accommodation facilities: five stars in the US and five stars in the Caucasus region do differ significantly. For a transparent rating, comparable standards are called for.

To illustrate the issues at hand, a typical example for a conflict that is linked to the tourist activities can be given from Kenya in the 1990s:

The development of lodges and hotels nearby and inside the boundaries of a national park led to several disputes with local communities. Near Amboseli National Park, for instance, the water resources which were used by the local Massai community were tapped to deliver freshwater to the lodges and hotels. In order to avoid disturbances for the wildlife and reduce the risks of conflicts between the cattle farmers and the "Big Five", wild animals every tourist expects to see in Africa, traditional grazing grounds were closed since they lay within the boundaries of the park. Despite the fact that the government agreed to compensate for the losses of water, grazing ground and some infrastructural investments, the core problems were neither solved nor did the people benefit much from the growing number of tourists in the region. Subsequently, some villagers went into the park and became poachers. Also a few instances of thefts and attacks on tourists were reported.

At first sight, the situation seems to be an internal problem between the Kenyan government and the local community. However, today it should be asked what role the tourist industry played and what its contribution to the conflict or any resolution attempt was. A strategic CSR approach might have helped to identify the risks before the conflict arose. In these days the situation has been improved but several issues are still pending.

3   CSR Solutions

There is no "one-size-fits-all" solution to the challenges the tourism industry is confronted with. But there are some generic approaches that can serve as a guidance to address CSR-related topics.

First of all, risk assessment and the identification of challenges and responsibilities form the basis for a strategic CSR policy. If the impacts are analyzed properly, risks and challenges can easily be identified and ways to handle the issues be mapped out. Many major tourist operators have started to integrate sustainability into their business strategy: they identify their carbon footprint, seek stakeholder dialogues and measure their local impact; they set up environmental management systems, issue sustainability reports and demonstrate to the public how they deal with emerging or hotspot topics. While all this is part of the equation, it can only be a first step. In order to fully integrate CSR awareness into a company philosophy, it needs to become a routine in the usual core business planning and development. This requires additional considerations: clients' awareness regarding environmental and social issues is rising; however, in practice this means that they still book the "best value offers". Thus, sustainability and CSR seem to be a cost rather than a return-on-invest. Moreover, an environmentally and socially aware hotel owner, who engages in CSR matters beyond legal compliance and "normal" operational procedure or cultural habits, needs to receive recognition for doing so. In catalogues or brochures, internet offers and ads, these hotels or tourist operators should be highlighted. On the other hand, a burden sharing regarding the additional efforts is unlikely to be offered. A public-private-partnership project may cover some of the additional costs. But this will not work for an overall industry policy on CSR. A possible solution could be that it has to be defined as good industry practice and become part of an overall Code of Good Conduct for the tourist industry to commit to CSR practices and sustainability. If this is done, all companies not fulfilling these high demands which in reality would be minimum requirements will perform negatively compared to those following the trend. On the other hand, if this is going to happen, CSR and sustainability minimum requirements can no longer be unique selling points for tourist companies. Either a race to the top needs to take place or a new topic found to distinguish one company's value proposition from the others'. For the time being, an investment in sustainability and CSR practices has no short-term return on investment. Clients do recognize the efforts a company makes and select it in a preferential way. But expectations rise and one holiday experience needs to be distinguishable from others. Addressed challenges need to be followed through.

Following through requires dialogue and involvement. Dialogues are needed with clients, with stakeholders in the destinations, along the travelling routes and – in a globalized world – also on the international level. An outcome of the dialogue needs to be communicated and the decision made transparent. And all dialogue partners should feel that their concerns, expectations or questions are catered for.

In addition, pilot projects may be a solution for immediate matters and potential conflicts. They require a thorough planning and need to be goal-oriented. Companies need to prepare themselves by clearly defining what their expectations and goals are: What can be achieved with this project? Does a tangible goal exist or is the project set up to appease a certain interest group?

At times the relationship with host governments can become complicated. Often, legal frameworks are lacking or can leave room for interpretation. This may open the door to corruption and malpractices in a number of areas in which the tourist sector is exposed to or in need for a stable framework condition. Leading by example, transparency regarding the financial transactions and contracts with governments may counteract bribery and extortion and could lead to slow but detectable change in the business culture of the country. Additionally, if CSR and sustainability projects are undertaken, they may stir up discussions and initiate a change.

Public reporting is another way to "spread the word" and to upscale local projects to a global level. It shows in a comprehensive way the level of commitment and can serve as a proof documentation if stakeholders require information or seek assistance. However, public reporting does have its limits and targets of the endeavour need to be clearly identified. The effort that goes into a sustainability or CSR report should not be underestimated.

Some stakeholders are in favour of a certifiable CSR standard for the tourism industry. In fact, certification goes hand in hand with the establishment of a management system, which is the prerequisite for certification. However, only large companies in the sector will be able to take the hurdle of the organizational challenges, namely to invest sufficient resources into the establishment and sustaining of the system. Despite these concerns, establishing a management system even on a small scale generates benefits many companies may not wish to miss out on. The reason being that quick wins are even possible in a small company and may lead to significant cost-savings and process optimization. The management system – whether it is an ISO-based quality, environmental management system or else – is a value and benefit in itself. Certification is only the icing on the cake. The question, whether a sector specific standard is needed can be debated. In general terms a CSR-standard per se does not exist yet and offers in this direction are often self-made standards by special interest groups or consultants.

Of course, a CSR "label" for a successfully audited company is very tempting. However, it should be considered that many labels for ecologically, socially or ethically appropriate behaviour exist and that by adding yet another, the efforts a participant in a certification scheme has made may be watered down. It seems to be more suitable to collaborate with a reputable third party which would add value by its reputation to a certificate or auditing process.

4   TÜV Rheinland: A Partner for the Tourism Industry

TÜV Rheinland is a leading testing and inspection agency with offices in more than 60 countries and a staff of over 13.000 employees. For years TÜV Rheinland has developed several tourist-specific products together with the tourism sector and for example the WWF. A range of services is offered in the areas of

- Service quality systems
- Environmental management ("eco hotel" and ISO 14001)
- Quality management
- Certification of Wellness-, Medical Wellness and Congress Hotels
- Certified Cruise Quality in River and Ocean Cruises
- Certification of Service Quality Systems
- Security and Safety in Hotels
- Sustainability Checks
- Food and Hygiene
- Training and Education
- Counselling on CSR-related matters
- Validation of non-financial reports, such as sustainability or CSR reports
- Mystery Checks.

Since TÜV Rheinland follows a partnership concept to exactly meet the needs of the clients the company was able to carry out various tests in the tourism industry. TÜV Rheinland tested or certified more than 60 hotels around the world according to the Hotel Eco-Standard and ISO 14001. Joint projects between WWF and local hotel owners in Africa have been implemented by the company. Among the tested operations were whale watching tours and diving bases. Together with tour opera-tors and the aviation industry, experts of TÜV Rheinland are exploring new ways of avoiding CO_2 or using CO_2 offsets in a variety of projects. All these services aim to improve the CSR performance in the tourism industry.

5 Conclusion

The tourism industry is becoming an increasingly important wealth generating business sector with global reach and impact. Managing CSR issues – risks as well as opportunities – is becoming ever more important. Consumers as well as not-for profit organisations will carefully monitor the activities in the tourism industry – in particular when it comes to labour rights and the environment. Decent CSR management requires thorough consideration of and recognition by stakeholders – clients and public advocacy groups alike. Independent third parties can measure and evaluate the performance of companies against standards and industry codes and thus assist in identifying weaknesses and strengths. Through this, potentials for improvements can be leveraged and a true CSR culture developed in a busi-ness sector that like no other has a unique opportunity to turn CSR investments into win-win situations. This will benefit not only local communities, the clients and the environment but ultimately will generate sustainable income opportunities and long-lasting prosperity.

Corporate Social Responsibility – Customer Expectations and Behaviour in the Tourism Sector

Wolfgang Adlwarth

1 Introduction and Methodology

This paper presents the results of a study, describing consumer's expectations regarding Corporate Social Responsibility in tourism in connection with concrete requirements regarding tourism offers as well the actual travel behaviour. To be more specific it is about holiday travels of German tourists with at least one overnight stay in the tourism year 2007/2008.

The data for the study was collected from three different analyses; however, these have been conducted single source analyses within the same sample.

- On the basis of the continuous consumer panel Travel*Scope, holiday travels of 20,000 households are being recorded. This representative sample of panellists describes month after month its holiday travels according to a wide choice of characteristics such as destination, duration, means of transport, type of booking, etc.

- With the help of the CSR-Profiler, surveyed in the same panel, it is possible to identify personal valuations of consumers as well as subject areas where consumers expect corporate responsible behaviour of organizations.

- Furthermore the need for action and the customer's intention to pay extra charges for concrete ecologically and socially responsible aspects of tourism offers have been identified via additional interviews with the CSR interested target group.

2 Quantification and Description of CSR Interested Target Groups in the Tourism Sector

2.1 Quantification and Classification

The CSR Profiler defined those consumers as "CSR interested" who scored disproportionately high in values such as environment and climate protection, devel-

R. Conrady and M. Buck (eds.), *Trends and Issues in Global Tourism 2010*,
Trends and Issues in Global Tourism, DOI 10.1007/978-3-642-10829-7_13,
© Springer-Verlag Berlin Heidelberg 2010

opment aid, compliance with ethic standards especially human rights and social commitment for disadvantaged. Because these value orientations correlate strongly among each other, this describes a cluster of households who consider this whole value bundle to be exceptionally important.

Approx. 22.5 million households out of 35 million German households (=65%) have been travel active in the tourism year 2007/2008, which means they have been on at least one holiday trip. Those travel-active households have been analyzed with the CSR Profiler. The result showed that approx. one third can be classified as "CSR interested", which amounts to a number of 7.5 million households.

In a closer examination of these households two further subcategories can be differentiated: 3.5 millions form the **core group** of CSR interested which is 10% of all German households. 4.0 million or 12% of all German households are the so-called extended group. These are people to whom these topics are also important, however they do not show such "burning" interest like the core group.

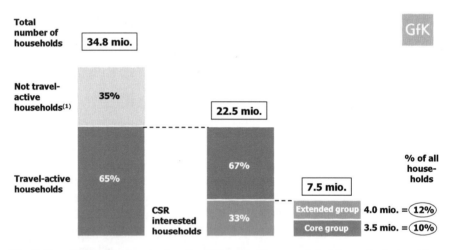

Fig. 1. Quantification: Almost every fourth household open-minded for ecological and humanitarian responsibility

[1] GfK TravelScope, 20,000 households, tourism year 2007/2008

2.2   Structure of CSR Interested

The 7.5 million CSR interested have a higher age focus: The group of people aged 60 years or older makes ca. 38% (vs. 32.8% total). Similar age focuses can also be observed in other areas of socially motivated spending behaviour. Over 50% of the revenue from donations for example is met by the generation 60plus.

On the other hand CSR interested show a more pronounced effect with high-income, well-funded households as well as a disproportionately high share in West Germany.

Altogether their structures resemble to the often described LOHAS.

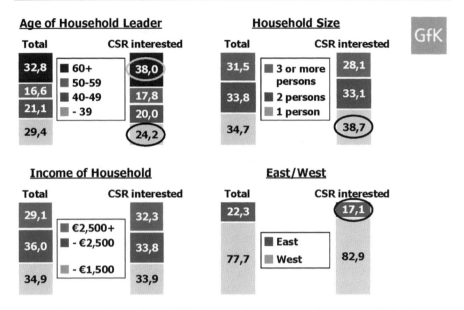

Fig. 2. Demographic profile of CSR interested target group in tourism: higher income, older and more in West Germany

2.3   Intention to Pay Extra Charges for CSR Aspects in Tourism

How does that CSR affinity result in acceptance and willingness to pay for ecological and social responsible tourism projects?

- 53% of CSR interested travellers—which is almost twice as much as with the remaining travellers—state social and humanitarian aspects at holiday destinations to be money-equivalent.

- 45% are prepared to pay extra charges for ecological commitment of their hotel or resort.

- 41% state they would pay an extra charge for the environmentally friendly construction of holiday resorts.

When asking "**how much** more" social and ecological compatibility would be worth, it becomes clear that 50% would spend up to 5% more money, the remaining 50% even 10-15%. This means every CSR affine traveller is willing to pay in average ca. 8% more money for a journey provided that CSR aspects, which are important to him, are being realized.

Admittedly, this measurement is still based on the level of intention. Even travellers who have not been classified CSR interested do state some willingness to pay extra charges—even though much less pronounced.

The question is now how strong the intentions of CSR interested households actually transfer into concrete actions.

3 Correlation of CSR Affinity and Actual Travel Behaviour

We took a look at the actual travel patterns in order to analyze behavioural relevance of CSR affinity and the involved intentions.

3.1 Choice of Transport

In 2007/2008 a significantly higher share of bus and railway usage can be recorded for CSR interested travellers. 9.3% of travel expenses fall upon railway and 8.7% upon bus journeys. In contrast only 7% of not CSR interested choose bus and 6.6% railway transport.

Now one may assume that this enhanced railway and bus usage is due to the higher age structure of the CSR interested. Though, keeping this influence constant by analyzing the transportation means within the age groups, it becomes apparent that the same significantly higher index values for bus and railway apply here as well.

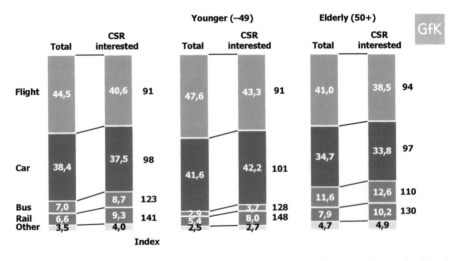

Fig. 3. The CSR interested target group takes significantly more frequently bus and railroad for holiday trips

Source: GfK Travel*Scope, 20,000 households, tourism year 2007/2008

This means that the choice of transport for holiday trips is significantly affected by CSR affinity.

On the other hand a considerably smaller share of air travel can be registered with CSR interested, which is for both younger and older travellers about 4 percentage points lower.

When going on a flight trip, 21.5% of CSR interested chose the more ecology-minded railway transfer to get to the airport. In contrast only 16.8% of not CSR interested travellers take the train to the airport. Thus, the abovementioned intentions do comply with the actual travel behaviour.

3.2   Holiday Destinations and Types of Travel

What are the preferred holiday destinations of CSR interested travellers?

- CSR interested German tourists travel significantly disproportionately high to countries such as Germany, Great Britain, France, the Benelux countries, Switzerland, Austria or Croatia.

- The classical beach destinations such as Turkey, Spain and Greece, in contrast, belong barely, if at all, to the preferred holiday destinations. On the one hand this is related to their renunciation of air travel. On the other hand these are countries that left a negative impression at CSR interested travellers regarding social and ecological standards.

  Therefore there is the chance for less classical, earthbound reachable beach destinations, for example Croatia, to prepare themselves for the target group of CSR interested travellers and to distinguish themselves from other destinations. For the classical beach destinations this means on the other hand that they have to work on their image if they do not want to discourage the profitable target group of CSR interested right from the start.

The preferences for certain destinations come along with the differently pronounced types of travel of CSR interested. CSR interested generate for example almost 38% of the turnover from culture trips, a value which is about one third above the share of sales of CSR interested from all holiday trips. Furthermore significantly disproportionately high are:

- city breaks (index 116)
- holiday apartments/homes (index 109)
- usage of rental cars (index 108)

and as an example for tour operators:

- holidays with Studiosus (index 131)

This means that especially for these types of travel social and ecological aspects will attract more attention at travel planning and decision making. Thus CSR measures should be communicated explicitly.

  Clearly disproportionately low sales shares are realized from packaged tours, club vacations or especially all-inclusive offers.

4   Evaluation of Concrete CSR Measures

How are different CSR measures or aspects evaluated by CSR interested?

Regarding **air travel** the wish for emission-reduced airplanes is expectedly very popular: 39% of all CSR interested consider measures in this area as very important, within the core group this share even amounts to almost 48%.

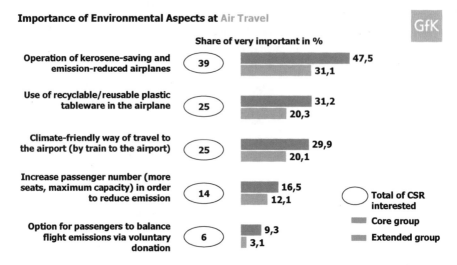

Fig. 4. Emission reduced airplanes most important on the other hand selling of indulgences not accepted

25% of CSR interested attach great importance to even more easily realizable aspects such as the use of reusable tableware and the opportunity for climate-friendly transfer to the airport (Rail & Fly).

The offer to balance flight emissions via voluntary donations for environmental protection organisations, on the other hand, is disapproved by the majority. It is probably regarded as some kind of selling of indulgences. Only 6% regard such donations to be important environmental protection measures for air travel. That is to say such offers have at least some need for explanation.

Hotels are in the position to fulfil the expectations of CSR interested guests to an even greater extent by simple actions:

- Every other person approves strongly to have towels changed only on guest request. As this is already implemented in many hotels this practice is approved alike by the core group as well as the extended group of CSR interested. Other measures with high level of acceptance, though more requested by the core group are:

Importance of Environmental Aspects at the Hotel

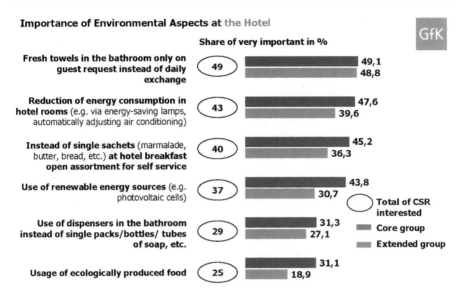

Fig. 5. For environmental reasons CSR interested travelers are prepared to abstain from some comfort at the hotel

- − to waive packaging
  - ○ at the breakfast table (open assortment for self service): greatly approved by 40% of all and 45% of core group
  - ○ as well as in the bathroom (soap dispenser etc.): greatly approved by 29% of all and 45% of core group
- − reduction of energy consumption in hotel rooms (e.g. via energy saving lamps, automatically adjusting air conditioning etc.): 43% of all CSR interested, 48% of core group

5   CSR Images of Tour Operators

Whereas many socially acceptable and responsible aspects and measures are being expected from holiday destinations and local hotels (such as environmental and nature protection measures, protection of children and youths from abuse and child labour etc., strict compliance and promotion of human rights, compliance of safety standards, etc.) the tour operator is presently credited little concrete responsibility for social/humanitarian/ecological measures. At best 34% of the CSR interested demand from the tour operator to get the possibility to become acquainted with the country's culture and its people in their everyday life.

Tour operators have lots of opportunities to increase their image with their own measures and to distinguish themselves by a choice of socially and ecologically acceptable travel offers.

This may be seen in the results from the direct question about which tour operator has already left a positive or negative impression regarding their support of CSR measures. The effects here are generally underdeveloped—and this, note well, with the target group of CSR interested tourists.

Most likely the tour operators GeBeCo (13%), Studiosus (11%) and Berge & Meer (10%) were awarded with positive perception, whereas especially the first mentioned may only draw upon the small target group of 8% insiders. The other two operators are only familiar to a good third of CSR interested travellers.

Vice versa no tour operator actually stands out in a noteworthy negative way: Terra incognita for CSR-related image building.

Besides doing something good, tour operators are given the great opportunity to approach and retain well-funded and influential target groups by straightforward and authentically communicated CSR.

Even smaller (low-cost or neutral) measures may already result in a positive perception within this target group.

The communication of such measures may be operated via target-group specific, well-definable media. Which types of media hit which target group specifically, without wastage, is revealed by the GfK Mediaprofiler. For instance, when looking at print media the usage of "National Geographic" lies about 50% above the average with the CSR target group, "Die Zeit" even about 80%.

6   CSR Aspects as Differentiating Additional Benefit for Travel Offers

With the results on hand we got to know Corporate Social Responsibility as an important and serious aspect for the target group of CSR interested tourists. Still, we need to classify CSR correctly regarding its significance during the purchase decision for a travel because nobody goes to a certain holiday destination just because human rights are respected and the environment is not affected.

Other criteria such as landscape, relaxation and recovery possibilities, culture and sights, the weather and safety are the crucial factors. Of course these aspects must first of all fulfil the demands and expectations of the consumers. After this, the compliance of social and ecological standards may be the decisive point to choose between otherwise equal offers.

Corporate Social Responsibility is certainly not a panacea regarding tourism marketing for neither holiday destinations nor the hotel industry nor the travel business. But provided the correct integration into the whole marketing mix it is an important component to enthuse the customer about the whole package. This applies especially for the target group of social responsible consumers and herewith for a group which we expect to grow in the future.

It is important to note that as this group consists of thoroughly critical and judicious consumers, credibility and authenticy of the measure are key aspects.

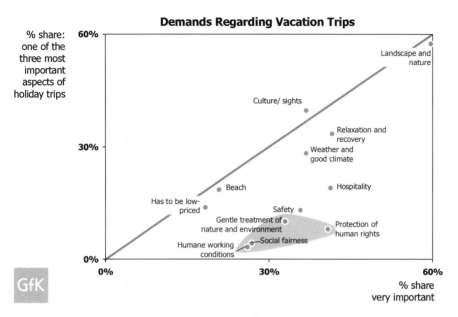

Fig. 6. Ecological and social aspects of holiday offers are important but not considered as core benefit

Sustainable Tourism: From Nice to Have to Need to Have

Erika Harms

The widespread and worldwide movement towards sustainable production and consumption is finally catching up with the tourism industry. Luckily policy makers, business owners, service providers, local, national, and regional industry associations, academic institutions, non-governmental organizations, and concerned travelers are all beginning to recognize the role they have to play in promoting sustainable tourism. As a result, they are looking for ways to inform their decision making and verify the credibility of the tourism products they support. There is great potential right now to think smartly about how the tourism market can be used to preserve the environment and change people's lives.

The powerful impact of tourism on the traveler and the local economy is borne on the face of every tourism destination in the world. And, if there is one thing that is even clearer, it is the impact of tourism on the world economy, its effect on the availability of natural and cultural assets, and its potential for poverty alleviation and as a mechanism to bring people from around the world together.

According to the United Nations, the tourism industry equals and even surpasses that of oil exports, food products, and automobiles. In 2008, the number of trips taken worldwide reached 922 billion, and worldwide tourism receipts reached $944 billion. While in some areas during 2009 tourism experienced slower growth due to the global economic crisis and the H1N1 flu pandemic, it is still expected that the number of tourists worldwide will grow every year over the next decade.

1 The Evolution from Nice to Have to Need to Have

"Sustainable tourism" is not a new idea. Thirty years ago, in a response to traditional travel, eco-tourism was created. This was an important step in the evolution of travel and in the mindset of the traveling public, but it was a concept that did not go far enough. It is really only applicable to a small subset of destinations and, philosophically, does not adequately address the development and sustainability needs of local population (not to mention cultural heritage aspects of tourism). Its application in the Galapagos Islands, one of, if not the first, eco-tourism destinations, is a good exam-

R. Conrady and M. Buck (eds.), *Trends and Issues in Global Tourism 2010*,
Trends and Issues in Global Tourism, DOI 10.1007/978-3-642-10829-7_14,
© Springer-Verlag Berlin Heidelberg 2010

ple. Though it is estimated that tourist dollars from the Islands provide one-third of all revenues generated by the government of Ecuador, the vast majority of tourist dollars spent are not benefitting the island or its inhabitants.

Then, the triple bottom line, an important concept developed through the United Nations to calculate the true cost of business endeavors, including the ecological and social impact, and the true birth of corporate social responsibility was born. The tourism industry did not immediately adhere to these principles and lagged behind others like the extractive industry, pharmaceuticals and chemical companies. The tourism industry, perceived as a service provider and a lesser threat to the environment did not come under scrutiny at the time. Some thought leaders eventually embraced the concept and translated the triple bottom line into programs around energy consumption and water and waste management. These programs were not only addressing environmental impacts but clearly demonstrated the financial benefits for the business. Today most companies have added some kind of social responsibility or philanthropic project or program. But we're still in the realm of NICE TO HAVE.

Sustainable tourism shouldn't be and isn't a luxury, a "nice to have" that can be dropped at convenience or when times are tough. It is a NEED to have. It rates up there with quality and health and is often directly connected. No doubt this is a tougher sell in the tough economic times we now face, when people are struggling with just keeping their business going. But there is really no other option. Fully embracing sustainable tourism is the only way forward and truly the only way through which stronger businesses can emerge.

2   Sustainable Tourism and the Bottom Line

The first inklings of the world really waking up to this idea can be seen in its slowly building awareness of the consequences of unchecked climate change. This is a primary concern of politicians, industry, and the public in general, as it should be. There is no doubt that the impacts of climate change on tourism destinations, on their communities' livelihoods, and on local economies is of equal concern. There are, however, other elements to this equation.

There are two major considerations that lead us to believe sustainable tourism is a NEED and clearly and directly applicable to an improved bottom line of the tourism industry, in addition to the environmental impacts that can be mitigated through more sustainable practices (which are clearly apparent to most of the industry). First, tourism businesses recognize that a healthy destination is vital to drawing in future customers and, ultimately, the health of their businesses. Collective efforts to sustain the integrity of irreplaceable tourism destinations and to improve the livelihoods of the local population can insure that these places will continue to act as a draw for tourists in the future. Keeping that sense of place is a NEED.

Second, consumers are beginning to recognize their own footprint on the planet and are becoming both more savvy in their ability to find new travel opportunities and more conscious of the effects their travel will have on the places and people they visit. By showing that they share the same concerns, more responsible service providers have seen an increase in this new – and fastest growing – tourism segment. Satisfying consumer demands is certainly not a nice to have; it is a NEED for survival of the business. By understanding how the mainstreaming of sustainable values will affect their business, they are in a better position to compete in the evolving consumer place.

3   Initiatives Leading the Way

While there are many noteworthy initiatives out there, following are some insights based on initiatives the UN Foundation has been involved with for the past several years to preserve World Heritage sites through sustainable tourism.

World Heritage sites are places around the world that have been internationally recognized for their outstanding value as natural and cultural treasures – and, not surprisingly, are often major tourism draws. Despite the protection provided by the 1972 UNESCO World Heritage Convention, signed to date by 186 countries, these sites still face challenges to their long term conservation, and increasingly sustainable tourism is viewed as part of the solution. The World Heritage Alliance for Sustainable Tourism, established under the guidance of UNESCO's World Heritage Centre, is a membership-based initiative that works to support World Heritage conservation, sustainable tourism, and local economic development for communities in and around UNESCO World Heritage sites. In 2009, the Alliance is working in six countries, in 20 World Heritage sites supported by more than 80 strong and growing members, recognizing the irreplaceable nature of the World Heritage sites, and, by working in a responsible way. The Alliance has helped to guarantee access for future generations and continued business for travel service providers.

One of the partners of this Alliance, the Hoteles con Angel in Puebla, Mexico offer a good example of what sustainable tourism looks like in action. The group is comprised of seven boutique hotels, drawn together by a mutual desire to preserve the Historic Centre of Puebla and the nearby Monasteries on the slopes of Popocatepeti, both World Heritage sites. These hotels go beyond the classical thought of sustainability – they still reduce their energy and water consumption and monitor their environmental footprint, and they support the community by purchasing local foods and supporting artisans. However, they do not stop there. These hotels are special because they also engage others. They invited the local municipal governments to help them build a holistic strategy to protect the World Heritage sites. They educate travelers about how they can travel responsibly to the world's cherished destinations and they even train other community businesses like taxi drivers and restaurant owners about sustainable tourism.

That is sustainability in action. The Hoteles con Angel understand the need to preserve places like the Centre of Puebla, but without reducing profit or potential for growth. By incorporating environmental and community responsibility into their business model, the Hoteles con Angel have driven the change toward sustainable travel in their geographic region. Hotels, tour operators, and trade associations all over the world are coming to a similar realization: they can no longer consider social good to be ancillary to their financial success.

4   The Tourism Industry as Free Market

It is increasingly clear that tourists and travelers are beginning to demand sustainable tourism options, that company employees want to be associated with companies that are doing the right thing, and that communities are opening up to amazing partnerships with the tourism sector.

The upshot of the democratization of global communication networks, online travel booking and advertising is that consumers are more empowered than ever to make decisions based on all of their needs, including those based on their concern for the planet, and are better able to find operators and destinations that speak to those needs. This speaks directly to sustainable tourism as a NEED TO HAVE. The widespread realization of the value of sustainable tourism through the public puts those operators and destinations not actively working to bolster their sustainable travel bona fides at a distinct disadvantage. Considering the even greater value placed on going "green" and on sustainability in general among the general public, and the even greater opportunity this offers for sustainable tourism, it is clear that disadvantages will only grow more pronounced.

Both Expedia and Travelocity have recently conducted surveys that directly show travelers' desires for sustainable options. Over half of Travelocity's customers said that a "green" rating would have some effect on their hotel choices in 2009, and 84 percent of Expedia customers expressed interest in sustainable hotels and said they were willing to pay more for them. Note that these interests have held through a devastating worldwide financial crisis.

Employee loyalty is also a sign that the concept of sustainable tourism really strikes people at the core. Expedia, a primary World Heritage Alliance partner, has created an employee community service program through which Expedia employees volunteer to help develop sustainable, locally-owned, and locally-managed tourism businesses in and around UNESCO World Heritage sites. In a survey of their employees, the Employee Program ranked as one of the top reasons to work for Expedia. And in a highly competitive space like online travel, employee retention is certainly good for the bottom line.

One of the Expedia employee programs took place in Sian Ka'an, a 1.3 million acre reserve and World Heritage site two hours south of Cancun. Expedia employees have partnered there with Community Tours Sian Ka'an (CTSK) – a local, predominantly Mayan-owned tourism cooperative. CTSK works to protect the delicate mix of coral reefs, mangroves, clear deep-water pools, and forests. Since the project kickoff, thanks in no small part to Expedia assistance with marketing, website design, and product development, CTSK has experienced revenue growth of more than 125 percent by drawing tourists southward from nearby Cancun and the Riviera Maya.

5   The Future of Sustainable Tourism

The biggest challenge for sustainable tourism is that, until recently, there was no clear and easily digestible definition with universal buy-in among the tourism industry, travelers, media and others. With no "common denominator" of what would be considered sustainable, there is inevitable uncertainty among travelers as to what they're actually embarking on and a certain inherit skepticism in the process. Clearly this artificially dampens the value of sustainability for operators and destinations. Until recently, there were hundreds of different measures for what constituted "sustainable tourism". Some were good; some were bad; none was universal.

And so, along with the Rainforest Alliance, the UN Environment Programme, and the UN World Tourism Organization, the UN Foundation reached out to over 80,000 people and engaged more than 30 organizations to help launching a global standard for "sustainable tourism" that would let everyone know that they are on the same page. And, at the World Conservation Congress in October, 2008, Ted Turner announced the launch of the Global Sustainable Tourism Criteria, a set of 37 criteria derived from certifications and best practices that are global in nature and feasible to implement.

Using these Criteria as a guide, tourists will know if they are traveling in a responsible way. And businesses, big and small, can profit from being able to certify their good works as they attract a growing number of people around the world who see personal value in this kind of tourism.

The Criteria's success depends on its universality, so great pains were taken to get everyone's input over the course of 18 months. Through this process, four main characteristics that define sustainable tourism were developed: maximizing tourism's social and economic benefits to local communities; reducing negative impacts on cultural heritage; reducing harm to local environments; and planning for long term sustainability.

The goal of the Global Sustainable Tourism Criteria is to help leverage and capitalize on the growing consumer interest by aligning all tourism stakeholders with a common understanding of sustainable tourism – from purchasers to suppliers to consumers. To facilitate this, the partnership, through the expert input of its working groups, is developing educational materials and technical tools to guide hotels and tour operators through the process of implementing sustainable tourism best practices.

Since the launch of the criteria in October 2008, the GSTC Partnership has taken off from theory to practice as major players in the tourism industry have applied them in recent projects. Partners have taken bold steps in the right direction to embed the Criteria within their own programs and initiatives. For instance:

- Travelocity launched a green travel website in January 2009 featuring third-party certified hoteliers that are aligned with the Criteria.

- Expedia launched a similar website in October 2008.

- The International Hotel & Restaurant Association launched a new sustainable hotelier recognition program, Emeraude Hotelier, based on the GSTC.

- The German Sustainable Development Cooperation Agency, in cooperation with Rainforest Alliance and others, is financing a project to build capacity among small tour operators in Latin America to align themselves with the Criteria.

- The Egyptian government, with assistance from a host of German allies including EcoTrans, launched a new eco-label in December 2008 called the Green Star Hotel Initiative that is aligned with the Criteria.

- The IDB launched a sustainability scorecard based on the GSTC to guide its large scale investment decisions in tourism projects in Latin America.

- And, 175 cities in the United States, led by the cities of San Francisco, Baltimore, and Miami, endorsed the GSTC as the minimum guidelines that lodging and tour operators should adhere to.

These companies, governments, and industry associates, among many others, have come to the realization that the "bottom line" is more complicated than they thought. The long-term viability of any industry is now directly dependent on its environmental and social impact and whether the public views that impact as positive. In order for the industry to provide a value proposition to the consumer, the tourism product must incorporate sustainability elements that not only save the consumer money but also demonstrate how they are contributing to a greater good.

To some this may sound like something that fits into the traditional mold of corporate social responsibility. But, it is becoming increasingly clear that tourists and travelers are beginning to demand sustainable tourism options. Embracing these values and practices early in the game will allow businesses to maximize their profits and become pioneers of sustainable tourism, a once in a lifetime opportunity.

Benchmarking Corporate Social Responsibility: CSR Is Still New Territory in the Tourism Industry

Klaus Betz

More and more businesses in the tourism industry are considering Corporate Social Responsibility (CSR). They are asking themselves how they can reconcile social responsibility with corporate transaction and combine value with merit. The idea of CSR becomes a mere label when businesses assume social responsibility only to ease their conscience or as a means to spruce up their image. This, of course, is going to backfire, and the businesses' aspiration for CSR as well as their credibility will be doubted.

Corporate Social Responsibility is more than just a promise to obey existing laws. It implies the thought of sustainability and requires replicable transparency, be it through a respective certification or through CSR reports of authorized neutral institutions. These steps lead to an acceptable and credible benchmark that is suitable for comparing one business with another.

Regarding this practice, privately owned and managed travel businesses in Germany – the so called German 'Mittelstand' – are quite a few steps ahead of corporations or, more specifically, publicly owned tourism businesses. There are, for example, the cultural tour operator "Studiosus Reisen München GmbH", who has a CSR orientated mission statement and built the charitable and non-commercial "Studiosus Foundation", and the "forum anders reisen e.V.", an association of tour operators committed to sustainable tourism, in which approximately 30 privately owned and managed businesses have been certified by now.

In short, 'Mittelstand' tourism companies have come to realize a lot earlier than other corporations that Corporate Social Responsibility is a process to safeguard the future. It implies not only economic but also social, environmental and cultural transaction.

Then again, there is an immanent crux to the matter. The tourism industry wants to sell freedom and pleasure, but, at the same time, cannot make use of all the associated possibilities. This seems to be a contradiction, but it is what responsible care is aiming for to safeguard the future, and therefore it depends on the cooperation of all involved parties. The tour operator is usually playing a key role in this because the way of presenting his offers can convince travelers of sustainable travel. On the other hand, he should be able to prompt travel destinations to align

R. Conrady and M. Buck (eds.), *Trends and Issues in Global Tourism 2010*,
Trends and Issues in Global Tourism, DOI 10.1007/978-3-642-10829-7_15,
© Springer-Verlag Berlin Heidelberg 2010

themselves with CSR profiles and standards regarding the development of their region.

Compared to other global sectors, the tourism industry is still not thinking laterally enough. Well-designed CSR projects can have a social effect and, at the same time, serve a business's self-interest. Examples in other industries prove it.

The Volkswagen Group, for example, established the Volkswagen Community Trust in South Africa, which supports adolescents living close to the Volkswagen factory with scholarships and training facilities. Volkswagen took into consideration that the better they train adolescents – who are possible employees – the better the quality of their cars will be. In the long run, everyone benefits from this concept.

But this is only one aspect. A global company like Volkswagen – and the travel industry is similarly global – cannot afford to apply different standards over the long term, such as implementing social measures in its home country that improve its image, while it is being criticized for its questionable practices somewhere else. For that reason, the VW Group, as one of the first great corporations, adopted a worldwide valid Global Labor Charter, which stipulates the same employment rights for all locations of its factories. But the VW Group does not blindly apply the same standards to everyone, because CSR is about finding the right measures for each location or choosing those that should be strongly promoted. That means that CSR – as shown in the example of Volkswagen – can focus on education in one country, health prevention in another and maybe road safety education in a third.

And why all of this? According to Dr. Gerhard Prätorius, Head of Coordination CSR and Sustainability at Volkswagen, the success of such measures is reflected on capital markets as well. "We strive to reach a top position in the Indices of Sustainability regularly. Every year, this is more and more appreciated and reflected in the expectations of great investor groups and pension funds." In short, the clearer and more directly a company follows such CSR strategies, the better its performance, appearance and reputation are on a national and international level.

However, a business does not necessarily adopt CSR simply for the sake of ensuring income return. The decision to commit to CSR can also arise out of the idea that income return that is already generated can be returned to society as a benefit. The privately owned and managed shipping company Beluga Shipping in Bremen, Germany is a respectable example. CEO Niels Stolberg equates "globally active" with "globally responsible". Furthermore, the ship owner sees social responsibility towards society as one of his duties. "Not only at a favorable balance", emphasizes Dr. Hans-Herwig Geyer, Director of Corporate Responsibility & Communications of the heavy-lift and project cargo shipping company.

Basically, the CSR activities of Beluga Shipping are divided into three strategic task fields. In the social sector, they want to offer help where the support of the government or the church is no longer enough. The second field focuses on the qualification and education of disadvantaged social classes; believing in the fact "that only education can enable people to live responsibly in (their) society", according to Hans-Herwig Geyer. The third field concentrates on giving people the opportunity of having cultural experiences "because only those who know their own culture know how to deal with cultures of other nations and see them as enrichment rather than a threat."

A project of Beluga Shipping in Thailand demonstrates how to combine all three fields. The Beluga School for Life is an aid project for children and their relatives who survived the tsunami in 2004. It started off as a school for 130 children who became orphans after the catastrophic flood. In the meantime, more and more children from lower income backgrounds have been attending this school while the tour operator Beluga School for Life Charity Travel (BSfL CT) takes care of all the touristic aspects of the aid project. They have built a guest area for visitors who are interested in exciting encounters and thereby contribute to the survival of the project.

It is remarkable that, of all companies, one in a different industry can prove – albeit on a smaller scale – that touristic entrepreneurship can be realized in such a way that both sides benefit from each other. The aforementioned 'Mittelstand' tour operators have already attended to this task. Treating local inhabitants with respect, considering their social and cultural interests and creating a win-win situation on an economic level are the very interests of the tourism industry. Therefore, it is about time that the tourism industry dedicates itself to pending CSR processes. Today – and more than ever, tomorrow – global performance is measured by sustainable and therefore responsible corporate transactions. Hence, associated benchmarking is increasingly becoming a quality feature in the tourism industry, especially in difficult times.

Links

www.studiosus.com
www.studiosus-foundation.org
www.forumandersreisen.de
www.forumandersreisen.de/aktuelles.php?id=5139
www.volkswagen.de
www.volkswagenag.com/vwag/vwcorp/.../de/.../csr_de.pdf
www.beluga-group.com
www.charity-travel-thailand.de

"Social Inclusion" – A Competitive Advantage for Tourist Destinations

Fritz Pleitgen

So far the Ruhr Basin has not been known to be 'a place to see before you die'. The region is chronically misjudged. Just as it was misjudged again when it entered the competition to become the European Capital of Culture of 2010. The Ruhr Basin has been primarily known for its industry and sports rather than for its cultural life. But we were able to show that the Ruhr Basin can offer more culture per square meter than many of the other European regions. We have more than 200 museums and over 1,000 industrial monuments with inspiring architecture. Furthermore you can find 120 theaters and 100 concert halls within a small area.

The Ruhr Basin is a region of sharp contrasts: you will find idyllic landscapes alongside a vibrant industry and cultural diversity. The Ruhr metropolis, as we call it more often now, may not be the largest European Capital of Culture, but the most heterogenic. Under the motto "Essen for Ruhr" Essen entered the competition for the European Capital of Culture, representing the entire region including all 53 cities. With this initiative the European Union pursues a long-term goal not only with regards to culture and a European conscience, but with respect to cultural industry and cultural tourism, as well. In addition we want to create concepts of social coexistence for the 170 different nationalities and more than 200 different religions living in the Ruhr Basin.

We have real-life proof of the successful realization of this goal: Recently, an impressive mosque has been built in cooperation with the Muslim, the Catholic and Protestant Christian and the Jewish communities. This mosque is not a traditional one. Its windows, for example, are very large, so that everyone can easily see from outside what happens inside.

What else do we have? In Essen there is the Folkwang Museum, "the most beautiful museum worldwide". Almost a hundred years ago the world premiere of Gustav Mahler's Symphony No. 8 was celebrated. Next year we will celebrate the 100th anniversary of this symphony that became known as the "Symphony of a Thousand" in an iron and steel works. More than 1,500 people will be part of this performance. Furthermore, we are planning a project on "singing" where arts and science merge. At the end we will gather 70,000 people from different countries who will sing as one big choir in the Schalke football arena. On July 18, 2010 the

R. Conrady and M. Buck (eds.), *Trends and Issues in Global Tourism 2010*,
Trends and Issues in Global Tourism, DOI 10.1007/978-3-642-10829-7_16,
© Springer-Verlag Berlin Heidelberg 2010

motorway A40/B1 between Dortmund and Duisburg will be blocked so that we can erect a banqueting area of 60 kilometers in length where different cultures and nationalities can meet. Of course, everyone is very welcome to participate and everyone should come with his or her personal understanding of culture. Not only should people perceive art and culture, but they should also play an active role in it. This is one of our key interests.

We want this to be the same for socially, mentally and physically disadvantaged people. Unfortunately for these people Germany is still a developing country, because many barriers still exist. We decided to develop concepts concerning this matter. England, the Netherlands and Scandinavia are our pacemakers and forerunners. If we want to be an open, democratic society, we will have to consider the needs of these disadvantaged people. Alas, as already said, here in Germany we are still very far from having an acceptable situation.

This concerns tourism, as well. What does it actually mean: tourism without barriers?

To many it might sound like a boring trip to places that need to spend a lot of money to guarantee accessibility for the handicapped. This image needs to be eliminated. For about 10% of the population a barrier-free environment is imperative. It is necessary for 30-40% and it is definitely more convenient for a 100%. A large number of people would benefit from a barrier-free environment. According to estimates of the national coordination unit "Tourismus für Alle" (*tourism for everyone*) more than 20% of the population are mobility-impaired, meaning that all in all 16.5 million people in Germany are affected. The German Federal Statistical Office (Statistisches Bundesamt) says that at the end of 2007 the number of seriously handicapped people was 7 million, which means that one person in twelve is seriously handicapped in Germany.

Here you already realize that the target group is substantially bigger than assumed. A handicapped person likes traveling just as much as an able-bodied person. The travel propensity of mobility-impaired people or people whose impairment substantially limits a major life activity however is only at 54% which is clearly below the all-German average of 75%. This difference mainly results from the poor infrastructure of this target group. 37% of all mobility-impaired people choose not to go on a trip due to the lack of barrier-free offers. 48% of the handicapped would travel more often, if there were barrier-free offers. The potential for this special target group becomes obvious. With about 1.3 holiday trips and 2.3 short breaks per year, handicapped people travel about just as much as non-handicapped people. With regards to the duration of the trip handicapped people even beat the non-handicapped. The type of trip is very similar, as well. 82% of the handicapped consider their time off as a vacation. Handicapped people usually go on city breaks during their short breaks and prefer the low season, because mostly they do not depend on school holidays.

The number of elderly people in our society will increase dramatically in the future due to the demographic change. In 2020 about 30% of the German population will be over 60. The number of tourists aged from 65 to 75 will increase by

40%. Elderly people prefer comfortable traveling which is why they embrace a barrier-free environment, as well.

So all in all we can say that mobility-impaired people have been a completely underrated target group, so far. Since the two groups are very much alike in their travel behavior, we realize that there are no suitable destinations for many people.

Now what barriers exist for mobility-impaired people?

Many obstacles exist along the chain of service in tourism starting from planning, organizing, arrival and departure, accommodation, excursions to lacking medical facilities. Accommodation and mobility at the destination are priorities for the affected. Arrival and departure as well as organizing the trip also play an important role. Due to the impairment of handicapped people certain basic offers have to exist and play a key role.

With all the mentioned activities, including arrival and departure, there is a particular discrepancy between their importance and how they are actually perceived in real life by the handicapped. Meaning: with all the above-mentioned factors they clearly feel disadvantaged.

- The biggest barriers are perceived when participating in cultural activities. A fact that hits the Ruhr Basin as a Capital of Culture particularly hard. Here 67% of the handicapped people find barriers, deaf people and wheelchair users in particular. However, for 61% of them cultural activities are important, if not crucial when booking the trip. They do not differentiate between trips in Germany or abroad.

- Planning the trip is absolutely crucial to more than 70% of the handicapped tourists, nevertheless it remains very difficult. The essential sources of information are: recommendations, special travel brochures, the tourist office (20%) and the internet (9,8%). Usually, an average of 51% use the internet as a source of information. However a sub market has emerged that provides information via special databases within handicapped-networks on barrier-free offers. But they are not linked with common tourist media. In standard tourist brochures, as well, you will find barrier-free offers specifically marked, for example with the pictograph "wheelchair user". The problem here is, that most of the time they do not provide any further information about what that pictograph actually stands for. Questions remain unanswered, so that the impaired customer when in doubt will decide against taking the trip. About 10% of German destinations offer special interest brochures, but they often get bogged down in detailed technical descriptions of their accommodation facilities. Only one third of the examined destinations with barrier-free offers were marked on the internet websites. The figures date back to 2004, so they could have increased by now.

The customer potential is constantly increasing. More than 50% of the target group is older than 65. Because the duration of their trips is above average and the time of year is unimportant to them, elderly and handicapped people are a very attractive tourist group. In most cases there is also an accompanying person traveling with them. The travel propensity can be boosted substantially with barrier-free offers.

The tourist industry has already made some progress, especially through the commitment of various organizations and funding agencies. Tendencies towards a special tourist market are becoming apparent, but here lies the danger of segregation.

We can sum up by saying that there are too few barrier-free offers along the touristic value chain, especially concerning accommodation. Existing offers lack effective marketing. In Germany elderly and handicapped are hardly ever perceived as a target group. The status quo shows that the supply is nowhere near being able to meet the demand.

The following figures, taken from a study of the Federal Ministry of Economic Affairs (Bundesministerium für Wirtschaft und Technologie), make it clear:

Because the target group of handicapped has been neglected, the economy loses a net turnover of 2.5 billion Euros. That is the amount that 6.7 million seriously-handicapped people would have spent in total on holiday trips and short breaks. 1 billion Euros would be in wages and incomes, and 65,000 fulltime jobs could be created. The macroeconomic consequences could have been at an estimated 5 billion Euros, 90,000 new jobs and a GDP growth by 0.25%.

It's basically: the more barriers are eliminated, the higher the rate of increase.

It goes without saying that concrete investments are necessary to realize this goal. A lot needs to be done. We want to push things into the right direction with the European Capital of Culture in the Ruhr Basin. We brought together all institutions dealing with handicapped people. Besides federal institutions like the Ministry of Labor, Health and Social Welfare (Ministerium für Arbeit, Gesundheit und Soziales), numerous organizations and interest groups as well as representatives of the civil societies, such as the Lions Club, were present. Some achievements have already been made: the infrastructure will be checked to examine the accessibility of all venues so that we can get an overview on what measures still need to be taken. All of our partners, as well, should be prepared in every way possible for the needs of impaired people. Our website is already almost barrier-free and currently we are building future-oriented visitor's centers. The project "Europa InTakt" (*Europe in step and harmony*), from the University of Technology of Dortmund, wants to promote the idea of people with or without handicaps being able to perceive and participate in culture together. We are trying to provide points of contact for handicapped people at every event. Many more ideas and measures are still being planned. We also discussed this topic with our cooperation and project partners, the shareholders and policy-makers, in order to pull out all the stops for 2010.

We all benefit from our concept of "Social Inclusion" and I hope that we can take a step towards it through our efforts for a world without barriers.

First ITB Berlin Forum on "Indigenous Tourism" Highlights Key Challenges Ahead

Imtiaz Muqbil

The first Indigenous Tourism Day on March 14, 2009, was a landmark event for the travel & tourism industry. It was the first time that the ITB Berlin Convention had expanded the range of topics to include this subject. The main theme of the session was the "Wisdom of Old Ways". Speakers from Canada, the United States, Bali and the South Pacific discussed at length the challenges they face in keeping alive their respective culture, heritage and languages in the face of globalisation and rapidly-changing societies.

Indigenous peoples are just as important to tourism as the environment. They are the last remnants of an era when nature, not money, was the real treasure. Time was measured by seasons, not seconds. For hundreds of years, they lived off the land, free of modern-day gadgets and gizmos. However, just as the world begins to realise the value of the ancient traditions in health and wellness, so too is it learning to value the original creators of those traditions. There is a growing realisation that losing species of wildlife, flora or fauna can be equally as damaging as losing traditions, languages, customs and rituals. These are the industry's real assets, and just as the "asset value" is a critical component of the real estate industry, so too does a similar "asset value" need to be established.

Indigenous peoples can be found all around the world. They are mainly tribes-people, rich with artists, musicians, writers, storytellers, and many more. According to the United Nations, there are more than 370 million indigenous peoples in some 90 countries worldwide. Reports presented at the UN 7th Session of the Permanent Forum on Indigenous issues in April 2008 indicate they hail from diverse geographical and cultural backgrounds, but also share challenges such as: lack of basic healthcare; limited access to education; loss of control over land; abject poverty; displacement; human rights violations; discrimination and economic and social marginalization.

Travel & tourism offers an opportunity to address some of these challenges. Indeed, promoting indigenous tourism offers a one-stop-shop opportunity to uphold a national culture and also address broader issues such as extinction of languages, preservation of ancient wisdoms as well as poverty alleviation, climate change and migration.

R. Conrady and M. Buck (eds.), *Trends and Issues in Global Tourism 2010*,
Trends and Issues in Global Tourism, DOI 10.1007/978-3-642-10829-7_17,
© Springer-Verlag Berlin Heidelberg 2010

In recent decades, the promotion of indigenous tourism has gained higher prominence in the product development and marketing policies of just about every country. However, indigenous tourism operators have a long way to go. Often divided amongst themselves and badly organised, many admit to having a hard time retaining their culture and transmitting it on to today's glitz-and-glamour younger generation.

Indigenous peoples and tribes stretch from Latin America to the native Americans of the North, the aborigines of Australia and Maoris of New Zealand and the numerous bedouins and tribes of Africa and the Arabian deserts. The website http://www.nativeweb.org/resources/native_travel_eco-tourism/ lists a large number of superb travel and eco-tourism opportunities developed by or for indigenous peoples. For example:

- A Bedouin experience in the high mountain region of Sinai, Egypt.

- Indigenous Tribes & Aboriginal Groups tours & eco tours in Panama.

- Native-owned and -operated tours in South Central Alaska, offering VIP tours on Alaska & Native history.

- Native-owned tour companies that teach visitors about Northern New Mexico and the history of the Pueblo people.

- Tours to Amazon Lodges run in conjunction with or wholly by indigenous people in Ecuador, Bolivia and Peru.

- Maori tours in New Zealand, where guests stay and trek with New Zealand's indigenous peoples.

- Inuit-owned and -operated Arctic sea kayaking adventure tours in Canada's high Arctic country of Nunavut.

- Customised tours to all Sioux Reservations in South Dakota, USA.

- Locally-owned and -operated ecotours specializing in homestays in remote (and not so remote) tribal villages in the Chittagong hilltracts of Bangladesh.

- Navajo-owned tours to over 2,700 archaeological sites in Arizona.

- At the Chief Bald Eagle Ranch in South Dakota, guests stay in tepees, learn Indian traditions and tour historic areas.

- In the Ecuadorian Andes, guests visit four indigenous communities, share in their ancient traditions, taste traditional foods, delve into their knowledge of medicinal plants and meet the shamans.

- Village Homestay accommodation in local indigenous Fijian communities.

- Fairtrade tours in Peru with the Quechua community (horse-supported treks to Machu Picchu).

1   The Issues They Face

Over the past few decades, the linkage between indigenous peoples and tourism has been intensely discussed. One recent publication is "Tourism and Indigenous Peoples" [Edited by Richard Butler, Professor of Tourism, Deputy Head of School (Research), University of Surrey, U.K., and Tom Hinch, Associate Professor, Faculty of Physical Education and Recreation, University of Alberta, Canada]. The publication defines Indigenous Tourism as "tourism activities in which indigenous peoples are directly involved through control and/or by having their culture serve as the essence of the attraction. Tourism attractions which are both controlled by indigenous peoples and which feature an indigenous-themed attraction clearly fall within the scope of it." The definition excludes other activities such as casinos owned and controlled by indigenous peoples.

The book uses case-studies to compare tours such as "campfire" programmes in east Africa, and the employment of indigenous peoples as guides, amongst other cases. It discusses host-guest relationships, conflicts within communities and contrasting strategies and results of tourism in indigenous villages in South Africa. It focuses on issues such as authenticity, religious beliefs and managing indigenous tourism in a fragile environment. Also covered are tourism education, tourism and cultural survival and examples of the policy and practice of indigenous tourism.

Professors Butler and Hinch argue: "Given the complexities of globalisation, indigenous cultures and tourism, the range of debate that surrounds indigenous tourism is not surprising. The reality is that there are a range of both opportunities and threats that indigenous peoples may encounter if they choose to become involved in tourism. The exact blend of these opportunities and threats tends to be unique in time and space, although some common patterns and themes exist. They are influenced by both external factors over which indigenous peoples have little control and by internal factors which indigenous peoples have at least some opportunity to influence."

According to the professors, "Western-based economic rationale remains the primary motivation for engaging in the businesses of indigenous tourism. The essence of this argument is that income generated through tourism will help eradicate the shackles of poverty and social welfare and lead to more cultural pride and economic self-determination." It is better for the indigenous peoples to develop tourism than, say, cut down timber in rainforests, the editors argue.

They stress: "A symbiotic relationship is possible to the extent that cultural survival contributes to economic success and economic success contributes to cultural survival." At the same time, indigenous tourism "also helps promote relationships between indigenous peoples and non-indigenous peoples and increases the mainstream populations' understanding of the plight of indigenous peoples, and hence creates a more just and equitable relationship."

However, the professors are realistic enough to note: "The travel trade is dominated by an increasingly global culture that operates at a worldwide scale and responds to shareholder interests. (Indigenous) operators who specialise in it present a very small segment of this group and must normally work within the parameters of the tourism industry as a whole if they hope to remain solvent."

The good news for indigenous peoples is that their fate and future has now become a global issue. August 9 is marked annually as the UN International Day of the World's Indigenous People, usually observed with panel discussions, art exhibits and cultural performances. This is also the Second International Decade of the World's Indigenous People, which runs from 2005 to 2015.

2   UN Declaration on the Rights of Indigenous Peoples

On 13 September 2007, the UN Declaration on the Rights of Indigenous Peoples was adopted by a UN General Assembly Resolution. Drafted and debated for more than 20 years, the landmark declaration emphasises "the rights of indigenous peoples to live in dignity, to maintain and strengthen their own institutions, cultures and traditions and to pursue their self-determined development, in keeping with their own needs and aspirations." A majority of 144 states voted in favour, with 4 votes against (Australia, Canada, New Zealand and the United States) and 11 abstentions (Azerbaijan, Bangladesh, Bhutan, Burundi, Colombia, Georgia, Kenya, Nigeria, Russian Federation, Samoa and Ukraine).

The Declaration affirms their contribution to the diversity and richness of civilizations and cultures, and expresses concern that "indigenous peoples have suffered from historic injustices as a result of, inter alia, their colonization and dispossession of their lands, territories and resources." Among some of its key points, the Declaration gives indigenous peoples the right to:

- self-determination in terms of their political status and free pursuit of their economic, social and cultural development.

- practise and revitalize their cultural traditions and customs. This includes the right to maintain, protect and develop the past, present and future manifestations of their cultures, such as archaeological and historical sites, artefacts, designs, ceremonies, technologies and visual and performing arts and literature.

- revitalize, use, develop and transmit to future generations their histories, languages, oral traditions, philosophies, writing systems and literatures, and to designate and retain their own names for communities, places and persons.

- maintain their traditional medicines and their health practices, including the conservation of their vital medicinal plants, animals and minerals.

- maintain and strengthen their distinctive spiritual relationship with their traditionally owned or otherwise occupied and used lands, territories, waters and coastal seas and other resources.

- redress, by means that can include restitution or, when this is not possible, just, fair and equitable compensation, for the lands, territories and resources which they have traditionally owned or otherwise occupied or used, and which have been confiscated, taken, occupied, used or damaged without their free, prior and informed consent.

- maintain, control, protect and develop their cultural heritage, traditional knowledge and traditional cultural expressions, as well as the manifestations of their sciences, technologies and cultures, including human and genetic resources, seeds, medicines, knowledge of the properties of fauna and flora, oral traditions, literatures, designs, sports and traditional games and visual and performing arts. They also have the right to maintain, control, protect and develop their intellectual property over such cultural heritage, traditional knowledge, and traditional cultural expressions.

3   Seventh Session of the Permanent Forum on Indigenous Issues

Not long after the UN Declaration on the Rights of Indigenous Peoples was adopted, more than 2,500 indigenous participants from all over the world, including Bolivia's President Evo Morales Ayma, met at the UN HQ in New York from 21 April to 2 May 2008 for the 7th Session of the Permanent Forum on Indigenous Issues. The session ended by issuing clear recommendations in a range of areas considered critical for the physical, cultural and spiritual survival, identity and well-being of indigenous peoples. Forum members heard from delegates on the multiple ways in which their countries could take measures to implement the Declaration.

The session's main theme was "Climate change, bio-cultural diversity and livelihoods: the stewardship role of indigenous peoples and new challenges". This is a subject of great relevance to the travel & tourism industry at large.

3.1   Effects of Climate Change on Indigenous Peoples

Papers and presentations at the 7th forum stressed that indigenous peoples are vital to, and active in, the many ecosystems that inhabit their lands and territories, and may therefore help enhance the resilience of these ecosystems. Victoria Tauli-Corpuz, Chairperson of the Permanent Forum, said that both the problem of climate change and its solution were concerns for indigenous peoples who – according to a World Bank report – contributed the "smallest ecological footprints" on Earth, but suffered the worst impacts from climate change and mitigation measures, such as the loss of land to biofuel production. Indigenous peoples are among the first to face the direct consequences of climate change, owing to their dependence upon, and close relationship with the environment and its resources. Examples include:

- In the high altitude regions of the Himalayas, glacial melts affecting hundreds of millions of rural dwellers who depend on the seasonal flow of water is resulting in more water in the short term, but less in the long run as glaciers and snow cover shrink.

- In the Amazon, the effects of climate change include deforestation and forest fragmentation, and consequently, more carbon released into the atmosphere exacerbating and creating further changes. Droughts in 2005 resulted in fires in the western Amazon region. This is likely to occur again as rainforest is replaced by savannas.

- Indigenous peoples in the Arctic region depend on hunting for polar bears, walrus, seals and caribou, herding reindeer, fishing and gathering, not only for food to support the local economy, but also as the basis for their cultural and social identity.

- In Finland, Norway and Sweden, rain and mild weather during the winter season often prevents reindeer from accessing lichen, which is a vital food source. This has caused massive loss of reindeer, which are vital to the culture, subsistence and economy of Saami communities.

- Rising temperatures, dune expansion, increased wind speeds, and loss of vegetation are negatively impacting traditional cattle and goat farming practices of indigenous peoples in Africa's Kalahari Basin, who must now live around government-drilled bores in order to access water.

- As sea levels rise, Kiribati and a number of other small Pacific island nations could disappear during this century. High tides and stormy seas have also caused problems recently in the Marshall Islands, Cook Island, Tuvalu and low-lying islands of Papua New Guinea.

3.2   Responding to Climate Change

Fortunately, UN reports indicate, indigenous peoples interpret and react to the impacts of climate change in creative ways, drawing on traditional knowledge and other technologies to find solutions. For example:

- In Bangladesh, villagers are creating floating vegetable gardens to protect their livelihoods from flooding. In Vietnam, communities are helping to plant dense mangroves along the coast to diffuse tropical-storm waves.

- Indigenous peoples in the Central, South American and Caribbean regions are shifting their agricultural activities and settlements to new locations which are less susceptible to adverse climate conditions. For example, indigenous peoples in Guyana are moving from their savannah homes to forest areas during droughts and have started planting cassava, their main staple crop, on moist floodplains which are normally too wet for other crops.

- In North America, some indigenous groups are striving to cope with climate change by focusing on the economic opportunities that it may create. The increased demand for renewable energy using wind and solar power could make tribal lands, such as in the Great Plains, an important resource for such energy, replacing fossil fuel-derived energy and limiting greenhouse gas emissions.

Other papers presented at the 7th Session of the Permanent Forum on Indigenous Issues highlighted more challenges facing the indigenous peoples.

Indigenous Languages

Linguistic diversity is being threatened around the world, and this threat is acutely felt by indigenous peoples. According to UNESCO, approximately 600 languages have disappeared in the last century and up to 90 percent of the world's languages are likely to disappear before the end of this century if current trends continue. Moreover, fewer and fewer children are learning indigenous languages in the traditional way, from their parents and elders. Hence, much of the encyclopedia of traditional indigenous knowledge that is usually passed down orally from generation to generation is in danger of being lost.

Migration

Deforestation, particularly in developing countries, is pushing indigenous families to migrate to cities for economic reasons, often ending up in urban slums. They often face double discrimination as both migrants and as indigenous peoples. For example, 84 percent of New Zealand's Maori peoples live in urban areas. Most are in the main metropolitan centres: a quarter live in the region, of Auckland, New Zealand's largest city. The urban migration of Maori has been described as one of the most rapid movements of any population. This also puts further pressure on the cities and urban areas with negative environmental consequences, including a demand on local resources.

4   Tourism Impact and Solutions

There is unanimous consensus that travel & tourism focussing on indigenous peoples can be a part of the solution. Considerable work is being done in Australia where organisations such as Aboriginal Tourism Australia and the Indigenous Tourism Leadership group engage with public sector agencies, training organisations, and the tourism industries to develop and deliver programs which encourage participation while recognising the need to address barriers and manage culture and community.

One recent development in 2008 was a new, improved web portal which offered Australian indigenous tourism companies the following: News stories, events and case studies; an 'easier to search' database of latest training, assistance and funding available to tourism operators; a comprehensive 'how-to guide' to visitor feedback; specific information for artists & art organisations, tour operators & tour guides, accommodation operators and tourism restaurants. It also offered a how-to guide on effective business management; a how-to guide on record keeping & administration tips as well as tools and tips on understanding tourism and industry associations.

At the ITB 2008, one of the To-Do! awards was conferred on the Perth-based Western Australian Indigenous Tourism Operators Committee (WAITOC). In his rationale, Studienkreis jurist Christian Adler noted that the Aborigines' contemporary history has been a long ordeal which is only gradually coming to an end. In 1967, the indigenous population of Western Australia was finally granted Australian citizenship, and legal equality was established. "Earlier, white Australians had been allowed to take children of Aborigine background from their parents, to take them to unknown places and have them grow up in missions and children's homes in order to subject them to forced assimilation.

"This practice, however, was stopped only in the early 1970s, and recently Prime Minister Kevin Rudd officially apologised to the Australian Aborigines for the many years of unworthy treatment. This helps forces in Australia who are intensively working to heal the wounds of the past and to build bridges to a common future, similar to the situation in South Africa," Mr. Adler wrote.

As the indigenous population of the Australian continent, Aborigines today constitute a minority of two percent of the Australian population. Of the roughly 400,000 Aborigines left, 70,000 are in Western Australia. Only five percent of Australia's tourism enterprises are managed by indigenous entrepreneurs, according to WAITOC. However, for 45 percent of the visitors to Australia surveyed, encounters with Aborigines constitute the main motive for their stay. 150,000 visitors per year book cultural programmes with indigenous communities, WAITOC reports.

WAITOC's goal is to improve the profile of small indigenous enterprises and to help Aborigines to get more employment in the tourism sector. It provides consultancy services for governmental institutions and organisations on all aspects related to indigenous tourism. In order to increase the share of indigenous entrepreneurs in the tourism sector, the state tourism authority Tourism WA also runs its own programme to promote indigenous tourism and supports the projects of WAITOC.

Another global group, Indigenous Tourism Rights International (ITRI), organized the International Forum on Indigenous Tourism in Oaxaca, Mexico in March 2002 as an alternative and necessary space for indigenous peoples to conduct a critical review of their experiences with ecotourism. Nearly 200 indigenous representatives and leaders from 19 countries attended and produced "The Oaxaca Declaration," which calls on indigenous peoples to "strengthen strategies of coordination and information sharing both regionally and internationally, in order to assert participation in initiatives like the IYE".

5   Highlights of the ITB Berlin Session

All these issues came together at the ITB Berlin on March 14, 2009. On the panel were Dominique Bearune, an artist, performer and writer from New Caledonia; Luc Collin, Quebec Aboriginal Tourism Corporation (STAQ); Kevin Eshkawkogan, Manager, Great Spirit Circle Trail, Ontario, Canada; Prof. Dr. Igde Pitana, Secretary General, Clan Warga Pasek, Bali; and Brian Zepeda, Seminole Tribe of Florida, AIANTA Board Member. The moderator was Imtiaz Muqbil, Executive Editor, Travel Impact Newswire.

The first speaker, Dominique Bearune, showed a video about New Caledonia and the way of life there. According to him, some key elements of the culture are the tribal lifestyle, the language, morality and respect for the earth, the high value of family kinship as well as respect for each other. Women rank very high in society.

He then discussed the major problems they face to preserve the culture, as more young people, influenced by the Western Culture, are moving to the city. As a result, fewer people live according to the old traditional ways, it slowly becomes extinct. Their tribe is not experienced in how to maintain a culture. They lack information about tourism projects and that is why consultation and help is needed in New Caledonia to keep the culture alive and share it with the world.

The next speaker, Luc Collins, said he is a member of the Inuit nation. Since completing his studies in Administration and Human Resources Management, he has been involved in the tourism industry for 14 years. He said that Quebec is facing economic problems, and has a high unemployment rate. More than 50% of the population lives close to Montreal and the percentage keeps going up. Thus the tourism sector is very important for low-developed areas that are further away. Mr. Collins' tribe already has a well-developed tourism concept that brings people to the area and allows them to see the culture without commercializing it. However, the tribes in Quebec are still encountering problems such as preservation of nature, lack of funding, and preservation of language and traditions.

The third speaker, Mr Kevin Eshkawkogan, described himself as an avid grass dancer from the Pow Wow Section in Canada. He is involved in developing the European Markets on behalf of Great Spirit Circle Trail in Ontario. He shared a story of how his people operate the tourism industry in their area, Manitoulin Island, the largest island in a freshwater lake in the world, and use it as a tool to educate the visitors. They are trying to get their youth involved and revitalize the culture.

After showing a video about how they live and share their culture with tourists via different activities, he explained how his people got there. In 1998, after seeing non-native tour guides bringing tourists into their community, some community elders decided that it was time to get involved in the tourism business. Rather than leave the interpretation of their culture to outsiders, they decided that they themselves should pass on this knowledge. After a long planning period they set up 2 companies: one to market the region and one to sell and promote their experiences and activities.

The first activity was developing cultural integrity guidelines, which is in accordance with their own teachings on how business is conducted. Everything the
tribe offers is educational and interactive, so that guests really learn about their
lifestyles and heritage. However, there are certain things they won't share with the
public, such as sacred ceremonies like pipe- or naming-ceremonies, because the
tribe believes that they would not be doing it for the right reasons if people pay
money for it. Tour operators and visitors are informed about these guidelines.
They also took an inventory of what they had in the area.

Today, students from their own first nation communities are working with them
to learn about the culture of the tribe. They can do research about the history and
then pass on their knowledge. Over time they developed a market-ready product
that provides guests with an educational experience.

The fourth speaker, Prof. Dr. Igde Pitana is Secretary General of the Clan
Warga Paset in Bali and also the Head of the Tourism R&D, Ministry of Culture
and Tourism, Republic of Indonesia. In talking about the "Local Wisdom of the
Balinese in Managing Development", he began with some geographical, economical and demographical background. Bali is a small island with 3.2 million people,
96% of whom are Hindu, and an agrarian-based culture. Being adaptive and flexible, it always welcomes aspects of foreign cultures, and has been in contact with
Chinese, Indian and Western cultures for more than 2,000 years. All these aspects
of foreign culture have become integrated into the local culture.

Balinese society is clan-based, not caste-based like Hinduism. It has 29 clans
and Prof. Dr. Igde Pitana is chief of the biggest clan, the Warga Pasek. He describes Balinese society as being "a modern society in a traditional environment"
with three main guiding values as applied in daily life:

- Living in harmony with God, community and nature
- Belief in Karma (you harvest the fruits of your own deeds)
- Focus on Balance: Balancing different elements of life.

The scheme of the balance of life is encapsulated in a triangular shape, with three
sources of happiness which are God, relationships with other humans and nature.
Happiness can only be found when these factors are in balance. This concept was
translated into a tourism concept:

1. The balance with God is shown by avoidance of sacred and profane things,
   including ensuring the sanctity of all sacred areas.
2. Maintaining the socio-cultural practices between people and empowering
   traditional institutions.
3. Preserving the balance with nature, which becomes a prerequisite of Sustainable Tourism Development. This is why buildings in Bali cannot be
   higher than 15 meters and must follow the 60:40 ratio, which means that
   only 60% of the land can be covered with buildings.

The fifth and last speaker, Brian Zepada, has been involved in tourism for over 20 years. His photographs, paintworks and woodcarvings can be seen in museums and private collections all over the world. Mr. Zepada reminds the audience that he is being able to share his information and knowledge with them via his voice, which has been given by the Creator, and a language that has evolved from that.

The Seminole tribe in Florida has been dealing with tourism since about 1920. At that time, he said, the U.S. Department of Transportation needed a road from Tampa to Miami and built it through the land of the Seminole tribe. The Seminole tribe knew since then that people would come through on a regular basis. So they wanted to take control over what these people learn about the Seminole culture.

Proactive steps were taken. They built little mock villages next to the main road to keep people away from the sacred areas. An eight-foot fence goes around the reservation. Over time, the Seminoles have learned to share their culture in pieces instead of giving away the whole thing. In these days of concrete jungles, tourists feel the need to connect with aboriginal people of the earth, because they want to see and experience what they don't see and experience on a regular basis. The Seminole reservation is all based on nature. Tourists want to know what it's like to live like aboriginal people.

However, Mr Zepada admitted that finding the balance between what they share and what they keep to themselves is a daily exercise. They now make enough money off tourism. Income is not an issue; it is now about how to protect their culture, ways of life and teachings from being commercialized. However, in the past 10 years, they have seen more of their children are getting involved in their culture, and attempting to find the balance between traditional life and modern lifestyle. Sometimes tourists get frustrated when they ask questions, because the Seminole tribe members are not allowed to share certain information with the public. Some things are very sacred. Tourists only see dances and hear songs, but the really spirituality is kept inside.

There is also an intercultural exchange with other tribes all over the world. For example, members of the Seminole tribe have been to New Zealand and shared their culture with the Maori tribes. Such exchange helps them to learn from each other about their successes and failures. They are always looking for opportunities to share with other natives.

Mr. Zepada cites the example of the Cherokee in North Carolina who had problems with keeping their language alive. Modern technology came to their assistance – the Ipod. They loaded their language and English on to the Ipod, so the kids could listen to it wherever they are and that way catch up with the language. The tribes have also held their first annual Southeastern Native American Cultural Preservation Conference, as a first step towards promoting intercultural exchange.

The discussion session that followed was dominated by the question of how the indigenous people are adapting to climate change, and how ancient wisdoms can contribute to the search for solutions. More importantly, how can these wisdoms be exported to the rest of the world?

Dr. Igde Pitana said that although the Balinese people are very close to nature and believe that if you cut a tree, plant two other trees, it is very hard to do this in practice, because the land is becoming more and more expensive in Bali due to tourism. Still, he said, 23% of the island is still protected forest. Modern machinery, appliances and vehicles are all contributing to climate change, and the response has to be greater preservation of lakes, mountains and forests. One regulation is designed to ensure no construction around temples, which preserves the surrounding environment and also spares that space from being over-run.

Kevin Eshkawkogan said culture is tied to Mother Earth and our way of life is very connected to nature. "We live our life based on a set of guiding principles called the seven Grandfather Teachings. One of them is respect, not only for the family, friends and other humans, but also for the earth. When we harvest things from the earth, we take what we need and that is it. The other teaching is about humility. The earth can survive without us, but we cannot survive without the earth. That is if the world could abide by that principle, which is actually designed to inculcate humility, it would go a long way towards staving off the damage to nature, which is the main cause of climate change."

Brian Zepada said the impact of climate change is noticeable in the tribe's Florida homelands. Not only have the temperatures changed and water levels gone up, but there's also change from Man himself. The US Army Corps has been trying to dig canals through Florida to get rid of the water, but in that process, "they are taking all that water from us, too. We have been fighting to re-establish the natural water flow through Florida, but we notice the change; the deer are gone, the fish catch is dropping. It has also brought more heat and this means that the water is evaporating at a higher rate than the clouds are dropping it down. We are impacted by this, as are all people, by global warming."

Prof. Igde Pitana said there is a basic principle which says that we have to acknowledge the local culture in developing tourism. In Bali, maintaining the balance of life is considered in all the local planning. "In 1971, we made our first master plan based on these principles. But we couldn't find a way of including the religious aspect but this is what Balinese values require. That is why we always fail in doing research on carrying capacity. We can learn from our tourism boards in Thailand or Malaysia or other countries (on how to promote Bali), but we don't have a proper criteria of measuring acceptable changes when it comes to the religious aspect. We can easily measure the need of water or power, but the acceptable change of religious aspect is impossible to measure. It is something we all need to probe further."

Kevin Eshkawkogan said his tribes' practices are very similar to the Seminoles in terms of retaining control. "We are not getting involved in mass tourism. This is the reason why we cannot develop our island very much. There is a lot of untouched nature in our area and we like to keep it that way. We are very conscious of the environmental practices on the tours or how many tourists come into the area at a certain time. It is limited. It is more effective and intimate that way. It's a one-on-one type of thing for the most part. Our culture is about spirituality and how you are connected to Mother Earth and to each other." He said he saw a lot of similarities across the panel on the need for maintaining the balance. "And the guidelines really help us to walk that fine line between sharing and giving our culture away."

Dawn Madabi, a female member of the Great Spirit Circle Trail, also offered a comment: "I truly believe that tourism involving indigenous people can be such a great opportunity to uplift the values and wisdom of indigenous people if it is led by them. When I listen to the presentations here, there is a fine line between sharing what we do and the exploitation of our culture. Visitors are becoming more sophisticated and it is really important to understand how tourism can be used for mutual benefit, and also to keep the area authentic."

She added, "Can you imagine a world that doesn't have the gift of all the different colourful cultures and the beauty of the different cultural experiences? This is a microcosm of the world when you see the participation of indigenous people and you can learn many beautiful things. We are all given gifts on this earth that we can share with each other." She thanked all the speakers for sharing their culture and heritage.

6   Conclusion

The first Indigenous Tourism Day at the ITB Berlin was a qualified success. Held on the last day of the ITB Convention, by when most of the senior industry executives had returned home, it nevertheless attracted a small group of very committed individuals who are conscious of the cause. If the ancient healing tradition of yoga is now in vogue, and the world is realising the catastrophic consequences of the ecological-economic imbalance, including the loss of biodiversity, the effort to rectify seek solutions is broadening to include those who realised the value of the old ways.

ITB Berlin's Indigenous Tourism Day made a small contribution to that effort.

Tri Hita Karana – The Local Wisdom of the Balinese in Managing Development

Igde Pitana

> "Culture is at the heart of contemporary debates about identity, social cohesion, and the development of a knowledge-based economy" (Universal Declaration on Cultural Diversity, UNESCO)

> [the Balinese] "creates new styles constantly, to inject new life steadily into their culture, which at the same time never loses its Balinese characteristics" (Covarrubias 1936:255).

Summary

Tourism has been developed in Bali for more than half a century, and hence it has become an integral part of Balinese culture. In economic terms, tourism is one of the most important contributors to the island GDP and employment.

The type of tourism developed is 'cultural tourism'; hence Balinese culture is directly exposed for tourist consumption. However, in this cultural commoditization, Balinese culture is conserved and revitalized, and the Balinese people hold their cultural identity firmly. This is associated with the local wisdom subscribed by the Balinese, that life must be in accordance with the changing environment, and that happiness can only be achieved if the life is in balance, a concept locally known as 'tri hita karana'. Augmented by other concepts taken from their traditions, the Balinese are successful in harmonizing tourism development and cultural conservation.

1 Introduction

Tourism is a very important sector in the development of Bali, Indonesia. The development of tourism in this island can be traced back to the 1930's, or even before. The type of tourism developed in this 'Paradise Island' is the so-called Cul-

R. Conrady and M. Buck (eds.), *Trends and Issues in Global Tourism 2010*,
Trends and Issues in Global Tourism, DOI 10.1007/978-3-642-10829-7_18,
© Springer-Verlag Berlin Heidelberg 2010

tural tourism. This is to say that the main capital used to attract tourists is Balinese culture, itself based on Hindu religion. This concept seems to put Balinese culture in a paradox, because the Balinese are forced to expose their culture for tourism, while at the same time they are dictated to conserve the culture as the main asset in tourism development.

Indeed, the relationship between culture and tourism is often awkward and paradoxical. On one hand, many argue that the use of culture as tourist attraction brings about negative impacts, conflicts, commercialization and commodification of the culture, and hence tourism tends to threaten the conservation of the culture in the destination. On the other hand, some put forward evidence that tourism is one of the best vehicles in the effort to protect the culture, whereby tourism can be a source of funding for conservation, increases awareness among the local, and motivates people to participate in the conservation process (cf. McKercher et al 2004).

This dichotomous views also holds true in analyzing tourism and culture in Bali. However, in the recent years the gulf of opposition seems to be narrowing down, whereby the use of the culture for tourism purposes is gaining acknowledgement as a mechanism for conservation (Pitana and Gayatri 2005). This paper will try to describe this situation in Bali, particularly in seeing how the indigenous people of Bali manipulate tourism for cultural conservation, and how at the same time they use their cultural aspects in tourism industry, all of which are guided by traditional teachings.

2   Bali, Its Culture and Society

Bali is a small island, of only around 5,632 km^2 in size, including its nearby isles such as Nusa Penida, Nusa Lembongan, Nusa Ceningan, and Nusa Menjangan. The island had 3.4 million inhabitants in 2008. Most of them (94.8%) are Hindus, while the rest are Moslems, Protestant, Catholic, and Buddhist (BPS Bali 2008).

Aside from the government's administrative structures as found elsewhere in Indonesia, there are also a number of traditional organizations in Bali, which are still functional, ie. the desa pakraman (customary village) and its banjar (hamlet), the subak (irrigators' organisation), subak abian (uplanders' organisation), seka (functional group), pamaksan (temple congregation) and warga (origin group or maxima-clan). These organizations are quite powerful in governing the daily interactions of the Balinese Hindus.

Balinese culture is very complex and dynamic, "a romance of ideas and actions …" (James Boon 1977: 7). Historically, Balinese culture is a hybrid of many cultural elements that have been in contact for thousands of years. An intensive contact between Bali and the world already took place thousand years ago. Almost all waves of external influence of culture had colored the history of Balinese culture, such as that of China, Egypt, Japan, India and Europe. But in taking these external cultural elements, history showed that Balinese society did not take them whole sale. The external cultural elements are filtered in such a way, modified in order to be fitted to Bali's environment, and then integrated into Balinese culture, so all absorbed elements become 'original Bali' elements. Mantra (1993) concluded that Balinese culture has a flexible and adaptive character. It can absorb and then manage all alien elements to enrich its own, without jeopardizing its own characteristics. In the context of flexibility and adaptive character of Balinese culture, Udayana University and Francilon (1975: 732) wrote:

> From one crisis to the next it has been able to keep its balance; more, it has been capable of making the best of most crises. The history of Balinese culture is that of syncretism; it has shown great power of resistance and adaptation to change. Indeed, the first contacts on record show that imported items were not taken-up wholesale, but were nevertheless assimilated.

The ability of Balinese culture to absorb other cultures without losing its identity, as mentioned above, is associated with the fact that the Balinese are so flexible in their interaction with the outside world. De Zoete and Spies (1973: 2) wrote that the Balinese "with suppleness in mind – had enabled them to take what they want of the alien civilization which have been reaching them for centuries and leave the rest."

This character has already been written by Covarrubias from his research in Bali in 1933. He said that Balinese culture "creates new styles constantly, to inject new life steadily into their culture, which at the same time never loses its Balinese characteristics" (1936: 255).

Balinese culture emphasizes the need of balance and harmony. This balance can be seen from the *tri hita karana* concept. This concept dictates that the real happiness can only be achieved if humans live in balance and harmony: the balance relationship between man and supernatural being; between man and environment; and among humans themselves.

The Balinese are tied to many socio-cultural institutions. Among the most important institutions that most Balinese are part of are desa pakraman (customary village), subak (rice-farmers' organization), subak abian (upland farmers' organization), seka (functional groups), warga (clan, ancestral-based organization), and pamaksan (temple congregation). To some extent, these socio-cultural organizations form a web where the Balinese are trapped and move within. This web strongly determines what a Balinese can, should, or cannot do. Of these socio-cultural organizations, desa pakraman (traditional village) and warga (clan or origin group) are the strongest, because they are detrimental in social-religious life of every Balinese, such as marriage, death and other life-cycle rituals (rite de passage). All Balinese-Hindus are members of these organizations.

In their life, the Balinese follow a number of tenets drawn from their traditional culture. Some important guiding principles in their culture among others are as follows.

1. Tri hita karana. This concept literally means 'three causes of happiness'. The concept dictates that the real happiness can only be achieved if there are harmonious relationships in the three components of the universe, i.e. (1) God (supernatural beings, parhyangan); (2) natural environment (palemahan); and (3) human beings (community, pawongan).

2. Rwa-bhineda: Balancing the contradiction. This term describes 'the two opposing things' that must be kept in balance. Even though the contradictory elements are so obvious in Balinese culture, this contradictory is united in a process, so they are ended up in a harmony, for example an individual in society, good and evil, material and spiritual, the real world and mystic world (skala and niskala), and so on.

3. Tri mandala: the three spatial zoning. The physical development must follow the spatial arrangement, which divides space into three parts: (1) utama mandala (the head zone, the sacred, for religious buildings, temple, etc); (2) madya mandala (middle zone, for people, housing, etc); and (3) nista mandala (the 'dirty' zone, for animal). By this zoning, the Balinese draw physical development of individual housing compound and a certain community in line with the sustainability concept, especially the focus that there must be an open space in every zoning.

4. Karmaphala. This principle dictates that any result from an action will be borne by the doer, or 'you will harvest the result of your own deeds'. This concept preventspeople from committing wrongdoing, and everyone tries to behave well.

5. Desa-kala-patra (time, space and circumstances), dictates that man must adjust themselves to time, space and objective situations in every action. This is a human ecology concept, in which man and society always try to adjust themselves to environments that influence their life.

3   Tourism in Bali

Tourism has become the main economic activity of the island province. For many decades, tourism has been the generator for economic development and motor for socio-cultural change (Pitana 2002). Wood (1979) and McTaggart (1980) stated that tourism nowadays is an integral part of Balinese culture. Talking about Bali today, one cannot separate it from tourism, because tourism has grown to be an inherent part of Balinese's life (Pitana 1993). Or, inversely, every time there is a discussion on tourism, Bali is inevitably quoted as an example.

The very basic concept in the development of Bali's tourism is that of cultural tourism. Cultural tourism in the context of Bali means that Balinese culture is the main capital in the development of tourism, and at the same time Balinese culture must be protected from the negative impacts of tourism. In other words, the development of tourism should accommodate the two opposing components at the same time; i.e. using Balinese culture as the main attraction in inviting tourists, and at the same time protecting the culture from bad influence brought about by tourism.

The decision to develop cultural tourism as the type of tourism in Bali is based on the supply and demand analysis of Bali. A research in the early 1970's showed that most tourists (61.78%) visited Bali because they were interested in the culture; tourists interested in nature, flora and fauna accounted for 32.8%; and the rest (5.37%) were interested in other aspects. The concept of Cultural Tourism has been adopted as a provincial act (Provincial acts No. 3/1974 and 3/1991).

In those acts, cultural tourism is defined as a kind of tourism which uses Balinese culture, itself is based on Hinduism, as the most dominant basic potential. It implies the ideal of mutual relationship between tourism and culture. The relationship is symmetrical, supporting each other, so tourism and culture will grow in balance and harmony or "interactive-dynamic-progressive relationship".

The development of Bali's tourism has undergone several ups and downs. This is clearly indicated by the development of direct arrivals to the island – direct arrival being one of the most commonly indicators used to measure tourism development. In 1970, the island received only 24,340 direct arrivals, and in 2000 this figures achieved 1,412,839. In 2001-2002, the island's tourism experienced a drop, attributed to the 9/11 tragedy in US (September 2001) and Bali bombing (October 2002). The years later, 2003-2004, there was a significant increase. After a downfall in 2006 (associated with the second Bali bombing), the international direct arrival increased in 2007, and in 2008 the arrival recorded 1.9 Million, the highest ever in the history.

Pitana and Gayatri (2005) concluded that tourism has already become the generator in the economic development of Bali, at least in the last two decades. It is further predicted that tourism will still be the leading sector in economic development of Bali in the future.

The role of tourism in Bali's economy can be predicted from GDP components. A study shows that 38% of job opportunities and 51% of people's income in Bali is directly associated with tourists' expenditure and tourism investment (Pitana 2005). If the indirect impacts are included, these figures would definitely be much higher. The sector called 'Hotel, restaurant and trade' alone contributed 33% of the island's GDP in 2008. From government side, tax earned from tourism, particularly 'hotel and restaurant taxes' is the biggest contribution for the regional income.

4 Balancing Tourism Development and Cultural Conservation

In discussing the impact of tourism on local culture, notably Bali, the most common train of thought is that of opposition or dichotomy, and in most cases, it is argued that tourism has a great impact in destroying local culture. This implies the assumption of a linear and one-way influence, in the sense that tourism brings about negative impact on local culture, while local culture has no impact on tourism. Furthermore, this also implies the assumption that local culture and community are passive objects that have no ability to redirect the influence (cf Pitana 2002). The above way of thinking was also very salient during the early stage of tourism development in Bali.

Theoretically, Cohen (1984) grouped socio-cultural impacts of tourism into: (1) impacts on the relationship and the involvement of a local community with community in general, including the level of autonomy or the level of dependency; (2) impacts on the interpersonal relationship among members of the community; (3) impacts on the foundation of social organizations; (4) impacts on migration from and to the tourism destinations; (5) impacts on the rhythm of socio–cultural life of the community; (6) impacts on the job distribution patterns; (7) impacts on social stratification and mobility; (8) impacts on the distribution of influence and power; (9) impacts on social deviance; and (10) impacts on arts and customs.

Impact of tourism on art, traditions, customs and religion may be the most interesting aspects to be discussed, because tourism developed in Bali is 'Cultural Tourism'. In its infancy stage, Ngurah Bagus (1975) already predicted that tourism would lead to a social disorganization process, either in community or family life. This would change the core of Balinese culture. Later, Ngurah Bagus (1989) was also afraid about the lost of social forms which have already been proven as the main key of Balinese societal integrity. Dalton (1990, in Picard 1990: 26) supported Ngurah Bagus, by stating that because of the commercialization, the social and religious network of the Balinese has decomposed.

In sum, it was said that Balinese culture has eroded, seen from (1) the emergence of the demonstration effect, that the local community tends to imitate the life style of tourists, without considering their own culture; (2) commercialization of culture; (3) the decreasing of crafts quality; (4) profanization of sacred arts, ritual ceremony and holy places; and (5) the decrease of Balinese willingness to maintain their cultural identity (Picard, 1990; Wood, 1979).

Contradictory to the above arguments, as a matter of fact, the Balinese do not put tourism and culture in a linear and one way cause-and-effect relationship. Instead, tourism and culture are seen in a mutualistic relationship, in a metaphoric of "tree analogy". In the "tree analogy", the root of the tree, as the main part of the tree's life, is Hinduism (religious values). The trunk is Balinese culture in general, both tangible and intangible cultural elements. The green leaves that look beautiful and motivating are Balinese arts. Tourism is the flowers and fruit, which can be harvested to increase the welfare of the people. The produces (flower and fruit) are marketable, but the income earned must be reinvested back to the root, to maintain the tree as a whole. In other words, the income gained from selling flower or fruit must be reinvested to buy fertilizer, to fertilize the root. Because if – and only if – the root is healthy, the trunk of the tree can stand rigorously, and only then can leaves grow well, resulting in a good harvest.

By applying the tree analogy, the Balinese delicately manage the balance between culture and tourism. Because of this mechanism, a number of sociologists and anthropologists are optimistic that Balinese culture will prosper in line with the development of tourism. McKean (1978: 94) stated:

> Even though the changes of social-economy is going on Bali ... all of them happened hand in hand with the conservation efforts for traditional culture ... In fact tourism strengthened the conservation, reformation and creation process of many traditions.

Tourism selectively strengthens local traditions through a process known as "cultural involution". Stephen Lansing (1974) said that Balinese traditional institutions have a high vitality and ability to adapt the new conditions. It is said that tourism impact in Bali is 'additive', and not 'substitutive' in nature. It means that the impacts do not cause transformation structurally, but integrated in the life of the traditional community.

Unud and Francilon (1975) also mentioned that even though there has been substantial change in Balinese cultural configurations, the change only happened in the external layer, while the core is still intact. History has already proven that Balinese culture has always been able to pass many crises and it was also able to maintain its harmony, and then produces the best result from every crisis. The history of Balinese culture is that of syncretism, and it has already shown high endurance and high ability to adapt many changes.

Bagus, amidst his worries of many negative impacts, also admits the fact that tourism has already given the consciousness about the value of art and culture which in turn, pushes Balinese to preserve their culture. Tourism even has already pushed the creativity in many fields (1989: 17).

Selo Soemardjan said that in the 1960s, he was so worried about the future of Balinese culture because of the Western culture and modernization brought by tourism. But, in 1987 (p. 322) he found that his worries did not become reality. Even though it is observed that the value of togetherness might decrease, it does not mean that this value is gone. Established social organizations such as desa pakraman (customary village), banjar (hamlet), subak (irrigation organization), Warga (maxima clan group) and pamaksan (religious organization) are still strong with their Balinese characteristics. In many tourism areas, traditional social organizations are even stronger and more dynamic, because of social-economic benefits brought by tourism invested to maintain social institutions (Pitana 2002).

A study by Pitana and Gayatri (2005) concluded that there is a strong ground to say that so far Balinese culture is still strong, as well as Balinese identity, and the worry that the culture is already loosen is not true at all. The social structure of Balinese society is still intact, dynamic, and has endurance and flexibility to adapt the changing environments. Social and cultural crises can still be controlled by the Balinese to return to its balance.

It is true, as Greenwood (1978: 136-7) said, that "culture has been packaged, priced and sold as other commodities". However, it is untrue that this commercialization has robbed the Balinese from their ethnic and cultural identity. Undeniably the arts have changed a lot, and the orientation of artists is not merely on religious, but also on economic aspects of the arts. Art becomes commodity, or there is a commercialization process, in which the value of art is measured by monetary terms (the market value), the same as other commodities. But the religious arts are not disappearing.

This phenomenon is in part relevant with MacCannell's theory, that the Balinese manage their culture by dividing their lives into "back-stage" and "front-stage". To some extent, in the backstage the Balinese continue to praxis cultures that are socio-religiously meaningful, away from the gaze of tourists, while in the front-stage they perform cultural activities for tourists' consumption. However, this is not totally true because in most cases, the Balinese do not separate their cultural praxis from tourists' gaze, but they seem to be undisturbed by the presence of tourists when they practice their cultural religious activities. Inversely, they are pride of their culture for being able to attract tourists' attention. In the commoditized parts of the culture, tourism even has become the new patron of cultural revitalization. Noronha (1979) aptly states this situation:

> The market is flooded with woodcarvings and masks. Many of these products may offend the purists ... but this does not mean that excellent art is unavailable or dying out or that tourist market has affected the quality of arts and crafts manufactured for religious purpose. These flourish, as careful observers note (1979: 192).

The advent of tourism in fact has significant roles in the conservation of Balinese arts and culture, to include the revitalization of the dying arts and the maintenance of various cultural aspects. This is in line with Cohen's theory, that:

> "the emergence of a tourist market frequently facilitates the preservation of a cultural tradition which would otherwise perish. It enables its bearers to maintain a meaningful local or ethnic identity which they might otherwise have lost. ... some of which have been salvaged or revived through demand by the tourist market (Cohen 1988: 382).

Internationalization and globalization of culture always attract questions on culture and local people's identities, because, as stated by Giddens, "transformation of self identity and globalization ... are two poles of the dialectic of the local and global in conditions of high modernity" (Giddens 1991: 32). There is a general assumption that in the process of internationalization, "the most firmly anchored identities are weakened, torn from their moorings and broken up, ... tradition and memory are misplaced" (Lanfant 1995: 8).

Tourism forces Balinese society and the culture to develop internationally (internationalization process). At the same time, however, there is a simultaneous process in a reverse direction, inward process, the process to search identity in the past, or commonly mentioned as traditionalization process. This process, among others, is indicated by the stronger movement to "back to the past", to the bond with the core of ancestral worshipping and traditional-village development.

From several indicators, it can be said that the level of Balinese religiosity does not decrease because of the economic development and transformation of Bali toward a touristic society. Field research in many tourist resorts show that traditional social organizations (especially banjar and desa adat) are even getting stronger and more dynamic, because of the prosperity brought about by tourism. The consciousness toward the self identity also increases, a process that might be called "indigenization" (Pitana 1991, 1995, 2002), or what Clifford Geertz terms as 'internal conversion'.

The success of the Balinese in balancing tourism development and cultural conservation can be closely attributed to the guiding principles found in their culture, as well as the strong web of social organizations where most, if not all, of the Balinese belong to, as stated above. It is also associated with the high level of people's participation, and the local wisdoms are already accommodated (and revitalized) in the development process.

As mentioned above, the concept of Tri Hita Karana strongly governs the Balinese in perceiving the changing environments. It dictates the Balinese to be always in harmony with their surroundings, physical and non-physical. There must be a balanced relationship between man as an individual with society (relationship among men), the balance between material and spiritual aspects of life (relationship between man and God), and the balance between the short term needs and the sustainable development (the balance with nature). The balance between man and their environment has already been written by Covarrubias (1936: 13), who said that the Balinese is the only tribe who has a perfect harmony with nature, and "no other race gives the impression of living on such close touch with nature, creates such a feeling of harmony between the people and its surrounding." He continued that the Balinese "regulate every act of their lives so that it shall be in harmony with the natural forces" (1936: 260). De Zoete and Walter Spies (1973: 2) who stayed in Bali since 1927 and became impresarios of the revival of Balinese arts, added that "the Balinese is so perfectly in harmony with his surroundings ..."

On the other hand, Balinese culture also recognizes the importance of the opposition or contradictory, as stated in the concept of "rwa bhineda" (two opposite things). However this contradictory is unified in a process, so they end up in harmony, for example an individual in society, material and spiritual, the real world and the unseen world (skala and niskala), black and white, purity and polluted, and so on.

In line with the above principles, changes occurring in their social-economic environments are 'manipulated' in such a way that a harmony is developed, avoiding conflicts and confrontations. The traditional concept of Tri Hita Karana and other traditional concepts have paved the way to the Balinese to adapt their life to a new environment without losing their own cultural identity, the 'Balineseness'.

5   Concluding Remarks

Cultural Tourism has long been developed in Bali, Indonesia. During the recent decades, tourism has become the main economic sector of the island-province, seen from its contribution to the province's GDP and employment structure. It has become the prime-mover of the development of the island and will be so for the years to come, indicated by its role in the making of the aggregate demand that is highly significant. From a socio-cultural point of view, tourism has become an integral part of the Balinese.

In the development of tourism, the main capital used as tourism attractions is its culture, aside from the nature. The use of culture in tourism industry theoretically put the Balinese in a paradox of two opposing worlds. The seemingly paradox is manipulated in Balinese context, that while exposing the culture for tourism, at the same time there is also effort to use tourism as an agent of cultural conservation. Hence, the development of tourism goes hand in hand with cultural development, and the two conflicting sectors are aligned in mutual-supporting nature to each other, in a progressive relationship. While utilizing the culture as capital/resource for tourism development, the sustainability of the culture is of no lower concern. There is a balanced attention given to the effort of preservation and sustainable utilization of the culture. This is possible by the guidance of traditional teachings, notably the tri hita karana.

Basing their practice to traditional teachings, the two sectors, i.e. tourism on one hand and culture on the other, are not composed in a dichotomy or paradox. Instead, a tree metaphor is developed. In this 'tree analogy', the root is Hindu religion; the trunk is Balinese culture; the leaves are arts; while the flower and fruits are tourism. Following this analogy, it is said that leaves, flowers and fruits can be sold but the money earned must be returned back to fertilize the tree, so that the root and trunk will be strong, which in turn will result in a good harvest of leaves, flowers or fruit. Employing this analogy into practice, it is proven at an empirical level that tourism has been the best vehicle for cultural conservation.

In a wider context, the use of culture for tourism should not be questioned because, as stated by Dradjat (2006), the management of culture must not be interpreted in a static way. Management or conservation of cultural aspects should consist of three interdependent components, i.e. protection/preservation, maintenance and utilization. Similarly, Adishakti (2005: 25) states that cultural conservation can be implemented in terms of "development and adaptation through preservation, restoration, replication, reconstruction, revitalization, and/or utilization for new functions".

Utilization is recognized as a tool to mobilize financial resource to be used in the conservation process. Tourism is also believed to play significant roles in the revitalization of intangible cultural heritages.

"... tourism is one of the many ways to experience cultural diversity
with the potential to create understandings of cultural difference and

the unity of the human condition. Furthermore, it allows the preservation of forgotten or threatened heritage resources, and the mobilization of these can generate economic wealth and feelings of collective identity" (Robinson and Picard 2006: 57).

References

Adishakti, Laretna T. 2005. Pelestarian Pusaka Budaya: Masyarakat sebagai Pusat Pengelolaan Perubahan. Paper in "Pra Kongres Kebudayaan, Denpasar", 28-30 April 2005.

Bagus, I. G. 1975. "Sanur dan Kuta: Masalah Perubahan Sosial di Daerah Pariwisata." Dalam I. G. Bagus (ed). *Bali dalam Sentuhan Pariwisata.* Denpasar, Fakultas Sastra Unud. h 95-109.

Cohen, Erik. 1988. Authenticity and Commoditization in Tourism. *Annals of Tourism Research* 15, pp. 371–386.

Cohen, Erik. 1984. *"The Sociology of Tourism: Approaches, Issues, and Findings".* Annal *of Tourism Research.* No. 30: 236-66.

Dradjat, Harry Untoro. 2006. Pelestarian Warisan Budaya dan Pembangunan Kepariwisataan. Paper presented in a seminar on The Development of Tourism and Cultural Resources in Indonesia. Jakarta, 30 August 2006.

Geertz, C. 1973. *The Interpretation of Culture.* New York: Basic Books.

Geertz, Clifford. 1997. *"Cultural tourism: tradition, identity and heritage construction."* In Wiendu Nuryanti (ed), *Tourism and Heritage Management.* Yogyakarta: UGM Press. H. 14-24.

Giddens, A. 1991. *Modernity and Self-Identity: Self and Society in the Late Modern Age.* Cambridge: Polity Press.

Giddens, A. 1990. The Consequences of Modernity, Polity Press, Cambridge.

Giddens, A. 1999. Runaway World: How Globalisation is Reshaping our Lives. Profile Books, London.

Hampton, MP. 2005. Heritage, Local Communities and Economic Development. Annals of Tourism Research 32(3): 735-759.

Hitchcock, Michael, VT King, and MJG Parnwell (eds). 1993. *Tourism in Southeast Asia.* London and New York: Routledge.

Lanfant at al. 1995 (eds). *International Tourism: Identity and Change.* International Sociology, London, New Delhi.

McKean, Philip Frick. 1978. *"Towards a Theoretical Analysis of Tourism: Economic Dualism and Cultural Involution in Bali".* In Valena L. Smith (ed). *Hosts and Guests: The Anthropology of Tourism.* Philadelphia: University of Pensylvania Press. pp. 119-38.

McKercher, B., Pamela SY Ho, and H du Cros. 2004. Relationship between Tourism and Cultural Heritage Management: Evidence from Hong Kong. Tourism Management Vol 26: 539-548.

Noronha, R. 1979. *"Paradise Revisited."* Dalam E. d. Kadt (ed), *Tourism, Passport to Development?* Oxford, Oxford University Press: 177-204.

Nuryanti, Wiendu. 1996. Heritage and Postmodern Tourism. *Annals of Tourism Research.* 1996. Volume 23, Number 2, pp: 249-260.

Picard, M. 1996. *Bali: Cultural Tourism and Touristic Culture.* Singapore: Archipelago Press.

Pitana IG dan PG Gayatri. 2005. Sosiologi Pariwisata: Kajian Sosiologis terhadap Struktur, Sistem, dan Dampak-Dampak Pariwisata. Yogyakarta: Penerbit Andi.

Pitana, I Gde. 1999. *Pelangi Pariwisata Bali*. Denpasar: Penerbit Bali Post.

Pitana, I Gde. 2002. Pariwisata Sebagai Wahana Pelestarian Kebudayaan Dan Dinamika Masyarakat Bali (Tourism as Vehicle for Cultural Conservation and the Dynamics of Balinese Community). Inaugural Speech for the Professorship in Tourism. University of Udayana, 15 June 2002.

Robinson, Mike dan David Picard. 2006. Tourism, Culture, and Sustainable Development. Paris: UNESCO.

Unud and G. Francillon. 1975. *"Tourism in Bali – Its Economics and Socio-cultural Impact: Three Points of View." Internaional Social Science Journal* XXVII (4): 721-52.

Wood, R. E. 1980. "International Tourism and Cultural Change in Southeast Asia." Economic Development and Cultural Change 28 (1).

Yunis, Eugenio. 2006. The Role of Cultural Tourism in social and economic development in the local communities. Keynote presentation in the International Conference for Cultural Tourism and Local Community. Yogyakarta, 8-10 February 2006.

**Product and Communication Strategy
in the Tourism, Travel and
Hospitality Industry**

What Comes After the Fun Principle?

Felizitas Romeiß-Stracke

After the events of September 11 2001, the self-indulgent hedonism of the "fun society" became a synonym in the German media for superficiality, commercialisation and Disneyfication; for what former German Chancellor Helmut Kohl referred to in 1995 as "theme park Germany". The peculiarly German fixation with work and the accompanying disparagement of everything that does not belong to work thus received renewed impetus. Writer Peter Hahnes' book, "Schluss mit lustig: Das Ende der Spassgesellschaft"[1] (the party is over: the end of the fun society) has been at the top of the German best-seller lists for months. It preaches a back to basics mantra, a return to tried and trusted values, to the old order, "new seriousness", more work and less leisured frivolity.

The perception of art and culture in this work-oriented society is also associated with work: one must educate oneself, be informed, able to face up to and deal with things. The more effort that is involved the better; on no account should it be shallow, entertaining or commercial. The language, too, is allowed to be a little incomprehensible, as befits a cultured discourse. "High culture" is, after all, the preserve of those and such as those. The others have either to make a bit more effort or rely on the cultural educators for "guidance". It is a situation that has led to the existence of a large and subsidised cultural scene promising "Culture for All" where the fun society is viewed as something superficial, commercial and actually rather contemptible.

But those who are currently involved in cultural policy are also going to have to adapt to the changed economic and social circumstances. The future is going to bring new concepts of work and leisure and a broader understanding of what constitutes culture. New thinking will be called for and that is going to mean the cultural establishment being shaken out of its familiar habits too.

A closer look at the current processes of social change will be needed in order to cope with this, something that political parties of all persuasions currently find hard to deal with.

They are still too much in thrall to an outdated model of industrial society or what the sociologist Ulrich Beck calls the "first modernization"; they would like

---

[1] St. Johannis 2004.

R. Conrady and M. Buck (eds.), *Trends and Issues in Global Tourism 2010*,
Trends and Issues in Global Tourism, DOI 10.1007/978-3-642-10829-7_19,
© Springer-Verlag Berlin Heidelberg 2010

to return to the parameters of success as it was measured back then (full employ-ment, growth etc.).

The German term for the kind of fun-loving, hedonistic society produced by the first modernization period, "Spaßgesellschaft" is a rather polemic and fairly crude concept. It is based on the development of what German sociologist Gerhard Schulze referred to as the "event society" (Erlebnisgesellschaft) in a book that pre-sented his analysis of what he believed was happening in German society in the 1980s and 1990s. According to this theory, for a considerable portion of German society at that time, the most important objective was to have a life that was as pleasant and as exciting as possible. The analysis related to a society that was rela-tively carefree and affluent. High levels of industrial efficiency and productivity meant that employees had a great deal of free time. Others referred to this period as the "leisure society" (always in a rather derogatory way and with more than a hint of anxiety attached). A "leisure industry" arose that conceived and sold ever more professional events and experiences, and these were by no means only of a superficial kind. "Experience Worlds" were created at the interface of consump-tion, culture and sport and began to compete with the established and publicly subsidised cultural institutions.

Some began to enhance the value of the experience they were offering with the addition of shops and restaurants, special events and new kinds of guided tours, and were doing so in ways that were certainly intended to thumb a nose at curators and other such guardians of culture. But against the backdrop of impending cuts in public funding at the end of the 1990s, many museums and theatres were left with little alternative but to change and adopt more flexible strategies in order to attract more custom.

Those potential customers had become hedonists, individualists and emancipated consumers, and that also applied to their consumption of culture. They were not, and still are not, prepared to be patronised by any abstract cultural ideals or an aesthetic or art historical canon. The latter are increasingly the preserve of only a small, edu-cated middle class elite, a means of providing them with social distinction.

Without a doubt, the experience society spiralled into a society where enjoyment and pleasure were primary. Everything had to be fun, and some sections of the Ger-man press even began referring to this as the "dictatorship of fun". Were one to at-tempt to reduce these behaviour patterns of the fun society to their essential charac-teristics, one might come up with something along the lines of the following:

- Extrovert: in the sense of always in a good mood, always cool, trendy, stylish and "in"

- Extreme: in the sense of more, higher, farther, faster, bigger etc.

- Exotic: in the sense of as way out and conspicuous as possible etc.

- Eclectic: in the sense of anything goes, no limits, breaking style rules, whether in clothes, behaviour etc. are here the order of the day

9/11 was not the first indication that the days of the shrill, narcissistic hedonism of the fun society were numbered. Back in the mid-1990s the first indications of the fundamental changes to come were already becoming discernible to trend analysts. But events in New York were to accelerate the process.

We are living through a period of transition that has been going on for at least fifteen years,

- From the firmly established nation state to overlapping communities, as part of globalisation

- From full employment to new forms of work and employment (The buzz words here being: New Work, Work-Life-Balance);

- From the nuclear family to new family forms (Multifamily, blended family)

- From thinking in rigid hierarchies, particularly in economy and management, to operating in networks;

- From the exploitation of nature as resource to an increased environmental awareness;

- From the idea of middle-class culture as an enclave of the educated and high-earning to a striving by many towards a more individual culture of living

This transitional phase may be faltering and inconsistent, but there is no denying that it is happening. Weaker economic growth and changes in the global political landscape are by no means all that lie behind this. In fact there are a whole series of factors which cannot be fully gone into here.[2] More and more people are coming to realise that the "logic of growth" (economic growth, increased structural and economic flexibility and acceleration) and the "logic of production" (ever more features for technical devices, still more production of goods that nobody needs, yet more choice in consumption) cannot give them what they really need. Gerhard Schulze talks here of a longing for "contentment with what one is".[3]

The driving force behind this change, along with the objective sociological, economic, technological and environmental conditions, and closely related to these, are the changing values in society and the increasing individualisation:

- All trend analysts are more or less agreed that this change in society's values runs from the values of duty and acceptance during the post-war reconstruction period, and Germany's 1950s economic miracle, via the "event" and "fun" orientation of the 70s to 90s (pleasure, money, self, atheism, sex and fun) to the search for meaning (experience, commitment, friendship, spirituality, eroticism, sustainability).

---

[2] For more on this see: Romeiß-Stracke, F. Abschied von der Spaßgesellschaft, Munich/Amberg 2003.

[3] Cf. Die beste aller Welten, Campus 2003.

- Individualisation, a characteristic of the modern since its precursors in the Renaissance, gives the individual opportunity and considerable freedom in shaping his or her own life. The struggle for personal freedom is one that has gone on throughout history, in particular in art and literary history. But individualisation also mercilessly increases the responsibility of the individual for his or her own decisions. In the "event" and "fun" society the project that is one's own life consists mainly in making individually appropriate choices from the many (consumer) options available, putting them together effectively and having a lot of fun at the same time – this, however, tends to be largely confined to the field of leisure. "Self-fulfilment" is the ideal to aspire to.

  For some time the variety of options has become rather a burden for many. It is not only the economic problems that arose at the end of the 1990s that have established limits, the sheer variety of options is also looked upon as being rather questionable and not a little stressful. A further complexity is added by the fact that individualisation is no longer just about private self-fulfilment, it also involves new demands on the individual in the working environment, which only the mentally, spiritually and physically healthy person will be able to deal with. He must invest in his personal growth and development, not only in fun for its own sake. Pure experience-orientation is being replaced by the need to constantly develop, to transform oneself. This goes far beyond the concept of "life long learning" that has been around for some time already. Above all it is also allowed to be fun. The contrast between work = (important) real life and leisure = (unimportant) pleasure and fun for its own sake, inherent in capitalism's protestant ethic, will be less marked in the future. Surveys of young people have long shown that they are of the opinion that work, too, ought to be fun! What is desired is an individual lifestyle, that meaningfully combines all aspects of a biography, career, creativity, emotionality, relaxation, etc.

Changing values and individualisation, in the form in which they are outlined above, give a special role to culture in all its guises. An ever-growing number of people for whom the sheer diversity of options has become just too much and the egomaniacal self-fulfilment more than dubious are turning to culture for orientation and meaning. That is the reason why millions visited the MoMA, why culture festivals and poetry readings sell out – an interpretation that many in the culture sector, museum curators and middle-class intellectuals would, of course, disagree with because it threatens their elitist monopoly on interpretation.

To put it simply, the hedonistic fun society is giving way to one that is in search of meaning. It is

- Introverted: in the sense that the individual looks out for what is good for him/herself – mentally, spiritually and physically, at all education and income levels

- Intimate: in the sense that it means a return to the familiar, though by no means only in the family, also in elective affinities and other spheres, and sensitivity to those who are socially very different

- Intensive: in the sense of "less is more," being selective but with real enjoyment as priority – and paying a bit more for the privilege

- Integrated: in the sense of "sorting things out for myself," seeking out course and direction for one's own culture of living.

These main characteristics of the "meaning society" also have their negative sides when pushed to excess, as everyone can see for themselves: introversion in hypochondria, intimacy in xenophobia, intensity in the arrogance of the connoisseur and integration in the worship of a guru.

This change towards a society that values meaning is in the broadest sense a positive one for culture and for those involved in the cultural sector. After all, all facets of art and culture satisfy the hunger for meaning, for ways of interpreting the world and for the deeper, more meaningful experiences that the superficial fun society seems to have neglected.

The role of the ego must not be forgotten, however. It leads to the rejection of art theory canons that are too narrow or too detached, as well as to scepticism about any imposed superstructure that goes beyond one's own sphere and beliefs. Even in spirituality, no return to the large denominational churches is to be expected. (The millions of visitors who attended the funeral of Pope John Paul II were it seems moved more by a very individually interpreted "free-floating spirituality" than they were by the Roman Catholic liturgy).

So it would be wrong for the culture industry to simply celebrate the revival of old canons in a meaning society and expect everything to return to how it was before.

The experience society that spiralled into a hedonistic fun society has permanently altered the perceptions and expectations of the culture audience. It is not just the museum shop or the original theatre restaurant, but also the professional organisation involved in cultural events, in high-quality architecture, in interior design and lighting that have now very much become an integral part of what these things are. After all, what has developed here is a highly professional "experience economy" and one able to create positive experiences for every occasion and at a high artistic level; the days of the Disneyesque here are a thing of the past. The modern museums with their spectacular architecture provide a good example of this, as does the recent "Erlebniswelt Renaissance" (Renaissance Experience) in the Weser Hills region of Germany.[4]

The general rejection of "commercialisation" on the part of many of those involved in the cultural sector and the slogan "Culture for All" have led to an outdated factionalism. This is not about pitting cultural hedonists and event freaks

---

[4] See below www.erlebniswelt-renaissance.de

against intellectual do-gooders and the educated classes. Cultural facilities are an integral part of the modern leisure and tourism industry, the "experience economy"[5] in other words, whether they like it or not. The realisation that modern contributions to personal growth and transformation are expected of modern citizens is one that opens up many opportunities beyond the subsidised cultural sector.

The "meaning society" is already clearly recognisable in its outlines. However – and this complicates the discussion – the "fun society" is not quite finished yet. They will co-exist for the next ten years, or so, though one will grow while the other will decline.

Those who bemoan the superficiality of the "fun society" and the dumming down of the masses are not entirely wrong, and the same is true of those who point to the growing search for meaning, especially in the challenging field of highbrow culture. But it is the task of trend analysis to look a little further ahead than is possible in everyday business.

[5] Cf. Pine, J./Gilmore, J.H. The Experience Economy: Work is Theatre & Every Business a Stage, Boston Massachusetts 1999; Rifkin, J. Access. Das Verschwinden des Eigentums, Frankfurt, New York 2000.

Best Practice Destination Management: Lessons from the Leaders

Auliana Poon

This session is based on the report "Successful Tourism Destinations – Lessons from the Leaders" published by Tourism Intelligence International. Three of the 25 success factors from 10 destinations are examined. In addition, 2 destinations are featured: South Africa and Costa Rica with interventions from the Directors of Tourism of these respective countries.

"Successful Tourism Destinations – Lessons from the Leaders" addresses the performance, constraints and success factors associated with the growth, development and transformation of tourism destinations around the world.

Success is not only measured in terms of growth, but also, on how well tourism destinations managed to achieve their specific objectives, and how resilient they have been in a rapidly and radically changing global environment. It is our objective in this report to demonstrate the critical factors underlying the success of these destinations. These success factors are best demonstrated by the destinations analysed – Australia, Barbados, Costa Rica, Dubai, France, Ireland, Jamaica, Mauritius, Singapore, South Africa and Thailand.

The report reflects both the wide geographical scope as well as various typologies of tourism destinations around the world. Old and new tourism destinations, small and large, emerging and mature, are analysed. Our selection of successful tourism destinations is not just based on their performance in terms of growth of hotel capacity and visitor arrivals, but also, the apparent resilience of some destinations and their sheer capacity to bounce back in spite of all odds (Jamaica, Ireland); those with strong sustainability objectives (Costa Rica); destinations that have virtually master planned or invested their way into existence (Dubai); destinations that have seen very rapid rates of growth as a result of changes in their political situation (South Africa); destinations that have consistently performed well despite external and internal challenges along the way (Australia, Barbados, Mauritius) and destinations, such as France, that boast one of the largest number of tourist arrivals in the world.

R. Conrady and M. Buck (eds.), *Trends and Issues in Global Tourism 2010*,
Trends and Issues in Global Tourism, DOI 10.1007/978-3-642-10829-7_20,
© Springer-Verlag Berlin Heidelberg 2010

1   Why Is "Successful Tourism Destinations" Important?

This research is particularly important for both old and new tourism destinations wishing to learn from the experience of other countries. Our selection of destinations is intended to expose the key factors contributing to the success of the destination and identify lessons that can be learnt from their experiences.

Every tourism destination or company wants to be successful. From managers and chief executives, to researchers and academics, there has always been an interest in what makes a particular destination or company successful; whether one can learn from these experiences; and whether in fact these lessons are transferable.

While it is true that success is a product of specific circumstances, *Tourism Intelligence International* demonstrates in this report that there are a number of determining factors of success that can certainly be learnt and are indeed transferable.

Tourism destinations and companies often benchmark themselves against competitors, or the most successful providers in their field. Knowing why some destinations are successful; understanding the key success factors; and adopting (copying) some of them, are key to improving competitiveness and profitability over time.

There are often a number of factors that contribute to success. These occur in a specific combination (for example political, social, economic, technological circumstances) that cannot easily be replicated.

But what makes a tourism destination successful?

While it is true that certain specific 'circumstances' cannot be replicated, specific strategies, actions and responses to 'circumstances' that have contributed to success, can certainly be replicated or at least learned from.

2   Key Questions

- Can success factors be replicated?

- Is there a relationship among the success factors? Must they occur together or in a specific order or combination?

- Are these factors specific to a region or country? And are they transferable?

- Do the same or similar factors contribute to the success of travel and tourism destinations across different regions of the world, different political systems, different sizes and levels of development?

- How important are factors such as leadership and vision, government policies, strategic alliances, Internet and Information Technology, human resource development, environmental conservation and sustainability as well as air access and marketing to the success of tourism destinations?

- Finally, what challenges do successful destinations face? And what strategies and actions are they adopting to overcome these challenges?

- Which destinations?
  - Australia
  - Barbados
  - Dubai
  - Costa Rica
  - France
  - Ireland
  - Mauritius
  - Jamaica
  - Singapore
  - South Africa
  - Thailand

3   What Are the Key Success Factors?

A number of factors contribute to the success of a tourism destination. These range from natural attributes to clever competitive strategies, forward-looking and visionary leadership, effective marketing campaigns and market segmentation, smart distribution networks, creativity and product innovations, dynamic national carriers, and more.

In the following sections, we list and examine the key success factors with a view to determining how important or relevant they have been for the destinations reviewed; the lessons that we can learn from them, and the extent to which they can be replicated.

Tourism Intelligence found 25 key reasons why these destinations are indeed successful. Today we will focus on three of these factors:

1. One key factor is 'Having vibrant national carriers': Singapore Airlines, Emirates and South African Airlines have all played key roles in the success of these destinations. So must a successful destination own a national carrier? The answer is: NOT necessarily. Barbados, for example, does not have its own carrier, however, but it is indeed a successful tourist destination. Nevertheless it is critical to be serviced by many airlines. Also important is the dynamism of the rest of the economy. A successful airline needs more than tourists on its plane, but it also needs the business travellers. In the majority of these destinations, whether it is Singapore, Dubai or France you have a nice quality clientele.

2. Focus on the wider economic development of the country in question: Mauritius, for example, has a dynamic sugar and clothing sector. Singapore is a vi-

brant trading centre, transport hub and home of thousands of MNCs (= multi national corporations). Costa Rica has a broad services sector, software development and environment services. As a conclusion you could say that tourism destinations cannot live from tourism alone. Developments in other sectors are key ingredients. The non-polluting services sector offers key opportunities that need to be exploited. In some of these successful tourism destinations, for example Mauritius and Barbados, real estate development and even health and wellness tourism are driving the industry. We should not be thinking that people are primarily travelling for sun, sand and sea.

3. An active and dynamic private sector: The example of Jamaica is critical: They have reinvented the holiday by building huge all-inclusive resorts, which are linked with the farmers, the other sector, the cultural providers and the entertainers. These places are the only places that offer jobs like playmakers, teachers of reggae etc. The tourist boards cannot do it alone, but have to work hand in hand with the private companies.

This is why the public-private-corporations are a key success factor. People have created an innovative and very effective marketing and should exploit distribution channels. With the recession also impacting the tourism sector the internet as a distribution channel will become more and more important. We can see that in Jamaica, in spite of the fact that everybody is forced to cut marketing expenditures, they are holding their own and have actually had an increase in travel in January/February. What counts is not what happens with the industry but what we do with it.

This makes a fundamental difference.

Today we will focus on two successful tourism destinations, which are chosen carefully. They have two critical features in common:

1. They care: In South Africa there is a fundamental caring about the local people and how they can benefit from tourism. There has been the first black empowerment charted that has been established for the tourism industry ever. Costa Rica cares a lot for the environment and the nature.

2. They act: We invited two of the best persons from both destinations, who will tell you exactly how they act.

3.1   South Africa

3.1.1 Key Success Factors South Africa

Among the key success factors underlying the success of the South African tourism has been the following.

Private/Public Partnership

The close working relationship between the government and the private sector has lead to a much better coordination and utilization of resources. Today, the private sector which includes nontourism stakeholders contribute about 50% towards SA Tourism's marketing budget.

Institutional Reform

Since the new government came into power, SA Tourism has undergone a major change. These changes include the appointment of a high profile CEO, making choices on the market segments that the country wants to target and closing down some of its overseas offices.

The Mandela Factor

South Africa is one of the few countries in the world that has a statesman that is admired across the world. This has helped boost the profile of the country. Mandela has been the driving force behind SA Tourism's successes.

National Tourism Policy

The National Tourism policy of the country is very clear on issues dealing with sustainable environmental development and addressing the imbalances that came as a result of the previous regime.

Adequate Funding

The key to any marketing effort is getting adequate funding to sustain SA Tourism's marketing strategy. Adequate funding is not the only reason for the NTO's success but is a major reason.

Smart Marketing

SA Tourism has appointed a research company to help identify which markets are strategic for South Africa. The overall objective of this strategy is to increase the country's return on its investment.

Regionalism

South Africa realizes that it cannot be an Island of success in a sea of failures. This has lead to several regional tourism initiatives. South Africa is a member of RETOSA which is a tourism regional body that represents 12 Southern African countries. RETOSA's mandate is to market the region as whole. Most successful economies are based on regional cooperation.

3.1.2 The South Africa Experience

Sindiswa Nhlumayo (S.N.), Deputy Director General, Department of Environmental Affairs and Tourism, South Africa:

"Tourism in South Africa is governed by a mandate that has been given by the government. The government wanted to invest in tourism so that it could contribute to the GDP growth. Other reasons were sustainable job creation and redistribution. Despite we are standing here talking about global economic crisis we in South Africa believe, that everything is possible. When we manage tourism we believe that 'If you can imagine it then you can do it!'. This notion is also underlined by the fact that our first black democratic president, Nelson Mandela, spent 27 years in jail. Other two very important personalities are Natalie Dudoit and Oscar Pistorius. They all fought and believed in themselves and said 'we will do it'. Focussing on that notion we have achieved a lot:

- In 1995 we hosted the Rugby World Cup and won it;
- In 1996 we hosted the Africa Cup of nation and won it;
- In 2002 we hosted the World summit on Sustainable development;
- In 2003 we hosted the Cricket World Cup.
- In 2010 we will as 19th country in 200 years be hosting the FIFA World Cup.

We are the 1st African country that has ever hosted this event. That is what we are proud of.Some dates: 20,000 media will be arriving, 3 million participants, billions of viewers. In 2006 we lost hosting the event to Germany, but we never gave up and now finally managed to host the event.

For us, hosting the event is not only about soccer but more about raising the profile and reputation of South Africa and Africa in general, it is about boosting tourism, trade and investment. It is also about building African pride and solidarity and strengthening South Africa's commitment to the region. Our mission consists in delivering a world class event, changing the perception of international communities about Africa and ensuring a lasting legacy for the people of Africa.

Before 1994, there were less than 500,000 people visiting our country. Due to the policies of the apartheid there was a limited movement by the people. However, in 2007 we recorded 9.1 millions arrivals. This did not just happen on its own, but it happened because we believed in what we were doing. Today tourism is creating 941,000 jobs. The contribution to the GDP increased from 2% in 1994 to 8.1% in 2007. South Africa has surpassed gold as a foreign exchange earner.

So how were we able to become a successful tourism destination?

1. It started with the political leadership: In 1994 tourism was identified as a key driver for reconstructing and developing South Africa economically and politically.

2. In 1996 we developed the White Paper, facilitated by Tourism Intelligence International, which talks about the idea of sustainable tourism development and promotion. Developing tourism we wanted to make sure that above all the local people would benefit. People talk about sustainable tour-

ism but we knew that it would not happen on its own. That is why we developed national guidelines for responsible tourism development. These were supposed to guide the private sector, the government as well as everyone in tourism about how to best manage responsible tourism. Tourism is about competing with other destinations.

Unlike doing nothing except waiting we undertook a Global Competitiveness Study in 2002, which enabled us to see our strengths and weaknesses. We are not scared of seeing where we stand. It also gave us an idea of which products we needed to develop in order to continue enhancing our competitiveness.

3. Tourism cannot be managed out of a vacuum, but is part of South Africa. Within the brand of South Africa there are many sub-brands, for example technology, diplomacy or trade. Tourism is also one of them, which we need to utilize to market South Africa. Our growth strategy is not just a strategy based on what we have. It is rather based on critical questions such as:

- What are our goals and aspirations?

- Where will we play?

- How will we win in chosen markets?

- What capabilities do we require in order to move forwards? (It is impossible to have a good strategy without good people who drive the strategy.)

- What will be the best management system to bring us forward?

4. When developing an integrated growth strategy for South African Tourism, trade-offs need to be made across three key dimensions: Time, resources and scope.

5. Which markets are we going to target? We developed a separate strategy for business and leisure tourism. Besides we created a strategy for events like the FIFA 2010. When doing marketing you need to understand who you are talking to. That is why we segmented the target markets: 60% of our resources are invested into our core markets, while we only invest 15% of the resources into our investment markets, which include markets with the potential to grow. 15% are invested into tactical markets and the last 5% in our watch-list. The message is that you need to allocate resources carefully in order to get the maximum profit.

6. We raved about tourism: In 1994 tourism was not taken seriously in South Africa but we made some noise. We showed everyone the potential.

7. Tourism can bring a socio economic magic to a destination.

8. Tourism has the ability to provide opportunities for all, which we made clear. Tourism should not be shed away in a cocoon.

9. We understood that tourism is a competitive industry and consumers are spoilt for choice. We defined our unique selling propositions.

10. There are new emerging destinations which are flavours of the day. That is why we needed to differentiate from the rest and play for gold.

What did we do with the segment markets?

- Selected them carefully,
- Made them come,
- Made them stay as long as possible,
- Spend as much as possible,
- Spread the benefits as wide as possible.

Our strategy consists of three pillars:

1. Marketing
2. Delivering on the ground: services must fulfil expectations and deliver what is promised in the marketing;
3. Conducive environment: proper legislations, proper policies and proper infrastructure and safety. It is critical for us to manage the relationships between the many players of tourism. Because if no communication between the players takes place, they will all spread different messages and do a different marketing strategy. We put in place mechanisms that ensure that all players are able to speak with one voice.

We wanted to address the challenge by building partnerships and clear role clarification. The public sector is the one to lead, whereas the private sector should drive the strategies. All work should be carried out very labour-based because those are the people that service the clients and create first impressions.

Summary of the lessons South Africa Tourism learnt:

1. You should have a plan, a winning strategy and clarify roles and responsibilities based on that strategy. Play as a team and pool resources.
2. Focus on USPs.
3. Touch the emotions. It is a business of selling a dream. Make people say 'I want to go there before I die'.
4. Clear communication and messaging to avoid confusion.
5. Speak with one voice.
6. Do more – talk less! Only good planners and doers will survive. Together we can do more. In Tourism each one of us is not as good as all of us.

The FIFA Worldcup will take place in June/July 2010. Developing the stadiums our intention was to create centres that even after the event will attract tourists. The flagship stadium is based in Johannesburg and will accommodate 94,700 persons. The stadium in Durban is right next to the sea. People will be able to climb on its roof, which is an arc, to see all of Durban city. Another one is situated in Polokwane. The stadium in Nelspruit has giraffes in its roof because the city is known for its wildlife. Each stadium reflects the image of the city where it is located. Standing on top of Capetown's stadium you have wonderful views of Robben Island and other surroundings."

3.2 Costa Rica

3.2.1 Key Success Factors Costa Rica

Costa Rica's tourism industry has excelled so quickly for several reasons:

Biodiversity

Costa Rica's incredible biodiversity offers foreigners a glimpse at mountains and volcanoes, as well as beaches and rainforests, all located within a relatively small region. Costa Rica's diverse flora and fauna are protected in 24 national parks, covering 21% of the country's territory (28% o the nation's Indian reserves are included).

Location

Costa Rica's proximity to the United States gives its tourist industry a clear advantage over the ecotourism adventures offered in Africa and Asia. Since the United States is the number one "tourist exporter" with American travelers making up approximately 20% of the world tourism market, Costa Rica's access to the North American market is a considerable advantage. The U.S. contributes nearly 40% of Costa Rica's foreign visitors with another 7% traveling down from Canada and Mexico.

Safety and Stability

Although Costa Rica has a long history of political and social stability, for a time its tourism industry was hindered by the violence, and guerrilla warfare exploding throughout Central America. Costa Rica does not even maintain a standing army, yet its reputation as a safe tourist destination was tainted by the turmoil occurring in neighbouring countries, El Salvador, Nicaragua, Guatemala, and Honduras. However, Costa Rica has since been able to distinguish itself from the rest of Central America, and its political stability, strong democratic institutions, and low violent crime rates are the nation's most important selling points.

Strong Environmental Lobby

Costa Rica's reputation among environmentalists is crucial to the successful promotion of their product, and this has incited the "green industry" to form an influential environmental lobby. Although the immediate costs of increased environmental regulations on travel services may initially injure profits, the long term benefits of maintaining an environmentally friendly image have swayed the eco-tourism industry to support most of the government's conservation initiatives.

Higher Standard of Living

Another advantage of Costa Rica's tourism industry is the nation's relatively high standard of living when compared with the majority of developing nations. Known as the Switzerland of Central America because of its high growth rates, economic stability, and low crime rates, Costa Rica enjoys a per capita GDP of US$6,700, literacy rate of 95%, and female life expectancy of nearly 79 years. By comparison, nearby El Salvador, boasts a per capita GDP of just US$3,000, a literacy rate of 71%, and a female life expectancy of about 74 years. When comparing Costa Rica with the developing nations of Africa, these differences are even greater. Thus, Costa Rica offers a look at a way of life distinct from the modernized world, while allowing tourists to largely avoid the sad realities of poverty in the Third World.

International Support

Finally, the development of Costa Rica's eco-tourism industry was both politically and financially supported by the IMF, World Bank, and the United States. For instance, the US Agency for International Development has long been active in promoting environmental protection and eco-tourism in Costa Rica by training park rangers and guides, funding conservation efforts, and setting up the Agricultural School for the Humid Tropical Region, or EARTH by it's Spanish acronym. For example, the World Bank had approved a $40 million loan for Costa Rica, a large portion of which focused on eco-tourism, including a unique program of paying landowners not to cut down their forests. This international support, along with a solid credit rating with international lenders, gives Costa Rica a degree of financial stability in handling the substantial costs of developing an eco-tourism industry.

3.2.2 The Costa Rica Experience

Maria Revelo (M.R.), Deputy Manager & Director of Marketing, ICT (Instituto Costarricense de Turismo), Costa Rica.

"First of all I would like to tell you about the long-term commitment of Costa Rica to human development and environmental protection. I will give you some surprising facts about our destination:

We have a life expectancy of 78,3 years, 48, 8% of our GDP is dedicated to education and 12% to health, 38% of our population has internet access and 12% have actually internet in their homes.

We have a tradition of peace and stability: The army was abolished in 1948. From then on that money was invested in health and education as well as creating a very big middle class.

According to an index of Latin America we are highest ranked in the absence of violence and political stability. Regarding politics we have more than a hundred years of democracy, three independent state powers, a 4-year term election with re-elections and a presidential system.

Which role has tourism played in Costa Rica?

Tourism is a rather new activity. It produced during less than the last 20 years more than double foreign income than our two main products coffee and banana combined. We have a population of 4 million people. In 2008 2.1 million tourists visited Costa Rica, which led to more than 2 billion dollars of income. In Costa Rica we have a very interesting combination of small, medium and large hotels. The average number of rooms per hotel is 16. During the years 2007 to 2008 the tourist arrivals growth increased from 5.2% to 12%. 56% of all air arrivals came from the USA, 16% from Europe and 28% from other countries. Tourism represents a 7.4% of the Internal Gross Product and 19% of exports.

So during the last 20 years the average growth of the tourism industry in Costa Rica has been 8%.

Most of the people that visit Costa Rica are very highly educated, wealthy and environmentally-conscious. They already have been to other countries and are now looking for another type of experience in Costa Rica. Within 10 years, from 1997 until 2007 our potential market has been growing, especially from the USA, from 4 million to 14 million.

Our commitment can be described in one word: Sustainability. 30% of Costa Rica's territory is protected in National Parks and reserves. The Government proclaims Carbon Neutrality for 2021 on our Independence anniversary. Costa Rica ranks 5 in the world (after Switzerland, Sweden, Norway and Finland) on the EPI (= Environmental Performance Index), which is a study done by Yale and Columbia University in 2008. Our country is number one in Latin America on the Tourism Competitive Index and 42 in the world.

We really believe that sustainability is not only A way, but it is THE ONLY way. It is the only way to make tourism successful for future generations and to stop global warming. It is the only way to make the tourist dollar have a good distribution in our countries. To ensure sustainability we put a lot of importance on quality. We have an eye on our private sector, which is a key success in our country. To make this happen we work hand in hand with the private sector. Governments cannot do it alone.

The type of products we are selling is a combination of nature, sun, sand and sea and adventure. We believe that sustainability does not only concern the tourism sector, but the whole country. We really need to embrace this word 'sustainability'.

That is why we, together with the other governments and the private sector, launched our Blue Flag Program. We encouraged more than 500 schools to participate in this program. We are working very strongly on the certification program, which certifies companies committed to sustainability (100 companies are already certified). The Blue Flag Program stimulates initiatives of the tourism private sector in the environmental protection, operation and social responsibility.

The four areas that we evaluate are:

- Physical-biological parameters: Interaction between the company and its surrounding natural habit;

- Infrastructure and services: Management policies and the operational systems within the company and its infrastructure;

- External clients: Interaction of the company with its clients in terms of how much it allows and invites the client to be an active contributor to the company's policies of sustainability;

- Socio-economic environment: Interaction of the company with the local communities and the population in general.

The rating of a company is the lowest rating on these four parameters. So the rating is very strict. Every one of these companies that has the certification for sustainable tourism is like a little sun that really warms up all the areas around it.

As a small country we would love to work with you for sustainable tourism."

4   About Tourism Intelligence International

"We are a well-respected research and consulting organization with offices in Trinidad and Germany. We saw the rapid change in tourism driven by more experienced and demanding customers and by new information technologies. We have been targeting the industry since 1994. We realize what makes the customers change in their way of feeling, thinking and behaving. We do research on how for example Germans, the British or Americans will travel in 2015. We do studies on the impact of terrorism and globalism in order to be able to give industry players and countries a real understanding of what happens in the industry. Tourism Intelligence has earned a reputation for research analysis and consultation that is often exhaustive. How we work: We are result-oriented, not task-oriented. We insist that good consultation needs a practical advice, clever competitive strategies, innovative solutions and well-defined problems as well as guidelines to put them in place. Since 1994 we have been involved in South African Tourism developing their tourism policy. We suggested them to adopt the strategy of Responsible Tourism because it was the only alternative for South Africa. The involvement of stakeholders and the process of sustainable tourism development are processes that we have been involved in.

Also we have consulted Abu Dhabi and delivered a tourism strategy that says 'Stay different'. That means to focus on the rich culture and create tourism for nationals and NOT just be another Dubai. Also we recommended creating a 'true capital with an icon'. So we developed the institutional framework for the Abu Dhabi Tourism Authority and led 10 Key Bankable Projects."

Megaresorts: Megaproblems or Megachances for Sustainability?

Klaus Lengefeld[1]

The tourism boom of the last decade, with Asia and the Middle East being its main drivers, has boosted a new type of developments, the so-called "Megaresorts". There is no common definition of that term, but it is usually associated with a sole investor developing a huge site which is appropriate for several hotels of different sizes and levels, private villas and apartments, shopping areas, a golf course and a marina (when in a coastal zone). Often, such developments are planned for areas which do not yet have the required infrastructure. Therefore the development of transport facilities (both roads and airports), water & energy supplies, telecom infrastructure, solid waste and sewage management facilities etc. is part of the project, and it is not unusual that the private investors take over roles and responsibilities which usually have to be assumed by governments from the public cofret. The investment volume for such Megaresorts frequently passes the 1 Billion US$ line.

Examples of Megaresort plans or developments are mainly to be found in the Middle East, such as Sama Dubai's Salam Yiti development in Oman, around the Egyptian and Jordan Red Sea Coast, Asia, North America and the Caribbean as well as Eastern Europe. And even in quiet rural places in the middle of Germany or Switzerland, such as the proposed 5000 beds resort in Beberbeck, a huge but under-used public farm in the north of the German Federal State of Hessen, or the Swiss Andermatt 1000 rooms/villas project of Egypt's ORASCOM.

Yet the tourism critics didn't take long to start denouncing such megadevelopments as a major threat mainly to the environment, even before taking a closer look at the foreseen precautions to control and minimize such impacts. Therefore it was a good moment to invite some major players in Megaresort development to the podium at ITB Convention's hospitality day, in order to bring some light into this debate.

Interestingly, a wide range of investors and projects presented and discussed at this forum showed that there is no "common denominator" for Megaresort devel-

---

[1] The statements made, and opinions expressed, in this article reflect the views of the author and do not necessarily reflect the position and policies of the *Deutsche Gesellschaft für Technische Zusammenarbeit (GTZ)*.

R. Conrady and M. Buck (eds.), *Trends and Issues in Global Tourism 2010*, Trends and Issues in Global Tourism, DOI 10.1007/978-3-642-10829-7_21,

opments besides the fact that those pass the limits of "normal" tourism investments in terms of size and scope.

1   Where Do Megaresort Developments Happen: In Untouched or in Already Developed Areas?

One of the panelists, Mr. Samih Saviris from ORASCOM has done both: What was a desert coastline on the Egyptian Red Sea north of Hurghada 20 years ago, has now become a Megaresort community for 15.000 residents, with 20 islands surrounded by lagoons, 14 hotels with 2700 hotel rooms, more than 100 restaurants and bars, a golf course, marina, shopping center, sports and recreation facilities, a hospital, schools, a university branch and even its own hotel school.

The good news about El Gouna is that it has been planned and built with very high sustainability standards in order to minimize its eco-footprint. More than 90% of solid waste is being reused or recycled in its own facilities or in existing recycling plants in Egypt. Water is not taken from wells but produced through desalinization. Bio-treated sewage is used for irrigation etc. In order to make these high eco-standards more transparent and credible, El Gouna has piloted the establishment of the country's first Eco-certification, the "Green Star" (see http://www.greenstarhotel.net/) which shall be taken over as the Egyptian standard.

Yet such megadevelopments are not only possible in uninhabited areas, what is shown by Mr Saviris last great "coup": The development of an integrated holiday resort in Andermatt, Swiss Alps, a 1 Billion SFr investment creating 6 hotels with 850 rooms, 490 apartments, 20-30 villas, a golf course, sports centre, congress centre and the required infrastructure. The foundation stone for this project has been just recently laid on 26 September 2009, and it shall fulfill the highest Eco-standards such as Carbon neutrality, a car-free village, environmentally friendly construction procedures etc.

But what is even more important: this megadevelopment shall create directly at least 1000 new jobs in a community of just 1,318 people that has suffered economic decline during the last decades and lost many people through internal migration. It was this huge positive local socio-economic impact in Andermatt and a very transparent approach involving all relevant stakeholders who paved the way to get this project approved and start building in – for Swiss conditions – a record short time.

The proposed Beberbeck development in Germany was less fortunate – although it was not even an outside investor who had proposed it but the mayor of Beberbeck, it encountered from the very beginning a strong rejection from environmentalists.

The TUI Toscana integrated resort project presented by the company's hotel director Karl Pojer has somehow started where Andermatt might have ended in the near future: in a nearly abandoned village in Italian Tuscany, that shall be revived by converting it into a big holiday village, the Toscana Resort Castelfalfi, with 3 major hotels, a golf course, restaurants and shopping area. Therefore this project has more elements of carefully conserving local buildings and culture and is not a huge new construction project. The eco-strategy of the Castelfalfi project includes investment in renewable energies, bio-sewage treatment and reuse of wastewater as well as the reconstruction of a diversified agriculture that was lost in the last decades, and that should supply the resort with fresh local produce. Although the 300 new jobs created are far behind the job balance of the other Megaresort developments presented here, for this rural Tuscany area it has a huge positive impact to cut unemployment.

The extreme opposite in terms of building concept is Singapore where the Las Vegas based Sands Company is reshaping the coastline and the skyline with its hypermodern Marina Bay Sands development: 2500 rooms and suites in three 200 m high hotel towers, with the roofs connected by a huge sky park, casino, shopping area, marina and a big museum that catches rainwater to create a huge waterfall in the museum and use it for water supplies etc. This project when finished shall employ up to 10,000 people. The company's principle, as clearly stated by Eric Bello representing them on the podium, is: We do what is profitable. So if good eco-practices are a business case such as energy, water or solid waste management, they would go for it, but not for eco-philanthropy.

Far ahead of that discussion whether additional investments into sustainable practices are profitable or not, nowadays the most advanced investors make zero eco-footprint *the* model for their holistic Megaresort development. Representing this latest trend, we had the Greek shipping magnate Achilles V. Constantakopoulos sitting on the podium, whose Costa Navarino development in Messinia, the southwestern part of Peloponnes peninsula is maybe the most consequent example. This more than one billion US$ total investment includes an incredible 100 Mio Euro for solar and geothermal renewable energy, not only to have a zero carbon and eco-footprint from energy generation for the Costa Navarino development with its planned 11 5-star hotels with 3,000 rooms, luxury villas and residences, 7 golf courses, 6 Thalasso spa centers, a marina and conference facilities, but to also make the whole region's energy supplies independent from fossil fuels.

Besides this "carbon positive" energy concept, the other stunning eco-investment is the construction of subterranean reservoirs to catch 650,000 cbm of rainwater, enough to supply the whole resort and irrigate all its green areas including the golf courses. Therefore this resort could also be called a "water positive" investment, because it not only doesn't exhaust the existing water resources, it catches lots of rainwater and keeps it by creating new green areas – similar to El Gouna with the only difference that there is no rainwater to catch in the Egyptian desert, but seawater to desalinize.

And if we would continue the list of eco- and socially positive investments such as a strong commitment with local recruitment for the thousands of jobs and local sourcing of supplies, undertaken by these Megaresort developers with an advanced sustainability concept, this would simply go beyond the size of this article.

In summary, the panel had 3 strong advocates for sustainability being a feasible, if not the only possible model in the future for developing Megaresorts, and with Las Vegas Sands' Eric Bello one strong skeptic.

However, when we take a closer look into the Marina Bay Sands development in Singapore, it has some strategies especially with respect to recruitment of local people that are hardly to be found in the sustainability performance of many other hotel developers: For instance, to fill the up to 10,000 job vacancies without relying on migrant labour, Marina Bay Sands together with the Singapore labour administration has started a campaign to motivate especially elderly unemployed people as well as women and housewives who might not have thought of having a chance to find a job. Such positive employment approaches from a private company are the dream of any public German labour agency, and therefore they should roll out the red carpet to invite Sands Las Vegas to build a Venetian in Berlin or Munich. Unfortunately I am quite sure that such an investment plan would encounter both huge bureaucratic barriers and strong rejection from NGOs in Germany – a rather "toxic" cocktail for such a megainvestment.

The essence: What are the messages on Megaresorts and sustainability?

2   The "Ecology of Scale"

Samih Sawiris spoke out one of the most significant messages on sustainability and Megaresorts: If you build just one or two or three hotels, you cannot invest in a wastewater treatment facility or a solid waste recycling system that fulfills the highest eco-standards. But if you build a complete village with thousands of hotel rooms, apartments, shopping centre, staff quarters etc., it makes perfect sense *and* is economically viable to include such investments into the project.

This positive **"ecology of scale"**: *"If you make it big enough, you can make it sustainable"* is the vision of those major investors that are on the forefront of sustainable / zero eco-footprint Megaresort developments.

On the other hand, big developments always generate also big risks for the environment, local people and cultures. If a small hotel has problems with its wastewater system, the negative impact on the environment might not be very big. But if the wastewater treatment for 10,000 people who are staying in a Megaresort fails, this might cause an eco-catastrophy. Therefore environmentally sensitive systems in Megaresorts need to be at the highest standards and must have double safeguards.

3   Megaresort Versus Conventional Destination Development

Conventional destination developments either start with a public initiative and incentives to invite investors to build hotels under a given tourism development or master plan, or with the private investor who discovers a pristine beach and builds the first guesthouse followed by many other private developers. Both might end in the creation of megadestinations such as Cancún (with 50,000+ hotel rooms) and Riviera Maya in Mexico, which was under a government plan, or Punta Cana in Dominican Republic which is a completely privately developed destination where even the airport, energy supply etc. was 100% private investment.

When comparing the sustainability of such megadestinations with the new Megaresort developments, the most evident issue is that those megadestinations have produced some very critical environmental impacts that might even put the whole tourism product at risk. Although all major hotels there do have wastewater treatment and some other eco-management procedures in place, everything that happens outside the fence of their hotel is not under their control. The most significant negative impacts in such megadestinations are the lack of a solid waste management system under the principle of "Reduce, Reuse, Recycle" as well as a sustainable settlement and community development policy, both issues that are under the responsibility of the central, regional and municipal governments.

In contrast, the advanced Megaresort developers such as ORASCOM's El Gouna or Costa Navarino with their holistic development concept take over these usually public responsibilities because they want it **"All under one control"**. Of course, this can only work if they own or control all the land and if the laws and regulations allow for it – in some countries for instance there is a public monopoly on waste and wastewater management or energy generation that wouldn't allow a private investor to build his own energy or sewage plant.

4   The "Licence to Operate"

The maybe most important challenge for a Megaresort developer is to convince local stakeholders that the overall balance of his project for local development is so positive that they would agree to accept the negative impact it would create for them especially during the construction phase. This process to get the local "Licence to Operate" is based on transparency, openness and mutual trust. In the ideal case, the investor starts what we call in modern development language a **"Multi-Stakeholder process"** to consult and involve all local interest groups and representatives from relevant regional and national public and private entities in order to take their criteria, expectations and concerns into account. Often an independent moderation of such a process from a renown outside entity is very helpful if not necessary.

All projects when local people are the last to know what others in the capital city have discussed and decided to be build in their area have encountered severe problems with an often unsubstanced local rejection and with the consequence that they could not be realized. Thus local people might lose the maybe best option for economic development in their area.

5   Outlook: Megaresorts Versus Investment in Other Sectors

Any major investment means a significant intervention in the local environment, social balance and cultures, even when trying to go for Zero Eco-Footprint and minimise critical impacts. Therefore small or even no development of tourism seems to be the most sustainable option.

However, when a region or a country needs economic development to generate jobs and income for thousands of people the question is very different:

> *Which sector or industry requires a minimum of resources to achieve the maximum output in terms of economic development, re-distribution and poverty reduction?*

Unfortunately the development impact scenarios of a Megaresort compared with textile or electronics factories, with oil palm plantations, mining or oil investments has so far not been done, although this would be the real baseline to discuss the sustainability of tourism development compared with other development options for countries who desperately need economic development.

And even for Germany, I severely question the sustainability of huge public support to attract some highly appreciated industries, such as the 7.7 Bio Euro subsidies so far to get AMD and other electronic industries into Saxony. One AMD factory costed 1.5 Bio investment and 1 Bio subsidies – and created 1000 direct jobs. With 2.5 Bio invested in Megaresorts along the beautiful Baltic coast or inland projects like TUI Fleesensee, at least 20 times more jobs would have been created …

Unfortunately, the negative scenario of no development is already there: In Egypt through tourism there is now (and after also having produced negative impact in the past) a certain chance to conserve the unique pristine marine biodiversity and coral reefs of the Red Sea. In many other places around the world coral reefs will long have disappeared through unsustainable fishing and erosion-producing farming and logging practices even before tourism discovers it, thereby finally losing the chance of conservation *and* economic development through tourism.

Branded Residences

Philip Bacon

The Branded Residence business is suffering on a global scale from the fall out from the credit crunch. Price premiums, seen consistently over recent years, are now hard, if not impossible, to achieve. In many markets people have simply stopped buying second homes. Financing models which have been valid for years are under scrutiny. A discussion during this year's "ITB Hospitality Day", held at ITB Berlin in March 2009 touched on the current difficulties and the effects of the actual crisis on Branded Residences. The following article covers some thoughts and principles of a business model that, despite the challenges of the current market, still has potential for branded hospitality developments.

"How can we create a lasting mixed use of hospitality-based assets that meets the needs of tomorrow?" asked Philip Bacon, Managing Director EMEA & Asia of HVS Shared Ownership Services based in Madrid, in a recent article for the "2009 Hotel Year Book" looking at trends in European mixed-use resort development.

For many, the mixed-use resort development simply involves the addition of residential units to a standard resort concept as part of a sometimes rather dubious way to finance the whole development. Off-plan sales are the key, coupled with a branded hotel and promises of rental guarantees for several years.

Years ago, hotel operators, especially at the top end of the market, found that their customers rather liked the idea of owning property where they could also enjoy the benefits of hotel-style service and even the chance to earn some rental income. The idea of premium branding was created (some leading exponents being Four Seasons Hotels & Resorts, Mandarin Oriental Hotels & Resorts and Trump International) and a marriage was made between the Condo Hotel model (by no means a new idea) and the world of exclusive private residences (which again have always existed, or at least for the last several centuries).

Something else that hasn't changed are the rules of the real estate business. It is important to repeat them for those who might have forgotten temporarily in the madness of the pre-crunch years.

Location – Location – Location. In Europe, this represents a significant challenge for those who have not been sitting on an undeveloped prime land bank for the last ten years, and even if you have, things have just got much harder than you ever expected.

R. Conrady and M. Buck (eds.), *Trends and Issues in Global Tourism 2010*, 179
Trends and Issues in Global Tourism, DOI 10.1007/978-3-642-10829-7_22,
© Springer-Verlag Berlin Heidelberg 2010

It is certainly easy to see that there has already been a major slowing down of new projects and a delay in the opening/completion of some that are already underway. Successful mixed-use resort development is a long-term subject and it pays to take your time to get it right, provided you have the patience and the pocket depth to wait for your returns over the medium to long term.

But will mixed-use resorts lose their lustre as real estate finance (both development and personal) becomes increasingly difficult to find? As long as the planners are in charge of our destinies, then perhaps mixed-use is here to stay and we should embrace it as the future of tourism-based development whether urban, beach, rural or anything else.

The reality for many is that the planners will often only allow residential development on the understanding that the project includes a decent chunk of transient accommodation to create 'life' and, perhaps more mundanely, jobs. As part of managing development risk, there will be a move away from off-plan and we will see the radical departure of handing over keys to a finished unit.

The economic upheaval will create some real market opportunities as the combination of a down-turn in spending and banking pressure may create some forced sellers of assets that you would not normally expect to come to market.

Don't discount fractional interests and other shared ownership models. In many ways you could argue that their time has come at last in Europe, through a combination of increased exposure and the impact of tightened belts and lower levels of disposable income. However, don't under-estimate the fundamentals of something that is not sold with a pure real estate pitch. Everybody understands capital appreciation of real estate, but making it cheaper by splitting it into smaller pieces doesn't make it easier to sell, it makes it much more difficult. And what's more, shared ownership models will not necessarily fix a poorly-conceived project.

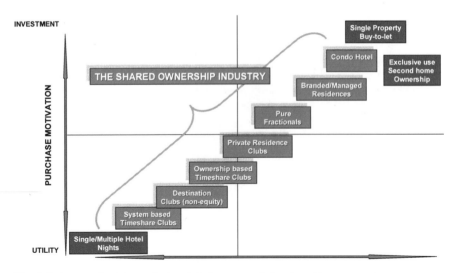

Fig. 1. Leisure real estate product matrix (accommodation-based)

In this article we focus on Branded Residences. Fig. 1 shows the position of this business model in a scheme of different shared ownership business models.

The shared ownership industry comprises a number of business models, each having at its core the ownership of an interest in leisure real estate assets by owners, including private individuals, within a resort-based environment. Increasingly, shared ownership products are frequently combined with traditional hospitality and exclusive-use real estate products in a mixed-use resort environment.

The chart shown above presents the approximate positioning of the various business models identified to date by HVS Shared Ownership Services that today make up the shared ownership sector, which in turn forms part of the accommodation-based leisure real estate industry.

Looked at it from a supply side or a developer perspective, this range of options starts at one extreme with the traditional, nightly-stay hotel business model, (i.e. the guest rents the key to the door and gives it back at the end of the rental period) and ends at the other extreme with the exclusive-use second home business model (i.e. the owner buys the key to the front door and keeps it) and the single property buy-to-let model (i.e. a stand alone property is placed within an external management company for rental and is not occupied by the owner).

Looked at it from the demand side in terms of the purchasers' motivation to buy, in all of these business models there will be a different mix of purchase motivation between the two main factors of:

1. Utility (i.e. use or enjoyment), and
2. Investment (i.e. some form of return on capital).

Set out below are brief definitions of these shared ownership business models. The list is not intended to be exhaustive, there are many variations on these basic themes, but the majority of products either currently on the market or being planned will fall into these categories.

1. System-Based Timeshare Clubs

This model covers the purchase by club members of an entitlement to use certain resort or similar assets during a pre-determined period of time (which may be long or short-term) without acquiring any interest, either a right of use or a right *in rem,* in any of the individual properties or any entity that owns the properties. Typically club members will pay an initial membership fee to cover the first period of membership and an annual membership fee to cover certain services. The facility to exchange between several properties of the same or similar nature is a key feature of this business model. There may be a separate charge for individual transactions such as exchanges between properties.

2. Destination Clubs – "Non-equity-Based"

A "non equity-based" Destination Club is a variation of the system-based timeshare club model. This model has been identified separately due to its relative prominence in the market, particularly in the USA. The differentiating factor of this model is that Destination Clubs are generally positioned very high up the quality scale and the properties tend to be individual homes rather than properties that form part of a larger resort environment. One additional difference is the practice of offering subject to certain terms and conditions, the return of a percentage (e.g. 80%) of the initial membership fee should the member decide to leave the club.

3. Ownership-Based Timeshare Clubs

This model is what is generally regarded as timeshare or vacation ownership around the world, made prominent by branded players such as Disney, Wyndham, Starwood, Hilton, Hyatt, Sol Meliá and Marriott. It is the most common variation of the timeshare concept. There are multiple legal definitions of this model, mainly because of the need of legislators and related regulatory bodies to find a place for a product that does not fall within traditional real estate rules.

In contrast to system-based timeshare clubs, in the vast majority of cases this model involves the acquisition by the purchaser of a long-term interest (usually more than 20 years) in a specific property or range of properties. This interest is normally an interval of time that covers seven nights of accommodation in a particular accommodation type and will either be a right to use the accommodation or a right *in rem* that can be registered publicly.

Because of the long-term nature of this model, the assets are normally subject to some form of protected legal ownership (e.g. a trust) so that the interests of the individual club members are protected for the life of their ownership.

In terms of membership services, exchange facilities and fee structures, ownership-based timeshare clubs are operated using the same principles as system-based timeshare clubs.

4. Private Residence Clubs (PRC)

This model is a variation of the ownership-based timeshare club model. The key differences are:

1. The nature of the assets and the members is consistently at the upper end of the price/quality scale;
2. The interest sold in the properties generally represents an interval of time of more than two and less than 12 weeks (often referred to as fractional interests).

One important aspect of these products is that the usage system over the course of a year will not be a function of a particular week, group of weeks or season, but rather an equitable, rotational system that offers the best possible solution to the maximum number of owners. It is the combination of physical product features, the nature of the real estate interest, the flexibility of the usage plan and the quality of the services on offer that add up to the value added above and beyond a simple interest in real estate.

Prominent examples of this model are offered by large branded hospitality companies such as Ritz-Carlton, Four Seasons, Fairmont and St Regis as well as within individual properties located in destinations that enjoy limited supply, high value real estate and a strong demand for repeat visitation.

5. Pure Fractional Interests

This model is more clearly part of the leisure real estate industry than the time-share sector. The focus is on the sale of a simple share (typically a ¼ share) in an individual property that may or may not be part of a larger resort environment. There is more expectation that the value of the fractional interest will fluctuate in value in line with the value of whole ownership properties.

Sometimes additional products are sold simultaneously (e.g. membership of an exchange system) but this is not always a major motivating factor in making the purchase.

6. Branded/Managed Residences

The Branded or Managed Residence concept is favoured by many of the major upscale hotel brands as they combine the provision of a luxury lifestyle with the development of superior real estate products for sale outright to an investor/user market. These products are often in very desirable destinations, not necessarily resorts, but always where the cost of prime residential property is high and will remain high for the foreseeable future. Whilst some residences may be offered for rental, this aspect of the business model is typically not a major motivating factor in the decision of the purchaser to buy.

Branded/Managed Residences are becoming increasingly prominent outside the USA and the Caribbean, where they are relatively well established, by branded operators such as Ritz-Carlton, Four Seasons, Mandarin Oriental, Banyan Tree, Fairmont, Starwood (St Regis) and Kempinski.

7. Condo Hotel

The Condo Hotel model can be applied to several types of property including ac-commodation types from hotel rooms & suites to apartments, townhouses and vil-las. The basic model involves the sale of property which is actively managed by a separate company that contracts the services of a management company to market accommodation and provides services to guests. In all cases there will be some split of rental revenues between the hotel operator and the individual property owner, either on a pooled or separate asset basis. In this way, the owner receives a contribution towards the costs of ownership as well as having, in most cases, some personal use of the property.

Many purchasers are more motivated by the yield on their investment than by the opportunity to use the property on a regular basis. This model is often em-ployed where the property represents the only hotel-based asset on the resort rather than where there are second home properties adjacent to a hotel.

Culture – A Tourist Attraction:
Importance – Expectations – Potential

Albrecht Steinecke

Culture is a tourist resource with a long tradition, a vivid present and a promising future. Already, for the Grand Tour of the English aristocracy in the 17th and 18th century, culture and education were the main priorities. Since then, millions of people have followed in the footsteps of their tourist ancestors by visiting historic buildings, cities and sites.

At the beginning of the 21st century, cultural tourism is extremely popular and, at the same time, omnipresent: cathedrals, art exhibitions and concerts are recording high numbers of visitors and the offers for events and festivals are vast. However, more and more providers of cultural activities are pushing into the lucrative travel market which will lead to increasing competition in the area of cultural tourism in the coming years.

In this situation, providers of cultural activities and educational travel need up-to-date market information to develop successful business strategies and target group orientated marketing operations. However, the current situation regarding data and research concerning cultural tourism proves to be ambivalent:

- On the one hand, tourism research has been concentrating on this issue in numerous case studies and at scholarly conventions since the 1990s. The results are documented in collected volumes, textbooks and bibliographies (Becker/Steinecke 1993; Robinson/Evans/Callaghan 1996; DSF 1996; Weissenborn 1997; Heinze 1999; Korsay et al. 1999; AIEST 2000; Dreyer 2000; Richards 1996, 2001; Steinecke 2007).

- On the other hand, specific data for this market segment are missing, because official statistics do not record cultural tourism (e.g. visitor numbers for museums are, at best, estimated). In tourist surveys cultural tourism is merely recorded as one out of many kinds of vacation travel.

Therefore, a specific representative survey concerning cultural tourism was carried out throughout Germany for the first time in 2009.[1] The survey focused on the following questions:

---

[1] The survey was conceived by Jens Hulverson (Gebeco, Kiel), Dr. Wolfgang Isenberg (Thomas-Morus-Academy, Bensberg) and Prof. Dr. Albrecht Steinecke (University of

R. Conrady and M. Buck (eds.), *Trends and Issues in Global Tourism 2010*,
Trends and Issues in Global Tourism, DOI 10.1007/978-3-642-10829-7_23,
© Springer-Verlag Berlin Heidelberg 2010

- How important is culture when considering a person's reasons for holiday travel?

- Regarding tourist activities, how important are visits to cultural attractions?

- What does it mean to tourists to visit cultural attractions?

- What do tourists remember most about a visit to a cultural attraction?

- What is the potential demand for (self-)organized cultural and educational travel?

- What do tourists expect from organized cultural travel?

The following article gives a short review of the survey's main results.

1   How Important Is Culture When Considering a Person's Reasons for Travel?

In recent decades, tourism research has compiled numerous surveys about the reasons for travel. On the one hand, there are theoretical surveys categorising one's wish for travel according to already established social science theories, e.g. travel as an anthropologic constant, as an ostentatious consumption, as a pilgrimage, as a game, as an exhilarating experience etc. Although explications of this sort seem to be logical at first sight, they can prove to be problematic, because of their one-dimensional character. They can, indeed, sufficiently explain the reasons for some kinds of tourism. Given the variety of reasons for travel, however, they prove to be insufficient (Hennig 1997: 72-101).

On the other hand, tourism motivation has been the subject of empirical research as well, e.g. in form of direct interviews as well as telephone interviews and mail questionnaires. But these methods are not perfect either, because the respondents' answers are based on voluntarily disclosed personal information. The respondents need to have a great ability to reflect and articulate. Furthermore, these methods involve the risk of receiving answers that are socially desired by the respondents, while those reasons for travel that need to be thought of ambivalently are not mentioned at all (Steinecke 2006: 49-51).

These methodological constraints have to be taken into account as well when looking at the following results. In each case, the data refers to the subjective view of the respondents. Therefore, no defined term for "culture" was given beforehand, because there is no absolute and interdisciplinary accepted definition of "culture" (Moebius 2009). Additionally, the number of statements was intentionally reduced

Paderborn). The telephone interviews (1,509 people over the age of 16) were conducted by the European Tourism Institute in Trier. The project was funded with the financial support of Gebeco (Kiel), a provider of educational and cultural travel.

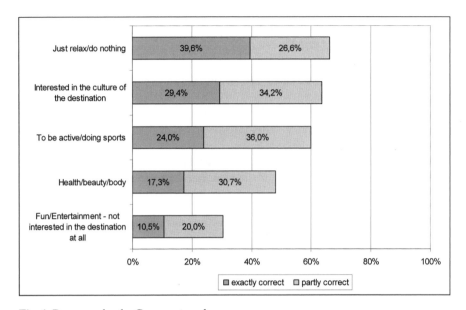

Fig. 1. Reasons why the Germans travel

Source: survey on cultural tourism by Gebeco/TMA/UPB 2009

to five central reasons for travel: relaxation, culture, health and body, sports, entertainment (see fig. 1).

For 66.2% of the respondents, recreational reasons such as relaxing/doing nothing are the most important vacation expectations. These reasons reflect the high physical and mental strain, as well as the restrictions, that the German population has to face in their everyday work (this is why recreation is particularly important to middle-aged, working respondents).

Interest in the culture of the travel destination comes a close second at 63.6%. This figure shows that culture is of great importance to Germans among their reasons for travel, regardless of whether the respondents understand culture as tourist attractions of a high culture or as cultural elements of everyday life. Older people especially show a keen interest in new cultural experiences (81.1% of the 65-74-year-olds vs. 37.5% of the 16-24-year-olds).

Usually, German tourists are more curious and open-minded about new impressions than is generally assumed. This fact also becomes clear in the relatively limited approval of the statement "During my last vacation, fun and entertainment were especially important to me – the travel destination did not matter". Although shown as pleasure-seeking, boozy and noisy in the media, especially on commercial TV stations, only every third respondent could be characterised as a hedonistic and solely fun-oriented tourist (predominantly younger tourists with a low level of education).

2   Regarding Tourist Activities, How Important Are Visits of Cultural Attractions?

Two thirds of all Germans want to learn more about the everyday culture of their travel destination during their vacation. The fact, that cultural attractions rate among the most popular activities during a vacation, reflects this great interest. In this ranking, taking a walk and hiking come first. However, a large section of the respondents visit historic buildings, an exhibition or take a guided city tour (see fig. 2).

Among the cultural attractions, churches and convents prove to be the most popular sights at 51.4%. From a touristic perspective, they have a diverse potential (Steinecke 2007: 103-104):

- As an architectural/ historical site, they represent different stylistic periods.

- Cathedrals are seen as especially spectacular buildings (landmarks), which impress with their great architecture and valuable inventory.

- Many churches and convents are religious sites which are still in use. Therefore, they offer visitors a special atmosphere of peace and tranquillity.

One proof of their great attraction is the high number of visitors some churches can record: Cologne Cathedral, for example, is the most popular of all German sites with 6 million visitors a year. About 1 million people visit the Aachen Dome

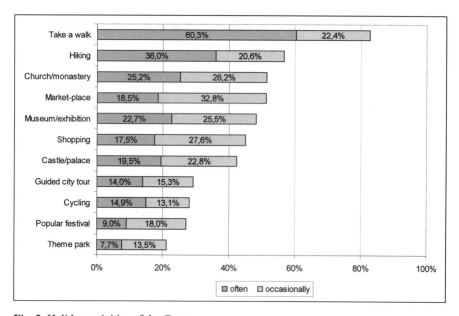

Fig. 2. Holiday activities of the Germans

Source: survey on cultural tourism by Gebeco/TMA/UPB 2009

every year and 600,000 visit the Ulm Cathedral (see German tourism association DTV 2003).

48.2% of the respondents stated, that they visited museums and exhibitions during their vacation. This type of demand is closely associated with the expansion of museums in Germany as well as in other European countries. The number of museums in Germany, for example, rose from 2,076 in 1981 to 6,197 in 2007 (Institute for Museum Research IfM 2008: 7). Besides the permanently exhibited art collections, special temporary events can attract visitors like a magnet, e.g. the exhibition of the Museum of Modern Art (New York) in Berlin, which recorded more than 1.2 million visitors in 2004.

Among the popular cultural attractions are castles and palaces (42.3%). Although they are now standard sites, they have been used as tourist attractions only since the 19th century (since the Romantic period – especially castle ruins, which are considered to be relics of a mysterious past). In Germany, Heidelberg Castle (1.2 m visitors/year), Neuschwanstein Castle (1.2 m) and Wartburg Castle (430,000) record the highest number of visitors (see DTV 2003).

3   What Does It Mean to Tourists to Visit Cultural Attractions?

In the survey, 85.6% of the respondents stated that they visited cultural attractions at some point. For the majority (82.1%), such sightseeing is a matter of course and is simply part of a perfect vacation (see fig. 3). Based on this evaluation, excursions and sightseeing can be described as habitual tourist activities, which have no particular importance for the holidaymaker.

This stance is the result of a historical learning process, which has been taking place since the beginning of tourism in the 17th and 18th century. During the Grand Tour of the English aristocracy, it was not the visiting of churches, castles and museums, but the training in dance, fencing and horseback riding, meeting important people and learning how to behave according to one's social standard that were on the agenda (Brilli 1997).

It was not until the 19th century, when the bourgeoisie was able to travel as well, that sites of interest came more and more to the fore. Given the short time and sparse funds available, tours had to be planned and calculated efficiently. Tourists wanted to be able to orientate themselves quickly and see those things which were especially worth seeing. The traveller's companions ("Red Books") of British John Murray and the guidebooks of Karl Baedeker provided a classification of sights (a valuation system with stars) and a catalogued order of sightseeing, influencing tourists' travel behaviour up to the present day (Steinecke 2007: 321).

Besides the habitual sightseeing behaviour, there are many, and sometimes very specific reasons, for visiting a cultural attraction: The desire to further one's professional qualifications plays a minor role (11.6%) similar to coincidental

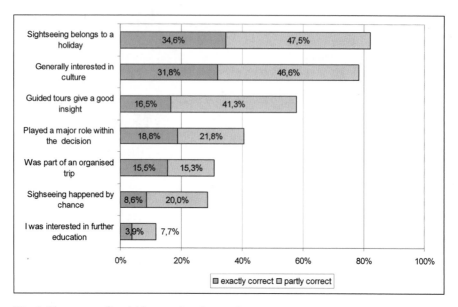

Fig. 3. The reasons for visiting a cultural attraction

Source: survey on cultural tourism Gebeco/TMA/UPB 2009

sightseeing (28.6%). On the other hand, 40.6% of the respondents said that the visit to a cultural attraction was already a central issue when deciding on a vacation. These holidaymakers can generally be described as cultural tourists:

- 18.8% are cultural tourists in a narrow sense (they regarded the statement as "exactly correct").

- A further 21.8% are cultural tourists in a wider sense (they regarded this statement as "partly correct").

These results agree with other studies of the cultural tourism sector (although the data cannot be compared directly due to different collection methods):

- In the 1980s, a survey carried out across Europe concluded that 23.5% of tourist arrivals could be attributed to the cultural tourism sector. 10% of which were "Specific Cultural Tourists" for whom cultural attractions were the main reason for choosing their vacation and 90% were "General Cultural Tourists", i.e. vacationers with an interest in culture but who also shared a broader range of reasons for going on vacation and shared a broader range of interests (Irish Tourist Board et al. 1988: 23).

- 16% of respondents of the travel survey "Reiseanalyse 2008", carried out by the research team for vacation and travel (Forschungsgemeinschaft Urlaub und Reisen, established in Kiel), stated that it was "very important" to them to do something cultural and educational whilst on vacation. This reason for a vacation can be found in the lower segment made up of a broad range which includes 29 statements (F. U. R. 2008: 86).

78.4% of the respondents claimed to be interested in culture at home as well as on holiday. This information may be important to the marketing departments of the providers of cultural activities and operators offering cultural travel. Through cooperation with adult education centres, theatres, museums and associations, communication strategies can be developed to reach prospective customers at their homes.

4   What Do Tourists Remember Most About a Visit to a Cultural Attraction?

The tourists are eager and curious visitors but at the same time they are no experts on the history of art and culture. They want to see something impressive, gain new impressions and be informed in an entertaining manner. This fact stands out clearly due to the respondents' answers to the question, what they remembered in particular about their last visit to a cultural institution (see fig. 4).

Even though classical learning experiences are significant, they are less so than general memories like a change from the daily routine (94.1%) and a good and in spiring atmosphere (90.1%). It is far more important to spend a pleasant day

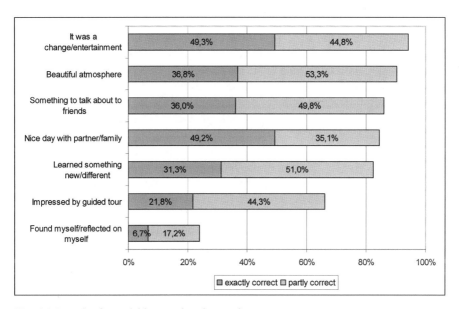

Fig. 4. Memories from visiting a cultural attraction

Source: survey on cultural tourism Gebeco/TMA/UPB 2009

with one's partner or family and to be able to have something to tell one's friends at home.

These results contain important information for providers of cultural activities and operators of cultural travel which helps them to design their products, because the demanding and travel-experienced customers do not simply expect dry data, numbers and facts – they expect an illustrated, lively and emotionally touching presentation. From the visitors' perspective, the sightseeing of churches, castles and museums is a collective experience which should include all senses, and not just the intellect. It should therefore be the central aim of culture and tourism marketing departments to produce such memories for holiday travellers.Therefore it is necessary to pay attention to a crucial factor that is typical for all cultural tourists: Selectivity. In the face of little time and money, holidaymakers are forced to select places and sights. They are not interested in getting a complete and systematic overview. Instead, they are looking for the extraordinary, the typical or the superlative. This selectivity forms a strong contrast to the aim of traditional providers of cultural activities (especially museums) who offer systematic, broad and thorough transfer of knowledge about collections, research and education.

5   What Is the Potential Demand for (Self-)Organized Cultural and Educational Travel?

The analyses of the reasons for travel showed that older people are far more curious about and interested in culture than younger age groups, who prefer to relax and have fun. Hence the aging of the German population provides an opportunity for cultural institutions and operators of cultural travel alike, as seniors constitute an increasingly important group in the tourist sector.

In order to record the potential demand for cultural and educational travel more precisely, the following question was asked in the course of the survey: "There are many ways to spend one's vacation. Which types of vacation are of interest to you during the next three years?"

Long-distance travel to exotic destinations (54.1%) and beach holidays by the Mediterranean Sea (52.2%) rank high among the most popular types of vacations (see fig. 5). Self-organized cultural and educational travel comes in third place (51.2%) and this is especially popular among the middle- and higher-age groups (above 45 years).

The potential demand for organized cultural travel, as offered by tour operators, accounts for 9.9% ("great interest") or 21.7% ("interest"). In comparison to other empirical data collections, this survey found a marked greater potential for this type of vacation: In the German travel analyses of 2008 quoted above, a mere 3% of respondents said that they were "fairly sure" they were planning a cultural holiday. A further 6% thought this offer to be worth "general consideration" (F. U. R. 2008: 102).

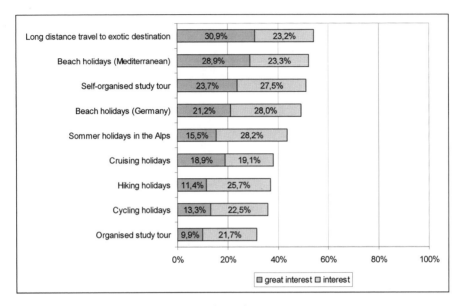

Fig. 5. Future interest in different kinds of vacation

Source: survey on cultural tourism Gebeco/TMA/UPB 2009

6   What Do Tourists Expect from Organized Cultural Travel?

The character of organized cultural travel has changed fundamentally in the course of history. The scientific expeditions of the 19th century, which were undertaken by professors and their students to get to know foreign countries and different cultures, became a touristic product in its own right in the 20th century (Steinecke 2007: 280-281).

Against the background of a changed definition for "culture" and new demands of the participants, cultural travel is undergoing constant change – away from the classical form which focused exclusively on the relicts of the high culture to a contemporary kind of vacation that also includes cultural elements of an everyday nature. Current trends of this market segment are: The thematic specialization, experience-orientated marketing, use of different modes of transport, designation of new target groups and product classification (luxury vs. low-budget cultural travel).

Notwithstanding these changes in organisation and content, this survey makes it clear that the (potential) participants are mainly interested in getting to know the holiday destination, its culture and people (94.5%). Additional typical expectations include furthering one's own education as well as gaining special insights through the tour guide (see fig. 6). On the other hand, comfort, the desire for social contacts and the interest in particular cultural institutions are of slightly less importance for organized cultural travel.

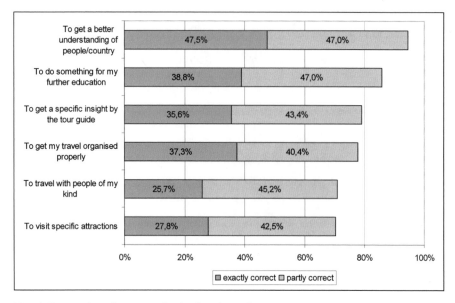

Fig. 6. Expectations from organized cultural travel

Source: survey on cultural tourism Gebeco/TMA/UPB 2009

The results show clearly that (potential) customers have a variety of demands for contemporary cultural travel. Tour operators are thus facing the challenge of combining the elements of classical cultural travel (transfer of knowledge, sociability, and safety) with new elements. This includes the individualisation of offers because participants place more value on flexibility and the realisation of their own interests. On the other hand, cultural travel should not just transfer cognitive knowledge but also facilitate sensual and emotional experiences (Treidel 2006: 367-368).

In spite of these changes, the core elements of organized cultural travel prove to be quite stable: An expert guide and a set program, based on a sound concept and good preparatory work.

7   Conclusion

This survey has generated current data on the general importance of culture as a tourist attraction, on the expectations of tourists and the future potential demand for this sector. The central results are as follows:

- The culture of the holiday destination constitutes an important part of the range of reasons for going on vacation.

- After walking and hiking, visiting cultural attractions is among the most popular holiday activities.

- Sightseeing is just part of having a great holiday; for 41% of the respondents it is a central reason for going on a vacation.

- Tourists do not just remember the educational value of sights, but above all, they associate general and positive memories with them (change from their daily routine, sophisticated atmosphere, pleasant day spent with their partner/family, having something to tell other people about).

- Great potential exists for self-organized cultural travel; 10% of Germans are interested in cultural travel.

References

AIEST (International Association of Scientific Experts in Tourism: 2000): Tourism and Culture, St. Gallen (AIEST Publication; 42)

Becker, Chr./Steinecke, A. (Ed.; 1993): Kulturtourismus in Europa: Wachstum ohne Grenzen? Trier (ETI-Stud.; 2)

Brilli, A. (1997): Als Reisen eine Kunst war. Vom Beginn des modernen Tourismus: Die "Grand Tour", Berlin

Dreyer, A. (Ed.; 2000): Kulturtourismus, 2nd ed. Munich/Vienna

DSF (Deutsches Seminar für Fremdenverkehr) (Ed.; 1996): Kulturtourismus: Besucherlenkung versus Numerus clausus. Studie und Dokumentation zum Fachkursus 258/95, Berlin

DTV (Deutscher Tourismusverband) (Ed.; 2003): Deutsche Touristenhits ziehen Millionen von Besuchern an, Bonn (Medieninformation)

F. U. R. (Forschungsgemeinschaft Urlaub und Reisen) (Ed.; 2008): Die Urlaubsreisen der Deutschen. Kurzfassung der Reiseanalyse 2008, Kiel

Heinze, T. (Ed.; 1999): Kulturtourismus. Grundlagen, Trends und Fallstudien, München/Wien

Hennig, Chr. (1997): Reiselust. Touristen, Tourismus und Urlaubskultur, Frankfurt a.M./Leipzig

IfM (Institut für Museumsforschung) (Ed.; 2008): Statistische Gesamterhebung an den Museen der Bundesrepublik Deutschland für das Jahr 2007, Berlin (Materialien aus dem Institut für Museumsforschung; 62)

Irish Tourist Board u. a. (1988): Inventory of Cultural Tourism Resources in the Member States and Assessment of Methods used to promote them, Dublin/Brüssel

Korsay, M. u. a. (Ed.; 1999): Heritage, Multicultural Attractions and Tourism, Istanbul

Moebius, S. (2009): Kultur, Bielefeld

Richards, G. (Ed.; 1996): Cultural Tourism in Europe, Wallingford (GB)

Richards, G. (Ed.; 2001): Cultural Attractions and European Tourism, Wallingford (GB)

Robinson, M./Evans, N./Callaghan, P. (Ed.; 1996): Managing Cultural Resources for the Tourist, Sunderland (GB)

Steinecke, A. (2006): Tourismus – eine geographische Einführung, Braunschweig (Geographisches Seminar; o. Bd.)

Steinecke, A. (2007): Kulturtourismus: Marktstrukturen – Fallstudien – Perspektiven, München/Wien

Treidel, R. J. (2006): Historisches Erbe und touristischer Markt. Geschichtsdidaktische As-
pekte der kommerziell betriebenen Studienreise. In: Geschichte in Wissenschaft und
Unterricht, 57 (5-6), 359-368
Weissenborn, B. (1997): Kulturtourismus, Trier (Trierer Tourismus Bibliographien; 10)

Culture – Tourism – Media

Norbert Bolz

Everyone is talking about the global economic crisis, and the best way to escape a crisis is to travel. But what is more important is that travelling is a concrete way of experiencing one's freedom and I don't think anyone is willing to give up this part of his personal freedom. We are all forced to cut back, save up and reduce spending, but travelling and mobility in general are among the parts of our lives that can be limited least of all. People won't accept it; they want to keep this specific freedom. There are two aspects of life that represent the utopian dreams of our modern existence: unlimited individual mobility on the one hand and communication on the other. Regarding our topic "Culture, Tourism, Media", the important thing about Web 2.0 is that its users cooperate – a cooperation that turns out to be incredibly simple. This is a fantastic feature of this new internet-based media that the mass media we are familiar with cannot offer. This cooperation, the participation in global communication, is going to become easier from one software generation to the next. I still have vivid memories of the first computers I had at home. You had to know at least some programming codes to actually be able to use the computers. Today, most people never think about that because now we have a user interface. This interface between man and media has been designed in such an ingenuous way that you do not even need a manual anymore to work and play with the new media.

For Christmas, I got two of my daughters an iPod because I was too stingy to buy them an iPhone. I bought it and thought it might be a good idea to set it up in advance so they could play or listen to music with it right away on Christmas. That was when I realized that it did not come with a manual. There was just a little note saying: everything is so simple, intuitive and user-friendly that you only have to twiddle with it and it will guide you to see what happens and understand everything right away.

I have to admit, it was not that easy. As an older person, I was not able to understand and to learn how to use the iPod just by playing with it. But that is not the point – what is really interesting about this is that it shows how the whole media industry is changing. It is now about exploring a new, fantastic, avant-garde world of media, in which we do not read manuals but simply play. There is no better way to understand this new kind of media than to play with it. To us older people, everything from the world of the new media is presented as a tool, whereas children

R. Conrady and M. Buck (eds.), *Trends and Issues in Global Tourism 2010*,
Trends and Issues in Global Tourism, DOI 10.1007/978-3-642-10829-7_24,
© Springer-Verlag Berlin Heidelberg 2010

view these innovations not as tools, but as toys. That is exactly why they like using them and trying them out, and that is the reason why they understand and use new media better than the rest of us. This is one of the most astounding conclusions in the world of new media in recent years.

The development of new media is very interesting. They are now so easy to use that the gap between experts and regular users has become so much smaller that now everyone can do what only experts used to be able to do. Just take a look at all the blogs and the whole world of platforms like YouTube and MySpace. What is all this about? It is all about citizen journalism. Nowadays, we don't really need real journalists anymore, because with these new technologies every single one of us is able to report on everything that is going on in the world. The German newspaper *Bild* took advantage of this concept by giving everyone the chance to appear on the front page with their picture. For example, if you see a celebrity, like the German actor Til Schweiger, somewhere in Berlin in a bar doing something improper and you capture it on camera, the *Bild* will pay you for the picture and may publish it on the front page. As trivial as it may seem, the changing relationship between experts and regular users is a revolutionary development and the idea behind the keyword Web 2.0. There are many polished phrases for it which, in the end, all mean the same. My favorite phrase is this one: "All together we are smarter than everyone", or "All together we are more creative than everyone". It means that all of us as individual amateurs naturally don't know as much as the actual experts. However, all together we are much smarter than each individual person. By the way, that is the concept behind the lifeline 'Ask the Audience' in the television show "Who Wants to Be a Millionaire". Most of the time, the audience is right – not because every single one is smart, but because all together they are smarter than each individual person. The same concept applies to creativity.

99% of what the internet has to offer is rubbish, but that doesn't matter. All that matters is what you actually want to see online and how you filter it out of all the virtualized drivel. Luckily, there are fantastic web content filtering solutions that make it possible to find some treasures the huge pile of internet junk. That is what makes the development of Web 2.0 so fascinating. Hence, the old dichotomies don't apply anymore, e.g. the dichotomy of experts and amateurs, teachers and learners, and of course of producers and consumers.

Many years ago, Alvin Toffler coined a term that has only now taken on greater significance: the term "prosumer". It is a coinage that blends the words "producer" and "consumer". This prosumer is the main figure in Web 2.0. People don't want to be assigned a mere receptive task; they are no longer satisfied with just being viewers, listeners, readers or consumers. More and more, we are rather dealing with a kind of personal union of consumers, users and citizens. But what are the specific effects of this personal union on economic life? Let us take a closer look at two effects that seem to be essential to our topic.

There is a fierce, predatory competition going on in all interesting areas of the market. To us, the non-experts, this predatory competition means the following: There are many offers for the product I want to buy, be it a sneaker, a TV, a car or a journey. From my perspective, the non-expert's perspective, the various offers cost more or less the same and seem to be more or less equally good. Here is the question: If different providers offer more or less the same product, why do I choose Product X rather than Product Y?

There are two answers to this question and one is the "linking value". It is the added value that you have to offer people nowadays to make them buy your product and not the competitor's. Here is an already historic example of a large German financial institution that created an internet portal, just like all the other institutions did before it. The big difference was that it didn't just advertise its own financial services, but those of the competition as well, even though some services of the competition were better than its own. With a shake of the head many people thought: "Why did they do it?" Well, in the age of the internet transparency is unstoppable. People know all the offers and everyone can get all the information needed. Since it is impossible to withhold information of any advantages, disadvantages, possibilities and options, the only sensible strategy is to say "Come to me and you'll get everything". My portal doesn't just show my products; it is a portal to the entire world that interests you. In this case, it is the world of financial services. That means that users can count on getting all the information they need right there. This builds trust – trust in the company's own brand, in their own business and thereby in their own products. That was the point, and by now, many companies have adopted this strategy. They build a link and in many cases that is all they do. What is eBay doing? eBay builds a link between two networks – between two amorphous groups – that have nothing to do with each other. The one group consists of those who own things that they don't need anymore, while the other group consists of those who have money but don't know what to buy. eBay came up with the idea to build a link between the two groups. The internet company doesn't need warehouses, because all it does is link the two groups that were previously separated.

There is an even more popular example: Google. All that Google does is building links between websites, which Google doesn't create itself, but which were created by others. Apart from that, Google has another added value to offer: it suggests keywords for navigation and a search evaluation. Users often wonder: What is important, what is unimportant? How can I navigate through the endless abundance of offers? How do I find the right information? Google – a search engine, not a person – offers the solution. There is a secret algorithm, the PageRank Algorithm, which ensures that links are not only built, but evaluated at the same time. Everyone who has issued a search request on Google before could see that it works. In short, the business model consists of nothing else but linking. The link is the added value. By now, this concept extends far beyond the field of software and search engines or online auction websites like eBay – there are plenty of examples. I want to summarize them with what Bernard Cova once said: "The link is more important than the thing". That applies to more and more areas of the new world of media and of the economy as a whole, since our economy is regulated and organized by these media. It is all about the added value that lies in the linking itself.

That leads us to our second concept: "The age of reputation and recommendation". What is Amazon doing? At first sight, it seems to be a mere bookstore working by means of the internet, but that is an egregious misconception. When you buy something on Amazon you will discover its secret. Once you have clicked the "buy" button, Amazon notifies you that "Customers Who Bought This Item Also Bought ..." Most of Amazon's sales are made by people following this link. An algorithm in the programme of Amazon evaluates how certain products correlate with respect to the customer's taste. As a matter of fact, this programme can figure out the correlation between all of Amazon's products. Basically, the mystery behind this company is once again the concept of linking. The more often you follow this link, the more specific the recommendations become. If you are in search of your own identity Amazon will put you out of your misery and – after only a few purchases – tell you exactly what you like and assign you to a certain group of like-minded people. Ultimately, this service is what Amazon is all about. In my opinion, a marketing expert might describe it as follows: Amazon and all businesses with a similar concept are focusing on a marketing of preference. That is the added value that Amazon has to offer.

But there's more to reputation and recommendation. Let's stick with our example of Amazon. On their site, you can not only buy products from Amazon directly; you can also access their virtual "Marketplace", which allows people to sell their books and other items for a commission online. But on the Marketplace, the buyer's interaction with Amazon does not end with the purchase. A few days later you will receive an email asking you to "rate your transaction". If you comply with "netiquette", you will dutifully oblige and provide a rating because you know how important that is to the seller's reputation. You rate a seller by moving the mouse over five white stars, which you colour gold – or not, depending on whether or not you were satisfied with the transaction. The more stars are coloured, the better the seller's ratings from buyers are and thus the more trustworthy he becomes. This is called karma in the world of the internet. Here, it has nothing to do with Asian wisdom but instead refers to the accumulated reputation that an enterprise, company or seller has built online and on which they can profit. If various sellers are offering the same product, it is pretty obvious that customers are going to choose the seller with the best karma. Especially since karma is quantifiable; so and so many people have rated their purchased products by a certain seller as "very good" within the last 3-4 months and hence that provider deserves your trust. And this is where the whole thing gets interesting, extending well beyond the realms of Google, eBay and Amazon. This now concerns everyone who makes an offer online in any way because they have the opportunity to build such a system of reputation. And my guess is that precisely this will be the currency that is going to decide between success and failure. Reputation is something immaterial and untouchable that is based solely on the evaluation of customers.

Booking your flight online is old hat, but the trend has expanded to generate links to hotels and car rentals. These links represent the concept of *linking value*. Clicking on a link will land you for example on a hotel's page on which they advertise the hotel. But this is by far less interesting than the "objective advertising", the karma that a hotel has online. You can find out: What do people who stayed in this hotel within the last three weeks say about its quality? Of course, this is a thousand times more interesting than what the hotel has to say about itself, and people are increasingly using the internet user recommendations to make decisions. That's an enterprise's karma or reputation. This "age of reputation and recommendation" concerns everyone who doesn't keep out of the virtual world completely; and honestly, who can afford to do so nowadays? It's all about reputation, recommendations and customers trusting other customers; "peers trust peers" as they say. Colleagues ask their colleagues; neighbours ask their neighbours. Of course, this has always been the case, but now it is globally organised and everyone can access this information instantly, with the possibility of accepting an offer right away or discarding it. Either way, this information is available immediately and with great ease.

My last focus on the topic of media, having discussed linking value and the age of recommendation and reputation, starts with a very technical aspect but one with far-reaching implications that will lead us directly to the world of tourism:the technical situation of virtualisation. Virtualisation has two dimensions. The dimension that is actually more important but less spectacular, thus getting less attention, consists of the internet being almost completely virtual. This is because you only ever have one web page refreshed – the remainder drowns in cyberspace. Thus virtuality is the normal condition of everything that's being offered on the internet and it's your own responsibility to refresh something, to take it to the foreground, i.e. onto the screen, in order to work with it.

First of all, the internet is almost completely virtual. When we speak of virtuality we of course think of something else. We feel that there's a kind of competing reality, a virtual reality on the internet that competes with the "real reality". Just think of the online virtual world Second Life, which is literally a parallel reality with houses, gardens and furnished rooms in which even conferences are held. The long-feared problem of people, especially youngsters, losing their ability to differentiate between what's real and what's virtual has long been discarded. The same fear had already spread when novels were first distributed to a wider audience, including those who were not supposed to read: young girls. So almost exactly 200 years ago, novels – romance novels – were unleashed upon young girls, resulting in the same outcries that Second Life and World of Warcraft have received in this millennium: that people can't distinguish between reality and fiction. Hence, theoretically, the young girls would lose themselves in the romance novels, preventing them from becoming dutiful mothers, or something along those lines. Today we can only laugh at this reasoning, but the argument, that youngsters would no longer be able to distinguish between what's real and what's not, was essentially the same one it is today. Now we see things completely differently. We've gotten the feeling that these worlds aren't mutually exclusive but instead complement each other. People don't usually have problems living and acting in both worlds simultaneously. There is a kind of adjustment to virtuality that is gaining more and more importance, and this has consequences. The real problem that exists here is that people can't keep up because of their own genetic makeup. Older people notice this faster than younger ones, but nevertheless, everyone falls behind at some point. Technology has a logic of its own and develops itself from itself, especially media technology. The idea that people develop technologies to solve problems is completely absurd. That's what we were taught at school, but hardly anything developed through media technology fulfils a need; instead technology does what it's capable of. It has a certain autonomy in its development and we as human beings increasingly find ourselves in a situation where we have to adjust to our own technology rather than simply letting it solve our problems.

A good example of this problem is media technology; there you have a certain social obligation to connect. I remember very well when I had my first business cards printed – nothing fancy, just University of Essen and my department, phone number and address. I had the standard information printed, just no email address. However, this attracted immediate negative attention on my first visit to a convention. Hence, I only realised my need for an email address when I was humiliated for not having one. The media don't respond to your personal needs; they're simply there and thereby create a social obligation to connect. And once you're connected to the latest media innovation, you wonder how anyone could ever live without it. But the most important point is that these new media technologies aren't tuned like people but accelerate with infinite power, thus making us feel overstrained by the technological advancements of the media. As I've mentioned before, youngsters and young people can handle stress and overstrain a lot better than the elderly, and because of that you will never hear a 14-year-old complain about today's culture. However, this doesn't change the facts. We are structurally and continuously overstrained and for that we need compensation. And that is my last point.

And it is exactly this kind of virtualization of our living conditions through which this compensation is achieved – a compensation through the actual reality. The realness factor is decisive. But what does that mean?

The more and deeper we dive into a virtual reality, the more we need cult places. A cult place is the epitome of realness, a place where you feel alive. It is the real, the true and the authentic that are the key elements to such a place. Therefore, I am convinced that we will be able to see a parallel evolution between the progressing virtualization of our living conditions on the one hand and, as compensation to that, the progressive upgrading of cult places on the other hand. A discussion on what conditions actually turn a place into a cult place would be lengthy. But surely all of you could name cult places and places that want to be called that off the top of your heads. Berlin is a prime example of a cult city. Why? Considered from an objective point of view, Germany's capital does not really have a lot to offer. If you travel to London, Paris or Rome, you immediately realize what a truly grand metropolis looks like. Berlin, however, is no more than an accumulation of several villages. But that actually does not matter. Berlin is truly legendary. It has had this legendary image ever since the 1920s or when Berlin was isolated and Americans flew in to see this cult place for themselves.

Luckily, it has preserved this particular aura to this day. Berlin is hence a great example for a cult place, whereas other cities lack exactly that special quality. Some places are sexy and some are just not. Some attract people, some don't, and this is essential in the future. You either visit cult places or you move there. Interestingly enough, you are more likely to move to such places, if you are part of the elite. This is not just a matter simply visiting a cult place: if you can afford it and are successful enough, you are willing to shift your whole life to a cult place. Richard Florida, a theorist who has attracted some in the past few years, has basically developed this one particular thought, the theory of the "creative class". He has discovered a pattern and persistently claims that creative people who are responsible for the productivity of the 21st century are not scattered equally around the globe, even though the internet enables us to work from practically anywhere in the world. In the past, people thought that it did not matter where they were; they could do their work from anywhere. Technically, that is true, but in regard to real life it is completely absurd. It is exactly this creative elite of our century that is marked by the habit of clustering. Hence, there are clusters spread around the globe. But a really interesting 21st century map of the world is not a geographical one, but rather a kind of Bucky Fuller map. Where can we find the most creative minds; where have the most patents been registered? Such a map is fascinating, because you can actually see the clustering in the world. You can see the most densely populated areas in terms of creativity, intellect and productivity. This is what I call cult places. I suspect that these destinations will become more and more important to a person's mobility and real freedom. People want to live out and make use of their individual freedom to the fullest. This explains why the way people travel today increasingly resembles the way people travelled in the past. The most ancient forms of travelling are pilgrimages and educational journeys; the way we once defined travelling actually changed quite a bit when we began to view journeys as relaxing holidays. But now "relaxing" has gained a slightly vulgar connotation, so instead, there is a kind of comeback to pilgrimages or educational journeys. If you go on a city trip, it is the culture that interests you the most. You want to experience something beyond just an ordinary holiday for relaxation. So we have to think of an additional term that describes the experience in cult places that are part of your trip. You also travel to cult places for educational reasons. These places then become personal destinations. They have a special meaning to you or at least to your holiday.

I mentioned the second added value earlier and it is the last term I want to introduce to you. I am talking about the "spiritual added value". But what exactly does that mean? As the term already implies, it is not something you can grasp with your hands. It is rather something beyond comfort, great hotel rooms, a luxurious pool or anything of that nature. When talking about a spiritual added value, we are talking about something impalpable. This implies that you can only outline its meaning through communication. It is only through communication that you can evoke the desire for a spiritual added value. Once again, Berlin is a great example provided that it is actually as legendary as its reputation. That would mean that Berlin is identically equal to its history, meaning the stories that are told about it. And whether it is about creating a cultural capital or advertising, selling or marketing one, finding a good story, an enchanting and mesmerizing story that you like to share, is basically the key. During my early days working in Essen, I once experienced something profound: when I arrived I was afraid that I was entering a cultural void. Then, however, I came to realize that I was mistaken and that a lot of stories existed, very fascinating ones that have formed the identity of an entire nation. After realizing this, I suddenly understood the actual meaning behind terms like "industrial architecture", "industrial monuments" or similar terms. It is really about a culture of reminiscence, about a cult site, about an identity formed by myths and about good stories. This is basically what someone has to keep in mind in creating a destination. Communication, production and finding or optimizing a good story lie at the core. And where there is a history in the actual sense of the word, you will most likely find good stories to tell about this place. The place becomes a cult place through its stories, and this is the spiritual added value that, in the end, actually sells when promoting a city.

Companies and Airlines: Negotiation Positions – Negotiation Options

Michael Schneider

Let me get one thing straightened out right at the beginning of this chapter: As soon as you have 2 professional people or more in the room you can be sure that there will be a negotiation. As a matter of fact all our life is full of negotiation: With your spouse, your friends, your children, your boss, your colleagues etc.

Are we aware of negotiations as they occur? Probably sometimes. Do we do well in the negotiation? Not at all times? In this we can be certain that the reason for it in most of the cases existed before the negotiation actually started.

In forums and associations, I had plenty of exchange with airlines sales reps who told me that actually they don't like much about the general position they find themselves in when selling to travel buyers. While the descriptions differed it always came down to the one point that it was ultimately the travel buyer who has the power and – with the exception of monopoly-like circumstances – finally dictates subject, pace, conditions and pricing in the discussion.

The very interesting part though is that at the same time travel buyers often state that they are feeling almost the same way. "By the end of the day, we have to get our people to our top destinations. However in the airline industry there is still not much of a competition if you look at individual routes with few exceptions. Therefore, the airline sales manager knows exactly that I have to buy from him and hence dominates the way the negotiation is going" one travel manager told me.

Indeed every negotiation includes risks and personal barriers to overcome on each side on top of the obvious negotiation targets.

Both sides run a number of personal risks associated with each negotiation:

- Conflict with interests and expectations of the company
- Reputation
- Image
- Career
- etc.

R. Conrady and M. Buck (eds.), *Trends and Issues in Global Tourism 2010*, Trends and Issues in Global Tourism, DOI 10.1007/978-3-642-10829-7_25, © Springer-Verlag Berlin Heidelberg 2010

At the same time they have to overcome inner barriers such as

- Fear of push-back and resistance
- Difficulty to find the right approach
- Missing the right moment for closing the deal
- Concern to damage a relationship
- etc.

What is the essence of the supplier – buyer – relationship in the travel industry? Well, to answer this question in one sentence we can say "the same as in any other industry" – at least in principal. We will come to the specifics and differences later, but let's have a look at the basic set, which we will do by defining the primary roles and responsibilities of the 2 main stakeholders in the process.

The buyer needs to buy for quite a number of reasons. The most decisive of those reasons are obviously:

- Ensure availability of goods and services needed for the operations of his organization
- Solve a supply problem
- Decrease cost
- Increase efficiency
- Improve related processes
- Secure quality etc.

Of course we could largely extend this list. However, already at this stage it becomes evident that purchasing is a fundamental element of the functional corporate organization. Hence, the comment of the quoted travel buyer is very right: He needs to buy *by definition* to achieve a number of results described above. Nonetheless the exact way how this is happening is very much defined by a number of criteria and techniques which buyers need to be "on top of".

Before we do that let's have a quick look at how sales people like to describe their role. You will often find following items:

- Help clients to achieve their goals by adapting the ways products and services are supplied
- Help the client to align his perception with the supplier's perception
- Ensure that concession of one party will mirror advantage of the other party
- Achieve agreement on a multitude of variables – between minimum of 2 parties, but in most cases many more
- Communicate with the customer supplier values

- Ensure a healthy and long-term customer relationship

- Secure revenue for the company

Sounds deliberate? The truth of the matter nonetheless is: if we would have a look inside the targets of sales persons you will not find much of the above in many cases. Indeed what you will find is usually about sales at its purest:

- Win a certain number of new clients

- Turnover volumes

- Sell a defined number of products

- Increase market share to x%

- Penetrate certain market segments

- etc.

Consequently much more than the buyer, the sales person is driven towards one ultimate goal: Close the deal! Over time however, sales managers have found that it is not possible to achieve their targets without satisfying the needs of their counterpart in the travel management departments.

While these needs can be very diverse – from factual to personal – they all can be addressed by negotiation management techniques of different kinds, many of those originating from the field of psychology. Nearly all of them are scientifically grounded and proven in practice.

The techniques enabling success in negotiations which are available today have not been brought up with sales people in mind in particular. Hence they do indeed work for both sides of the table and can be applied and adapted as needed.

1   The Road of Negotiation

In contrary to cycles where you would re-enter into step #1 each time you completed the last step of the cycle, negotiations are a closed process which does not renew itself. Consequently, we would rather use the metaphor of a road having a start and an end point to it. One would probably want to argue that in travel management the existing base deal is about to be renewed to each year so that we could also speak about a cycle. However in reality we need to differentiate between the contract and the negotiation: While you can renew a contract you cannot renew a negotiation. This consequently stipulates the fact that each negotiation is a solitary organic process. Of course the professionalism and quality of a current negotiation largely impacts any following negotiation as it positively enhances and creates rapport and personal relationship, which is one of the 2 major success factors for excellent negotiation management. The other one is preparation.

Let's slice up the negotiation road for a moment to see how we can get the best out of each step. The vast majority of negotiations will cover following elements regardless of the negotiator's position (buyers/seller):

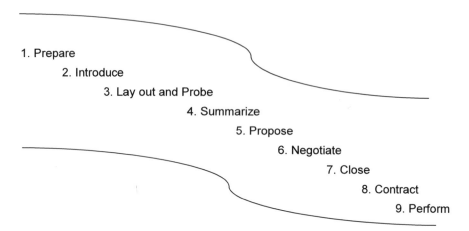

1. Prepare
    2. Introduce
        3. Lay out and Probe
            4. Summarize
                5. Propose
                    6. Negotiate
                        7. Close
                            8. Contract
                                9. Perform

Fig. 1. The negotiation road

The combination of this negotiation road and the fact that both parties – seller and buyer – *need* to come to a conclusion leads to a very positive and logic consequence: Unless either party makes a severe mistake the closing is unavoidable. Even more positive is the fact that the way and result of the closing is largely defined at the beginning of the process. We will have a look at an example in the next paragraph.

Whenever I had conversations with travel management professionals on negotiations which did not successfully lead to the result they had desired beforehand, the majority of them advised that it boiled down to 1 major reason: A "surprise" had occurred during one of the late steps of the above process and negatively affected the following conversations. Repeatedly it had been reported to have led to confusion and irritation in the negotiation. We will have a much closer look therefore at the most important process step of all, "Prepare".

Within this essay we will focus mainly on the 3 most important parts of the process being "Prepare", "Negotiate" and "Close" as you will find that those are the ones which predominantly can make your deal "fly or die".

Looking at travel management today, negotiation professionals would want to achieve following fundamental goals alongside the process:

- Achieve their individual goals in a win-win situation
- Increase efficiency to reduce negotiation amount over time
- Build trust and relationship
- Be tough on facts but soft in tone

2   Are You Prepared?

Often we will find that negotiation parties have a certain tendency to be self-centered when it comes to facts. They are rather well prepared and equipped with knowledge on "their own facts". For instance will the airline sale person (hopefully) always be excellently aware of the product features offered as well as available price structure. On the other hand the travel buyer usually is well aware of the needs of his internal customers, origins & destinations, number of trips, existing fare levels at different suppliers for top O&D etc.

It is on the contrary rather likely that not enough preparation time is spent on the other party and the criteria might influence or even steer the negotiation process into a certain direction. For each of the above steps of the negotiation cycle we will find that in the vast majority of cases challenges which occur later on in the process date back to lack of preparation at the beginning of the process on either side:

- Did we know enough about the targets of the other party?
- Did we know enough about the key personal motivators of the other party?
- Did we know enough about the internal decision making process?
- Did we know enough about the different persons involved in the decision making process?
- Were the right questions asked?
- Did we take into consideration alternative scenarios?
- Etc.

Failing to prepare is preparing to fail.

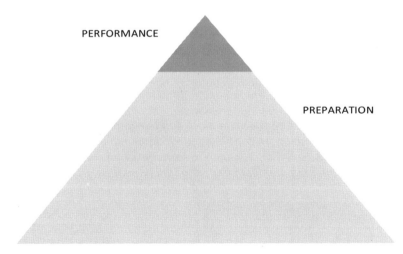

Fig. 2. The pyramid of negotiation success

To say it in the words of Jeffrey Gitomer, author of "The Sales Bible": "In sales it all boils down to one word … *YES*". How easy it will be for both sides to get to "yes" entirely depends on preparation and adaptability.

3   Digging the Information

How crucial preparation is – especially information on the other party – becomes obvious when we remember one important fact: Everything our companies do – from strategy over product to price – can be copied by any competitor. And it most probably will be copied over time. The only constant differentiator is the negotiator and her/his ability to adapt to the other party to achieve superior results for her/his company. In other words: prepare or save the time for something else.

Let's have a look at 2 examples:

The Airline Sales Manager Who Got Too Laid Back

The sales manager of a major European airline alliance is about to negotiate next year's corporate negotiated rates and bonus program with a global leading pharmaceutical company based in Germany and subsidiaries in 60 countries around the globe. Like every year, he goes and meets the global travel manager to talk about services and routes. Over the next weeks the negotiation progresses until the global travel manager advises that he and his US colleague had decided to go for an preferred airline deal with a competitive airline alliance so that our airline sales rep is only offered the back-up option.

What seems to be a sudden event with no particular obvious reason for this unfortunate end of the negotiation could have been avoided had the sales manager known more by better preparation: Due to the almost equal share in total flight volume the US travel manager of the company has become a fully equal co-decision maker with the German based global travel manager and convinced his German colleague to try the competition.

The Blue Eyed Travel Manager

A European travel manager of a medium sized pan-European company negotiates with the preferred airline on fares from each destination. The sales manager of the airline finally insists on only offering corporate net fares for Germany but the much higher published fares for all other markets, even for those with the same volume as in Germany, explaining that you cannot negotiate net rates for other markets out of Germany. The travel manager finally gives in and accepts the offer leaving his other European markets with air fares far above market average.

What often is still accepted as an "airline rule" indeed could have been overcome by investigating on the organizational structure of European sales management responsible staff within the airline and of course inclusion of those parties.

Preparation has become so much easier with the arrival of the worldwide web. It is amazing how much you can learn about your negotiation counterpart if you visit their website:

Lately I met an airline sales rep of an Asian carrier, who was still embarrassed because the nice golf book he had bought for the (golf-crazy) travel manager of an oil company had been refused by that person: His corporation did not allow any gifts at all nor invitations whatsoever for compliance reasons. Not a too big surprise for those who had checked out the chapter "Ethical Sourcing" of this company's website, where it is clearly stated that staff are expected not to accept any – in words: any – gifts. Never.

The least you need to do is to check out their website to understand the background and strategic principal of the other negotiation party. Googleing the name of your counterpart will most likely tell you even more: Facebook and the like will tell about hobbies, family etc. and hence give you valuable information on the motivational set of the person.

More information regularly can be found with usually well informed sources: Travel Management Companies typically link both parties (travel supplier and buyer) operationally and are in permanent contact with either side. Therefore, establishing a close relationship and calling on your counterpart within the TMC will most likely result into useful information. The same eventually can be true for sales staff of other suppliers i.e.

- Airlines
- Car rental companies
- Hotels
- GSAs
- Independent travel management consultants
- Travel Insurance Companies
- Payment Providers
- GDS
- OBE Suppliers
- General Travel Technology Suppliers

Like in any industry, especially in the German travel industry almost everybody is a member of networking organizations. If you're not yet a member of any association become one a-s-a-p. Being a part of and using those networks will help you to find out more information. In particular those can be:

- VDR
- ACTE
- BARIG
- DRV
- IATA
- ASRA etc.

Especially when it comes to strategic and complex negotiation it is of utmost importance to find and use available sources for information on the other party. A very helpful approach is to view this phase like a brainstorming: One would eagerly collect any type of information not evaluating yet. Hence, any information is equally valuable and will be saved. Once the collection of information is completed it is typically saved in a matrix for a general overview:

Table 1. Corporate master data

Corporate Information	Corporate Environment Information	Personal Information
Shareholders	General Market Conditions	Age
History	Industry Trends	Status
Size	Competition	Income
Products	Suppliers	Hierarchy Level
Countries	Customers	Reputation
# of Staff	Strategic Partners	Personal Preferences
Vision	Legal Framework	Value Set
Strategy	Political Framework	Motivational Factors
Compliance	Stakeholders etc.	Hobbies
Regulations		Activities
Purchasing Process Decision		Interests
Making Process etc.		"Character"
		Expectations etc.

4   The Multi-SWOT

Once we have found enough "raw material" through our network channels we would like to consequently run this information through some more sophisticate analysis methodologies: The Multidimensional SWOT Analysis is a perfectly structured way to use available information to analyze the negotiation counterpart. It allows each negotiator to view not only their own strategic position within the negotiation from various perspectives but also gives a good insight on the positioning of the rivaling parties.

1. My company in my eyes

Strengths	Weaknesses
Opportunities	Threats

2. The supplier's competitor in my eyes

Strengths	Weaknesses
Opportunities	Threats

3. My company through the eyes of the other negotiation party

Strengths	Weaknesses
Opportunities	Threats

4. The supplier's competitor through the eyes of the other negotiation party

Strengths	Weaknesses
Opportunities	Threats

Fig. 3. Multi-SWOT

1. *The reflection of my own position:* In this sector you would need to list all of your own company's strengths, weaknesses, opportunities and threats related to the upcoming negotiation with the other party. What we are talking about is *not a general strategic* overview of your company in its market environment as a whole but a very specific pinpointed analysis how *you* see *yourself* and your company tactically positioned for *this very negotiation specifically*. If you are a buyer then of course you take the buyer's perspective. In case you are the seller then this is about you as a seller.

2. *The reflection on the seller's competitor:* Regardless whether you are the buyer or the seller you would fill this anyway to analyze the alternative supplier – the competitor of the seller – from your point of view. If we are the seller it makes perfect sense, but why would we do this from a buyer perspective? Because it will give you as a buyer a much clearer picture of what your negotiation party, the seller, is facing and potentially scared of: In case the competitor turns out to be particularly strong then this would tell a buyer a lot about the balance of power being more on his side than on the seller's side.

3. *The assumed reflection of how the other party sees me*: This will be very helpful indeed. You would now put yourself in the shoes of the other party assuming their background and know-how. Now you start evaluating the

SWOT from this angle. So, if you are the buyer you would need to assume for a moment that you are the seller looking at the buyer to analyze his areas of strengths, weaknesses etc. Of course, if you are the seller you do it vice versa.

4. *The reflection on the seller's competitor – but seen through the eyes of the other party*: That means in a buyer's position you would again assume that you are the seller but now evaluate the competitor of the seller from this angle: What does the seller usually comment on his competitors? How would he rate the product quality of his competitor with his own underlying philosophy? etc. And vice versa, if you are the seller assume that you are the buyer: How would the buyer see the competitor? What would he like about the competitor? etc.

Regularly with this tool negotiators find the level of transparency on not only their own but also the other party's strategic positioning options most surprising. Interestingly enough it also allows a prediction of optional moves of competitors – no matter on which side of the table you are seated.

5   The Decision Making Map

Looking at strategic and complex negotiations retrospectively you will often find that at different stages of the negotiation process different people were dominating the process. As a simple example we can think of the yearly negotiation between airline and corporate customer: In the initial phase the sales manager might start off discussing with the travel manager on the subject but later on a sales manager of the corporate customer's travel management company gets involved. At again a later stage the travel manager might bring in the purchasing manager for individual processes and conditions before finally the legal counsel have a look at the contract document.

Sales people are regularly very target-driven personalities and hence it is not surprising that the final result is often more in focus than processes. Very often you will find that especially in the travel industry sales persons try to identify what they consider their counterpart. Even in cases where those sales managers are indeed aware of a network environment within the prospect organization they prefer to have one person to talk to. The reason behind this are multitude, but sure driven by the "one face to the customer philosophy" most of the travel industry supplier organizations pursue. While it seems to make life easier for sales staff it is indeed contra-productive when applied vice versa. In this case it will conceal the network of decision making within the other organization. Of course the same is true for the buyer side due to the "one face to the customer philosophy" with the suppliers.

Indeed not taking into consideration the fact that decisions in professional organizations are made within networks bears a significant risk of failure. Frequently you can find decision making networks of up to 10 or more people within one local organization. Evidently this number can be significantly higher when it comes to multinational negotiations.

Alongside the sheer number, roles and responsibilities of decision makers and influencers you will certainly find that their importance for the negotiation process profoundly varies. In a negotiation between an airline sales manager and corporate travel manager the influence of the purchasing manager on a successful result is often stronger than for instance the influence of the legal counsel. Moreover, you will often find a specifically defined level of affinity towards/against the supplier for each player of the network.

Below you will find a generic sample of the Decision Making Map. Now you will start to fill it in 4 steps a-d for each field:

a) It will always have your key negotiation partner centered in the middle. So, if you are the seller then you would list the buyer with whom you are negotiating in the center of the map. In the fields around the center field with your negotiation counterpart you list each and every other staff within the other organization, who has a direct influence and / or decision making power in the negotiation and its result. In any case you need to find out the decision making structure without exceptions. Otherwise you will definitely face sever challenges later on: A decision influencer, who was left out of the process or is only drip-fed by your negotiation counterpart will always develop a bad feeling about not being taken serious in his role. Therefore, she/he will oppose the outcome of your negotiation wherever possible – unless that person had explicitly asked not be directly involved for specific individual reasons. Attention: You will as well find constellations where players outside the organization have influence on the decision. This is primarily the case with every consulting function such as TMC's, independent travel management consultants etc. How can you find out about all of this? Go back to the section "Digging the Information" and read carefully. Then start digging.

b) Now you will start enriching each field showing the decision influencers with the first of the 2 indicators being the% level of influence on the final decision: E.g. 80% for a strong buyer in possession of a lot of decision making power. You will find that the bigger and more complex the organization of your negotiation counterpart is, the more influencers/decision makers are involved and simultaneously the lower their individual decision making power. Therefore be aware: You might come across discussions with a central person to talk to who however is not the main decision maker. In this case make sure that (as mentioned above) you have the real decision making structure on your map! How you would find out about the assumed decision making power? Digging the information is the key.

c) 3rd step: Now you would indicate the perceived level of affinity to-wards/against your own organization influence within the negotiation using the 3 dimensions "+", "o" and "-" i.e. positive, neutral and negative. It is crucial to make yourself aware of the fact that those co-decision makers – even on the supplier side – always have an attitude, affinity and opinion on the other party. Positive, neutral or negative – either way it will strongly in-fluence the quality and flow of the negotiation. So dig that information.

d) Last step: In case you discover that 2 decision influencers are somehow connected to each other by function or sympathy mark it accordingly as shown below with #1 and #4. This might typically be within an airline or-ganization the pricing manager and the revenue manager. On the other hand in the buyer organization you often find that external parties are in-volved: In almost all cases the travel agent will play an important role. Not rarely, specialized BTM consultants are additionally contracted to guaran-tee a professional negotiation result.

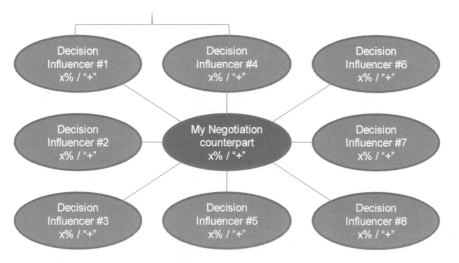

Fig. 4. The Decision Making Map

Particularly in consensus oriented cultures like the German, negotiations and deci-sions are usually made in teams facilitating extensive discussions aiming for a common understanding and high level of agreement within the specific network.

In the case where you find yourself in a negotiation with a team on the other side of the table there is another very important yet helpful step: Once you have completed the Decision Making Map you will need to list for each influencer the key information and expertise necessary to answer the typical questions of the per-son. Usually it is very easy to assume and anticipate the most likely upcoming questions per player. For example you will make sure that you have all the financial figures together for the finance manager whereas you would have a generic sample of the contract document including terms and conditions with you for the legal counselor etc. We will come back to this point in the paragraph "Expertise" in section "Ingredients of the Professional Negotiation".

In general, the advantages of having a Decision Making Map are obvious:

- Clear understanding of the decision making process within the other party's organization

- Realization of additional decision makers and influencers in the process

- Comprehension of each decision makers/influencers roles and responsibilities

- Understanding the affiliation with the supplier of each involved party

- Option for individual / collective negotiation strategies and action plans

- Faster and easier access to additional information as each player can be a source of input

- More precise and efficient negotiation

- Taylor-made results satisfying all needs

- Significantly reduced risk of barriers at a late stage, specifically shortly before contract signature

- Help the other negotiation party to achieve their targeted results / Support the buyer

- Establish long-term relationships based on commonly achieved understanding and success

Thus, inquiring the decision making map is highly recommended and will definitely save a lot of resources later on as the negotiation progresses.

6   Travel Industry Decision Making Maps

A closer look at a typical decision making map of a real example of an airline/corporate relationship will give us more insight (cf. Fig. 5).

In the above case the airlines sales manager was negotiating on the foundation of the "one face to the customer philosophy" and relied on his established relationship with the travel manager who had been the major decision maker with originally 55% influence on the decision. In this relationship the travel manager had naturally facilitated the interaction with all other internal departments. Additionally, the airline sales manager could largely rely on his airline's very good reputation as well as his excellent relationship with the travel manager's boss.

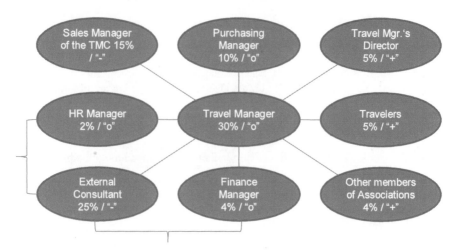

Fig. 5. Decision Making Map of the travel buyer's organization drawn by the airline sales manager after the negotiations failed. The figures in % indicate the perceived level of influence within the negotiation process while "+", "o" and "-" (i.e. positive, neutral and negative) represent the general perceived affinity to / against the supplier organization.

However, with increasing need for travel cost reduction the travel manager had asked his TMC, who were not particularly in favor of our airline, for consultancy service to identify additional savings opportunities. The TMC had brought in an external specialized consultant with whom the TMC was in cooperation and who was as well not in favor of the airline. As a result the originally 55% influence on negotiation and decision power were now 30% with the travel manager and 25% with the consultant. Unfortunately the airline sales manager fell short of this information still focusing on the travel manager alone. Within the activities and focus of the consultant of course also air fares were under review and this finally resulted into a new preferred agreement with the airline's competitor leaving our airline as a secondary supplier with significantly less business. The relationship and reputation with travelers and travel manager's boss did not save the business of the airline in a scenario where 40% of the decision making influence were against the supplier.

Needless to add that all about these developments and changes could have been easily discovered by investigating the network and probably even more importantly the underlying roles, drivers, needs and expectations of each player: Only if a negotiator is aware that there is an additional decision maker/influencer she/he can start integrating that specific player into the negotiation.

Of course the above example is not necessarily representing the basic structure of each buyer's organization; however it is a good starting point to draw an individual corporate buyer map from. It goes without saying that it is equally important for buyers to be aware of and pay attention to their own decision making structure to avoid internal barriers, push-back and resistance to buyers' decisions and direction at a later stage.

In order to illustrate the importance of a decision making map for both sides let's have a look at a map of a typical airline with the airline sales manager centered.

It is elemental for buyers to recognize that their negotiation position also highly depends on their own understanding of the decision making process within the organization of their counterpart, the sales manager. Therefore the meaning of the principal is of equal importance regardless of the position. If you are a travel buyer ask yourself how often you have taken the time to investigate whether you really understood the decision making process, its involved parties on the supplier side, their roles as well as a negotiation strategy per player.

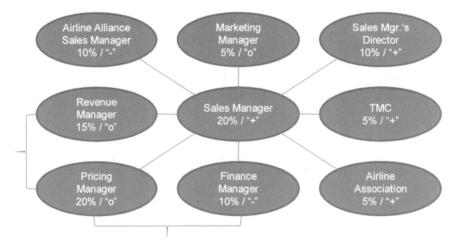

Fig. 6. Decision Making Map of the airline sales manager's organization drawn by the travel buyer after the negotiation failed. The figures in % indicate the perceived level of influence within the negotiation process while "+", "o" and "-" (i.e. positive, neutral and negative) represent the general perceived affinity to / against the buyer's organization.

In our above example the responsible person for travel management is a purchasing manager of a medium sized industrial tool company. He is negotiating with the sales manager of an US Airline on negotiated rates for certain O&D's as well as a general rebate program. The travel buyer assumes the decision making power on the airline side with the sales manager. Nonetheless, a look at the decision making map of the airline organization would have shown our travel manager that indeed the sales manager's ability to make independent decisions is considerably limited. Let's have a closer look at the really decisive constellation in this scenario:

As a matter of fact, the sales manager is confronted with a very high pricing competence bundled in revenue related departments i.e. Pricing, Revenue Management and Finance. On top of it – in our example – the finance manager shows a comparably negative attitude towards this specific customer as they have shown a rather mediocre payment moral.

Another delicate point to be taken into consideration is the airline alliance sales manager, who closely watches the sales & pricing actions of all alliance partners in the specific alliance across the Atlantic. To the travel buyers' disadvantage, the airline alliance sales manager has developed a rather hesitant opinion on this specific corporate prospect as a result of the fact that other alliance members had unsuccessfully tried to develop business with this company before. In his eyes, considerable resources had been spent with no return.

Now in his negotiations with the airlines sales manager, the travel buyer has requested significantly reduced fares on specific routes across the Atlantic as well as a 10% tiered rebate at the end of the year. As a benefit to the airline our travel manager promises to bundle the attractive flight volumes, which are currently spent on other airlines, on our airline.

Not surprisingly the airline sales manager has a tough stand now in his internal discussions with Pricing, Revenue Management and Finance as well as the airline alliance sales manager to explain why to reduce fares plus offer a rebate to a company that has not yet shown what those players would call much of support to the supplier, the airline. Finally, the maximum offer submitted to the travel buyer is a slight reduction in fares – just matching the competition – and no rebate.

Remarkable? Indeed, but at the same time could have been easily anticipated and at the same time gives us an idea on how decision making structures are impacting our negotiation positions. Many times the reason behind those constructions can be found in the focus within the Marketing Mix of suppliers: Amongst those who put significant emphasis on Pricing and Revenue Management you will find airlines, rail and car rental companies on the top of the list. The sheer amount of distributed airline fares speak for themselves: IATA publications mention more than 10.000 fare actions per day and close to 2 Million fares (public and net) in total. No question that pricing & revenue management have an important share in decision making.

7   Retrospective Success Factors

This is an excellent little technique I learned when our team had to go for a negotiation on a subject we had never dealt with before. Also we had to meet a type of negotiators we had not come across yet. To prepare of course we had described the "Negotiation Road" with an exact story line, we had put together a "Multi-Swot" as well as the "Decision Making Map" and we had equipped ourselves with as much information as possible. Still, we felt we could do better when suddenly one team member proposed to brainstorm: We counted down what we thought were our most successful negotiation cases during the last 2-3 years. In addition we listed to each case the maximum of 3 ultimate factors, which were the main drivers for the success of each respective negotiation. Soon we had about 15 which we called the "Retrospective Success Factors". Most of them had been listed more than one time – which we thought was good as we interpreted this as a sign of plausibility.

The positive aspect of this exercise was that all of those success factors were proven in real cases and probably even more importantly: They were all highly individual and relevant for our company in our environment.

Finally in our group of 3 we condensed them down to 9 ultimate success factors and each of us had to come up with suggestions how to ensure that those factors are covered in our negotiation strategy by specific actions.

You will also find this technique very helpful in cases of newly composed teams.

8   Negotiation Rehearsal

I am a very big fan of Al di Meola and Joe Bonamassa. I really like to listen to their guitar music and I read plenty of stuff about them. Every time I ask myself how one can play the guitar in such an overwhelmingly expressive way and at the same time I sense the answer: Work, hard work. The same hard work and training that made a Boris Becker. Those who are at the top of their bunch are not there because someone carried them to that point, but because of years of training and rehearsal, which they didn't stop since they are best in class but continue day by day.

The message is simple and logic: if negotiating is an important or regular part of your occupation you need to rehearse. The more complex, unusual and tough your next planned negotiation the more important it is to practice. You can train in a team with someone playing the counterpart or you can video-tape your performance. You can even go through your points on your own counting them down and envisioning the scenario. When we once had an important negotiation with a Chinese delegation of about 20 managers we rehearsed our greeting ceremony, our presentation, our arguments and counter-arguments over and over. The best thing about practicing is that it makes the real scenario become a known field as you saw it all before in your rehearsal. This is a great way to minimize unwanted surprises.

9   How Airlines Became Experts in Pricing and Revenue Management

Logically negotiations in any industry are ultimately centered on price: To successfully negotiate prices however it is elemental to understand how in any particular industry prices are being made up. Like all strategies also the pricing strategies of suppliers in the travel industry, especially airlines, are driven by the underlying market environment conditions. Looking at the market environment from an airline's perspective we will see some major elements with significant influence on our pricing methodology.

In general we can state that airlines see themselves confronted with a number of monopolies and oligopolies. As many of those are themselves suppliers to the airlines for their strategic sourcing they are the main cost drivers for the aviation industry in general:

- Airports and Airport Ground Services
  As an integral part of aviation it is not possible for airlines not to use the services of airports. However still today with the exception of the pure so called low-cost carrier segment there is little to none competition between airport companies within one single catchment area. Even between different catchment areas it is limited compared to other industries. Needless to mention legacy carriers that do not have the flexibility to change airports or even hubs on short- or mid-term. Hence within the balance of power it is rather difficult for airlines to influence this cost in their own favor.

- Aircraft Manufacturers
  Looking at this category of airline suppliers it is obvious that in each market segment there are usually not more than 2 suppliers who dominate the market and hence the prices (e.g. ultra wide body: Boeing & Airbus). Entertaining major fleets is a huge investment binding significant financial resources of airlines.

- General Distribution Systems
  In the past, for professional electronic airline distribution, there was not a way around the GDS' for airlines. Even though there is a number of suppliers in the markets one would find that usually in most markets especially in Europe there exists one dominating system e.g. Amadeus in Germany. This often goes back to historical development: When GDS' where originally invented the owners of those GDS' were primarily the airlines. This way airlines controlled their most important electronic distribution and of course also the pricing policy of this supplier. Over the years however most of the GDS' had been sold to other private companies by the airlines, which did not see this as core business any longer. From that time on the dominating GDS of a country started to dominate the pricing for their customers of the airlines. In the past 5 years the increasing importance of web-based distribution applications has decreased the dependence of the airlines on the GDS. Lufthansa's recent preference pricing model clearly shows the influence of a changing power of balance between a supplier (GDS) and its customer (airlines) as well as its significance for the end user pricing (corporate customer).

- ATC
  Air Traffic Control as a governmentally controlled security function is a mandatory part of aviation as is its pricing. Usually DFS Deutsche Flugsicherung as well as Eurocontrol would publish their pricing rather than to negotiate it with their customers, the airlines.

- Aircraft Fuel
  OPEC as the oil cartel clearly is a monopoly dictating the prices which drive the fuel price. The fact that many airlines are hedging on fuel is a

clear indicator that there is not an option for airlines to effectively negotiate the price of this supply.

- Competition
  Historically aviation only in the last 35-40 years has been increasingly considered to be a pure business. Still today the ultimate instance over aviation in most countries sits within the government. Legally regulated aviation is equally seen as an elementary part of a country's mobility infrastructure, military system, political framework – and only then as a part of the economy. Even many airlines who were often calling for free competition between airlines happily received government aid further influencing competition after September 11 as well as during the world bank crisis of the years 2008 / 09.

Taking the above aspects into consideration it becomes evident that the cost situation of airlines is very difficult to influence in their own interest due to the mono- and oligopoly structure of suppliers and conditions. Over the years this environment has led to the airlines conclusion that they have less possibility than other industries to influence their profit/loss situation on the cost side. Consequently this left airlines with prices and volumes.

Another driver in understanding airline pricing is the fact that in the travel industry you usually find a time gap between booking (i.e. reservation of a seat on a individual O&D), the purchase / payment (buying of the ticket) and the actual consumption of the product (actual trip). As a result an airline can never be sure that the customer is really travelling even if he booked and paid as the traveler could eventually cancel last minute and refund the ticket. For the airlines the combination of those elements resulted into the conclusion that they had to become experts in managing their pricing as well as the revenues.

10 Understanding Airline Pricing

The general mechanism of how price is built in principal in the travel industry does not differ from other industries and follows the logic described by Simon (cf. Fig. 7).

This suggests that airlines indeed can influence the way the customer perceives the value of the product and hence indirectly mold pricing.

Accordingly there is not such a thing as "The Price". The reason is that the airlines publish hundreds of thousands of air fares during the years driven by many different market segments.

- Business / Economy fares per booking class

- Negotiated Rates

- Published Fares

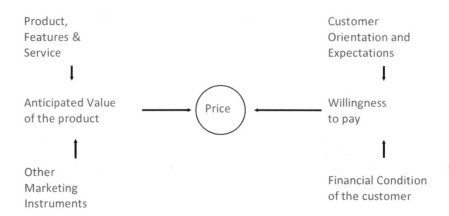

Fig. 7. Key factors of how price is formed

Source: Compare Hermann Simon, Preis Management, page 4

- Preference Pricing
- Rebates
- Incentives
- Corporate Loyalty Programs
- Bulk Deals
- Price Bundling
- Taxes
- Transaction Fees
- Etc.

The International Air Transport Association IATA estimates that worldwide there are more than 15.000 air fares published each day. GDS' at peak times during a year will show close to 2 million available tariffs of all kinds. Most of those different fares are part of distinctive marketing mixes designed for specific customer segments and various demand scenarios.

Ultimately, airlines also follow the general mechanisms of trying to exploit or "milk" the market at times when demand is greater than availability e.g. months of June and September for business travel ex Europe outbound. Equally they would try to stimulate customer demand when it's lower than availability.

In order to do this with the highest level of flexibility and effectiveness airlines have invented an extremely versatile system to put an infinite number of different price tags on the same product i.e. an aircraft seat flying from A to B. Needless to say that airlines and other travel industry suppliers are not capable of managing the above mentioned multitude of available tariffs manually so that an electronic system was mandatory.

This system is called Revenue Management. It is the reason why negotiating prices in the travel industry is a deliberately delicate task as many other suppliers of travel services have adapted this system for their own benefit e.g. car rental companies, railways, hotels etc.

11 Understanding Airline Revenue Management

The ultimate goal of revenue management is the maximization of revenues per each available seat by accurate forecast of the unconstrained demand. Ideally this will happen at flight, date and class level.

In order to achieve this target, airlines would identify those times when demand exceeds availability to make a conscious decision to accept or deny any given customer requests for a seat at a certain price: By opening and closing booking classes which represent certain price bands airlines accomplish a precise selection of "wanted" customers. Instantly with this system airlines are in the position to apply electronic multiple pricing to an extent at which it becomes increasingly non-transparent for the customer. In principal revenue management in the travel industry follows a number of easy steps as follows:

1. First fill the seats.

2. Identify opportunities where demand exceeds capacity

3. Once the customer we want the most comes along to buy – will we have a seat left for him?

4. The customer who comes first is the one we want the least!

The heart of revenue management is the assumption based on Simon's model that each buyer has a different perception of the value of our product and hence a different willingness to pay a certain price level. Consequently we would under all circumstances like to sell primarily to those who are willing to pay the highest price. In reality it is very unlikely that anyone would precisely tell us what price level he/she is willing to pay. However we can look at indicators in absence of prove.

The indicator used in the case of revenue management is travel pattern found in historic data: For each individual flight sector on any given date the airline is in possession of a significant amount of information. This includes name of the passenger, date, exact routing, service class, booking class, time of booking, price paid etc. Consolidating this data we find that travel buying habits and price sensitivity are underlying clear patterns.

One of those patterns is that business travel and leisure travel demand are congruent: At times when leisure travel demand is high business travel demand is low and vice versa. A manager who is spending his holidays with his family using a leisure flight cannot at the same be on a business trip and use a business flight. Consequently business travel demand is notably low during holiday seasons and notably higher during the rest of the year. Of course a lot of other factors will drive demand such as business peaks, trade shows, conferences, etc. Further scientists found that this is not only true throughout the year but even on a daily basis: Business travelers want to fly out/arrive at a destination early and fly back in late to spend as much time as possible at the destination. Of course these patterns are molding what airlines would call demand.

Based on these findings airlines are regularly categorizing their customer segments by 3 main criteria: Price sensitivity, network value and market. Of course the most valuable customer would be typically the customer, who is willing to pay the full fare price, uses an extensive portion of the offered network and is part of the main strategic target market.

So now that airlines had roughly defined, who the customer is they want, they are faced with a second challenge: They would not necessarily know when this customer will knock on their door with the intention to purchase the ticket. Hence the airlines run the risk of selling their inventory on a first come first serve basis and being sold at once the adored high-value customer decides to purchase. In light of the unfavorable market environment conditions described before, such a practice would not enable airlines to survive. Therefore, airlines have invented another element of revenue management called bid pricing:

Based on the available historic data the revenue management system will mathematically predict likelihood of demand for any given flight sector on any date. In addition it will also forecast the price sensitivity of the next anticipated customer:

Y – $999

H – $655

K – $425

B – $362

V – $303

$254 = Bid Price LGWLAX

Q – $233

In the above example I have listed the economy class booking classes (airlines like to call them "buckets") from high down to low value. Behind each bucket you will find the minimum value in USD, which our revenue management system would expect any customer to pay if he wants to enjoy the availability of seats matched to this respective bucket.

The current expected bid price (i.e. the price which the next given customer is willing to pay for a flight on this routing as estimated by the system) is set at 254$. Consequently the revenue management system will shut down Q class as a result. Why?

Because the system has calculated the next customer to be willing to pay more than the value of Q class. Basically we could go as far as to say that the airline takes the freedom to deny any customer at a value below 254\$ – even if there are fares at lower levels published in the market.

Based on complex mathematical formulas comparing the available historical data with the various forecasting models the airline revenue management system has calculated the future demand plus price sensitivity not only for each bucket but also for the next given passenger.

The interesting part of this system is that airlines have managed this way to split the pricing completely from the availability of the product in order to specifically select to whom they want to sell at which price in any given moment before the actual trip date:

Very often we find that there is a low fare listed in the system for a given routing however there is no seat availability for the respective booking class of this particular fare in the GDS' (Q class in our example).

Of course it does not necessarily mean that this particular flight is sold out. It only means that the airline does not want to sell it at this price, but most probably at a higher fare – for which there would be availability indicated in the respective booking class (V class in our example). The reason behind this is again the same: The airline revenue management system "knows" that it can expect higher value passengers at a later time hence it saves that seat for this wanted high yield passenger. This is going back to rule #3 of revenue management as mentioned earlier on: Once the customer we want the most comes along to buy – will we have a seat left for him?

Why is this so important to take into consideration? Actually buyers as well as sellers in the travel industry usually have a strong tendency to focus their negotiations on price. However as laid out before airlines have found a highly sophisticated way to agree on a price in principal based on negotiation but then to sell at a totally different price at the moment of ticket purchase by applying revenue management. This of course leads to a couple of ultimately crucial aspects for the negotiation between airline and corporate customer. For the corporate purchasing side following questions are essential to ask before entering into a negotiation with the supplier:

- How many seats on any given routing are needed during the year?
- When exactly are they needed?
- What is the expected/acceptable price range not only on the airline side but also from corporate customer's point of view?
- What exactly will be the availability at the needed travel times?
- How many prices for each routing will both sides have to agree upon in order to cover all booking classes which might have to be booked at time of travel?

- Which are the booking classes?
- Which terms and conditions will apply for each booking class / fare type?
- What are the alternatives?
- Is the seller capable to influence/agree on those aspects?
- Etc.

It is obvious that aspects like the above are very unlikely to be satisfactorily discussed by an airline sales representative alone as he will not have an influence on most of those items. The general environment in the travel industry indeed call for the extensive usage of Decision Making Maps hence the involvement of more decision influencers on the seller's side as mentioned in chapter "Travel Industry Decision Maker Maps".

12 Negotiating Price

Assuming that both sides have prepared themselves well and satisfactorily clarified the above mentioned questions they unavoidably will have to discuss about price. At this stage it is very important to bear in mind the psychological mind set and targets of each party:

The seller's challenge is to get to yes. Derived from the logic of revenue management he first needs to fill the airline seats before worrying about the value of the transaction. As a result we will often find that sales people are much better at navigating their prospect customer to finally sign a contract than to actually negotiate the optimal price for the airline. The reason for this is pretty clear: As the conclusion of a contract in theory has a 50/50 chance the sales person can never be sure to win the customer. Therefore logically he is willing to give in on price (as far as this sits within his area of responsibility). Also the sales targets of a typical airline sales manager consist rather of figures like load factor, number of passengers, revenues than of yield, profitability etc. and hence support this trend. Nonetheless, airlines and other travel industry suppliers have found an elegant and effective way to solve this problem by assigning the responsibility for the conclusion of the contract with a customer to their sales force. The responsibility for the actual pricing ranges however is sitting with the pricing and revenue management departments. Those will provide a certain bandwidth of pricing flexibility to the sales force while still maintaining the major decision over price in their own area of responsibility. This way, airlines and other travel suppliers can easily avoid that their sales people would trade off at any price just to successfully get a signature under the contract. However, it evidently also shows that the sales person's ability to negotiate on price is considerably limited.

The buyer however indeed is focused on the best value for money. Accordingly, a buyer looks at comparing product fit, conditions, benefits etc. to the requested price. For the buyer the "yes" is inevitable as the purchase is of strategic importance for his organization. Hence he must buy. His main question is from which supplier at which price. As a result, by precondition the focus of the buyer is more on the price as the ultimate conclusion of a contract with one of the suppliers is already a given fact from the very beginning. On pricing however he is not limited for his preferred direction being the lowest possible price.

In the below illustration we can see a typical example of the basic setting before and during the negotiation: Both sides will have at least a rough picture of what their optimal price would be. For the buyer logically this will be the lowest available price. For the seller the optimal price is the highest possible price at which he still would get the customer to sign the contract. As we can see while the buyer's optimal price is unconditioned the sales person has a condition attached to his pricing position: The optimal price from seller's perspective will always be limited at the level at which the buyer would not want to buy from him anymore.

Typically both sides would also know which would be their least desired price negotiation outcome. For the buyer this would be the maximum he is willing to spend, whereas for the seller it would be the minimum price as defined by his pricing and revenue management department.

Last but not least you will find that both sides usually have a desired price level on an individual basis. Needless to say that of course the desired level of the buyer is normally different from the seller's.

Fig. 8. Negotiation options

In our example consequently the available area for agreement between the purchasing manager and the airline sales representative is defined by the buyer's maximum and the seller's minimum i.e. between 1.200€ and 1.700€ (shown in green). It is very unlikely that an agreement can be reached outside this area unless changes are made to the offer in regards to volumes, product features etc. We will come back to this aspect at a later stage.

As a result it becomes evident that neither negotiation party will achieve their optimal price in this constellation. Mathematically, 1.450€ is the most likely result of the negotiation. Hence the main challenge for both parties is to find ways how to move the price into the desired direction. The way how to achieve this is applying negotiation techniques.

As mentioned in chapter Decision Making Maps it is important to ensure that the negotiation is actually taking place with those parties, who are responsible for the decision. Below I am illustrating the same negotiation, but now the buyer has requested the airline to involve not only the sales person but additionally the decision maker on price and availability – in our example a pricing manager. As a result, the potential area for agreement has extended down to 1.000€ favorably for the buyer.

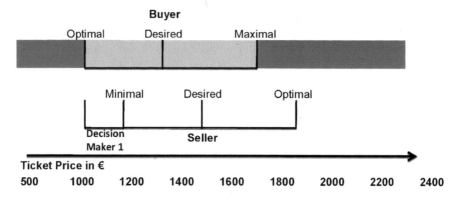

Fig. 9. Negotiation options

13 The Golden Rules of Negotiation

Even before the negotiation starts it is possible to put together a clear strategy for it and many elements and techniques of how to put that strategic approach together have been discussed. However, in order to successfully carry out that strategy once the actual negotiation is taking place it important to stick to what is called the Golden Rules.

1. We must have the courage to set a very ambitious target. Throughout the negotiation we must focus on this set target.

    For the airline sales representative this should normally mean to start with the published full fare. For the buyer however theoretically there is not a limit to go down to: Hewlett Packard's travel management recently came to the conclusion that being a supplier to HP is of such a high value in terms of image transfer (from HP to the supplier) that the price for the air ticket should be 0 in general. Of course this strategy will not work with all suppliers; however it indeed is a perfect example of a very ambitious target.

2. Once the other party is challenging our position we must have the courage to defend it.

First of all of course this is a credibility issue: If you start a negotiation on price and decrease you position by x% after the first argument you will probably not be perceived as a strong negotiator. This will potentially diminish your negotiation position. Moreover, experienced negotiators are aware that there have to be several rounds of argument and counter-argument, each of which bearing the risk of decreasing your position. Hence, standing firmly to your original position over as many rounds as possible will reduce the erosion of this position significantly.

3. We must have a predefined list of our own possible concession steps as well as a list of possible contribution steps of the other party.

This rule is largely underestimated as it is one of the most important tools to protect and defend your original position: Once there is no way around starting to offer concessions to the other party it is elemental to have a clear vision of what to offer, how much of it and what we ask in return. Very often we would negotiate on price not thinking about what other aspects of the relationship might be of high value. In workshops I have seen sales teams list up as many as 40 additional items they would potentially request from prospects in return for decreasing the ticket price by one step.

Example: An airline sales representative should always be interested in items like receiving further sales leads such as other contacts in the customer's industry, having the customer become a reference customer, being permitted to use the customer's logo for reference to new prospects, etc. Buyers might ask for free samples, additional credits in loyalty programs, upgrades, free reporting etc.

4. If we have to make concession to the other party we will ask for a concession in return.

This is the essence of negotiation: If I do a favor to you then I will expect a favor in return. The more items we have in the pipeline to ask for the less we potentially have to compromise on price. My absolute favorite sentence of all times is: "Unfortunately I cannot do anything on this end, but if you would be able to offer "xy" I would be willing to "..."

In case there is no way around compromising on price in the respective round, then it is very easy to adapt this sentence to something like "If I would be willing to meet your request for a reduction in price by x%, will you be able to guarantee me 10% more passengers?"

With this technique we will definitely make sure that for whatever we give away (and by the way, this is always the money of our employer by the end of the day) we bring something back in addition to the deal itself. No matter whether you are the seller or the buyer, your company would consider it normal that you come back with a signed contract. Hence limiting the bottom line cost of this contract will also change the way you are perceived in your own environment.

5. If we have to make more than one concession we will do this in increasingly smaller steps.

This would mean that in the role of sales in the first step why might lower the original price suggestion by e.g. 5%. After another round of negotiating we would go down further but this time only by another 3% mentioning explicitly that this now reflects already a total reduction of 8%. This way you keep the focus on the "high" number of 8% rather than on the "low" figure of 3%. Next step in our example would then be a further concession of another 1.5% totaling into 9.5%. Of course we would lift the 9.5% in a final step to a 10% now (hence a last 0.5% contribution) – signaling that this is the bottom line to your flexibility on price. The essence of this technique is to send a clear message about the foreseeable bottom line in order to entirely keep in control of the process as well as of what you give away. Note: Always remember to ask for something in return for each concession.

6. Once we have come to an agreement we will write down the agreement in order to protect from re-entering into price negotiation at a later stage

This is an aspect which we have to be aware of: Some negotiation cultures believe in a win-win situation for both parties while other negotiation cultures rather aim at the maximum benefit for their own side regardless of the result for the other party. Hence it is indeed possible that shortly before contract signature one party might bring up another round of negotiation on price and conditions. Also often other cultures do not share our very process oriented understanding of the negotiation process in which you would not re-address a subject on which there was already consensus. You will often find that jumping back and forth revisiting points discussed and apparently agreed earlier is a part of the other party's negotiation tactics.

Having an original agreement in written format – even if it is only in minutes of the meeting – will not necessarily prevent this incident from happening. However it will make it much easier to first insist on the original agreement and then question everything which was compromised on your end as needed. Especially in international negotiations the more consensus oriented German negotiator might be surprised with this habit which in some areas of the world is not at all unusual (Asia, Middle East, Africa etc.). Of course this is equally valid for the case that either party changes other substantial elements of the agreement (e.g. product, volumes etc.). In this instance we will challenge the original agreement on price – potentially going back to our original position.

14 Closing

The more agreement both parties have developed on price the closer the negotiation gets to its final point. The negotiation parties would now start contracting as shown in chapter "The Road of Negotiation".

Experienced negotiators can tell by certain indicators if the negotiation is close to entering the next level:

- The number of open subjects is getting closer to zero
- The level of agreement grows and finally reaches its maximum
- The seller starts highlighting the specific areas of agreement
- Both parties start discussing
  - Volumes
  - Terms and conditions
  - Customer service
  - Implementation
  - Testing
  - Payment processes
  - Time plan
- The negotiation parties start discussing templates of contracts

This phase is particularly interesting as psychologically both parties now start to go back into two different directions:

This is the moment at which the seller senses himself very close to his most important goal: to bring back home the signed contract. The buyer however will ask himself whether this really is going to be the best possible deal he could get – not only with this particular seller but also with any other supplier.

As a result very often we will find that shortly before the deal is ultimately closed another round of questions, objections or negotiation will occur. These might be within perception, expectations, needs or any other driver individual to the negotiation party.

Often, this can cause frustration and irritation on either side as it is regularly perceived as a break in what at least one party had considered the natural flow of the negotiation. As mentioned earlier especially outside of Europe negotiators will not necessarily follow any rules on certain steps which have to be followed. Therefore it is quite natural to go back and re-discuss items which had seemed closed earlier on. Of course this has nothing to do with lack of professionalism. On the contrary it is an expression of a remaining area of uncertainty for which there is a need for clarification. This can be:

- Lack of information
- Areas which are too vague or unclear

- Perceived benefits do not exactly match the needs of the other party
- Redefined perception of the offered value
- Compliance questions
- Need for more security and "ease of mind"

As a result it is crucial that both negotiation parties will not refuse the specific concerns. In practice it has proven to be successful to address those in a fact oriented and positive way:

- Negotiation parties should actively listen closely to the points of concern
- Understanding and accepting the particular need for more clarification is of high importance
- The objecting party should not need to justify his objection
- Objections need to be taken as a positive sign and invitation for further clarification
- It indeed is an indication that again both parties have come a step closer to the final agreement
- Many times the objection can be overcome by a variation or adaption of the original offer
- Inappropriate objections however need to be rejected

Experienced negotiators are well aware that naturally there is a high probability for crucial points on which both parties have strongly different opinions. As a result and long before the negotiations even start he will therefore remember the most important rule for negotiations which is to be prepared: While collecting the necessary information on the other negotiators it needs to ensured to also find out about the main areas of concern. This will allow the negotiator to put together alternative scenarios, to ultimately overcome objections – and successfully conclude a new contract.

Forecasting the Future of Tourism and Travel

Scanning the Horizon

Future Trends and Concepts for the Global Travel
and Tourism Industry

Rohit Talwar

1   Introduction – Winning in a Turbulent Era

In the space of a few short months at the end of 2008 and the start of 2009, the travel and tourism sector went from great optimism to a state of shock and complete disbelief. This state of extreme discomfort was brought on by the speed with which the economy served up a multi-course menu of unpleasant surprises. The downturn has demonstrated that virtually no one can assume they will be immune from global economic uncertainty. At the time of writing, the uncertainty has by no means ended and there remain concerns over further possible shocks in the financial system. In financial services alone we expect more bad news in the form of further large scale losses on sub-prime and prime mortgages, problems in the corporate mortgage market, credit card and personal debt defaults, large payouts on credit default swaps and problems with a range of other complex derivative products about which there are growing concerns.

In the travel and tourism sector, we have seen declines of between 5-25% in visitor numbers for different regions and destinations. In the face of such challenges, continued economic uncertainty and market turbulence, travel and tourism investors, operators and managers could be forgiven for wishing for a time machine to either take them back to the 'good old days' of constant growth or to take them forward to the end of 'down' and the return of market optimism.

Whilst time machines remain in the realm of science fiction, what is very real is the understanding that many of the problems faced by the industry were self-inflicted. They were bought on by an excessively short termist focus on current profits and near term targets. This was exacerbated by a failure to either track or act on the trends, forces and signals that told us the world might be changing.

Perhaps the single most important lesson from the downturn is the need for an 'early warning system' to help us spot and understand the patterns of change, ideas and developments that are shaping the future. In what most expect to be an era of economic turbulence, we need to develop the skills of managing in an un-

R. Conrady and M. Buck (eds.), *Trends and Issues in Global Tourism 2010*,
Trends and Issues in Global Tourism, DOI 10.1007/978-3-642-10829-7_26,
© Springer-Verlag Berlin Heidelberg 2010

certain environment and the courage to challenge trusted but outdated assumptions and beliefs.

To help map out some of the key future trends and issues that we need to be tracking, in this chapter I have outlined critical 'future drivers' the sector needs to be mindful of, highlighted the potential implications for the industry in the short and medium term and provided practical ideas on how to develop a future focused organisation.

The chapter is broken down into 10 key sections which address the following:

- Section 2 explores the current economic downturn and the potential sources of future turbulence.

- Section 3 outlines a set of four scenarios for how the downturn might play out over the next few years.

- Section 4 examines key themes for 2010 in the travel and tourism sector.

- Section 5 looks at ten major patterns of change that will shape the global outlook and hence the industry over the next two decades.

- Section 6 seeks to paint a picture of the world in 2030.

- Section 7 focuses on the way in which customer expectations and technology solutions could evolve over the next decade.

- Section 8 provides the results of a global survey on the travel industry in 2015.

- Section 9 sets out some practical actions for building a future ready organisation.

- Section 10 concludes by identifying critical questions for leaders in the sector.

To help the reader's personal learning and action planning, I have identified key questions for reflection at critical points in the chapter.

2   The Economic Downturn

The credit crisis and resulting global economic downturn which started in 2008 highlight how integrated the global economy has become and demonstrated how quickly shockwaves can spread across the system. The crisis has also highlighted how the pain has not been evenly distributed. While developing economies like China and India experienced a downturn, they did not go into a recession. In contrast, at the time of writing, while most European Union economies have emerged from recession, it is the more developed economies such as the US and UK that are taking the longest to recover.

The travel industry around the world has felt its share of pain. Indeed, in many countries and sectors of the industry the problems have been more pronounced than in the overall economy. The new reality is that we must prepare for perhaps a decade of economic turbulence and accept that uncertainty is now the new central planning assumption. Despite the current signs of recovery, tremendous volatility still exists and there are many potential sources of future challenges:

- The IMF Global Financial Stability Report[1] estimated total losses on loans and securities of up to US2.7 trillion for the USA and around US$4.1 trillion globally.

- The IMF also forecasts that the rich G20 economies will have a cumulative net debt of 100% of GDP by 2010. The cost of dealing with public sector debt could lead to cuts in public spending, higher taxes, rising inflation, higher interest rates, lower spending across the entire economy and job losses in both the public and private sector. These factors could in turn depress spending particularly on activities such as corporate travel, international in-company meetings, conference and exhibition attendance and leisure travel.

- The total value of outstanding potentially high risk derivatives contracts are estimated at between US$60 trillion and 600 trillion dollars – e.g. between four and forty times the size of the US economy.

- Informal estimates put the total of 'at risk' debt from Easter European economies at between US$500 billion US$1 trillion.

- Credit card debt in the US is expected to top US$1 trillion in 2010 and default rates are expected to rise to 10-12%.

- Most developed countries are experiencing jobless recoveries.

- Despite the downturn, there is still a strong expectation that increasing economic power will be exerted by the BRIC economies (Brazil, Russia, India and China). Current forecasts from the OECD (Chinese Economic Performance in the Long Run, 2008)[2] suggest that China's GDP could overtake that of the US as early as 2015. The adjustment pains for the developed world could be felt for at least the next two decades.

Key Questions

What assumptions are we making about the economic environment over the next decade?

Do our management processes support the speed and manner in which we need to evaluate the operating environment and make strategic decisions?

---

[1] http://www.imf.org/external/index.htm

[2] OECD
     http://www.oecd.org/document/11/0,3343,en_2649_33731_40277515_1_1_1_1,00.html.

3   Scenarios for the Road to Recovery

I believe there are four main scenarios for how this downturn could play out over the next few years. These are driven by two key drivers – (1) the level of economic growth in the developing economies led by China and India and (2) the level of growth in the so called developed economies of Europe, the US and Japan. The implication is that 'plan A' is no longer enough – we can no longer just have a single set of economic assumptions. We also need plans B, C and D because none of us can be sure how the future will play out, so we need to prepare for a range of viable scenarios for how the global economy could evolve from where we stand today:

- **Scenario 1 – Love is in the Air** – under this scenario, the recovery is underway in most economies by the middle of 2010 and we see a return to 2008 growth levels by 2013. Some economists call this a 'V or J shaped recession'.

- **Scenario 2 – Suspicious Minds** – The decoupling between developed and developing economies begins. China and India recover faster, Europe, the US and Japan don't complete their pull out until later in 2010 and do not get back to 2008 growth levels until 2014. Some call this a 'U shaped recession'.

- **Scenario 3 – Dancing in the Dark** – the short term recovery that started towards the end of 2009 fades away as more shocks emerge in the system. By the middle to end of 2010 many economies fall back into a much deeper and longer lasting recession – pulling out sometime in 2012 or 2013 with zero net growth over the period to the end of 2014 for Europe, the US and Japan. Some call this a 'Double Dip or W shaped recession'.

- **Scenario 4 – Road to Nowhere** – here, following a temporary recovery in 2010 we go back into a long and deep downturn in Europe, the US and Japan with little sign of recovery by 2014. Many economies would fail in this scenario. Some call this an 'L shaped recession'.

Key Questions

What strategies might our main competitiors and our larger customers adopt under each scenario?

What would be the impact on our current strategies under each scenario?

What new strategies can we adopt to cope with each scenario?

How can we ensure our business can remain profitable under even the worst case scenarios?

4   Key Themes for 2010 in the Travel and Tourism Sector

So what might the short term implications be of the economic turbulence outlined above? In the section I highlight ten key emerging trends for the sector that will be prominent in 2010:

- **Air Today, Gone Tomorrow.** As airlines continue to struggle, airports will be under intense pressure to diversify their business models and ensure they can survive under even the worst case economic scenarios. IATA forecasts that the airlines globally will lose US$13Bn in 2009. In addition the pattern of airline closure continues – airline update.com lists 90 airline failures and 7 mergers for 2008 and a further 31 failures and 6 mergers to date for 2009. We can expect 30-40 more failures and further mergers by the end of 2010. This will result in further reductions in schedules and flight frequencies – particularly for routes in Europe and the US. This could lead to airports having to close and will create major challenges for some destinations in attracting sufficient travellers.

- **Staycationing.** Nervous consumers in western economies in particular will continue to exercise caution in their spending decisions for fear of a double dip recession. The middle classes of Europe will stay at home in large numbers and vacation in their own country.

- **Asia Asia.** The speed with which Asian economies are recovering from the downturn is highlighting their increasing power and importance. This will see a significant rise in business tourism as foreign firms tour the region in search of partners and opportunities.

- **Rail Reborn.** The arrival of more high speed trains in Europe and environmental considerations will see a significant rise in people taking vacations by rail.

- **Cruise It or Lose It.** A massive recent increase in capacity coupled with sluggish demand will result in continued bargains for cruise passengers – particularly in the US.

- **Mind the Gap.** Rising numbers of people of every age group will choose to take a year, half-year or a few months off to pursue extended vacations – possibly combining working opportunities and volunteer work on their travels.

- **Agent Seeks Model for Profitable Relationship.** The desperation to find a viable business model for high street travel agencies will intensify. As airline commissions continue their inevitable slide to zero, agents will find themselves squeezed as they struggle to compete with internet travel booking services for straightforward transactions like airline ticketing. Only those who can provide a truly exceptional service will be able to charge their customers a fee for the value added. Otherwise they will have to choose between turning the customer away or doing the airline booking for free in the hope of building customer loyalty and then charging the customer fees for other more complex bookings in the future.

- **We Love Grandma.** Stresses in the workplace and concerns over job security will see increasing numbers of parents chose to stay at home and work while their children take vacations with their grandparents.

- **Ethnocations.** The quest for authenticity means people will increasingly seek out the opportunity to visit and live with tribal people in their indigenous habitats.

- **The World in Your Hand.** 2010 will be the year when we see an explosion of take up in the travel applications that are emerging for smartphones such as the Apple IPhone. You'll be able to get background information on every cultural site you visit, see animations or videos of how people used to live in ruined cities such as Pompeii, check out what every seat looks like on a particular plane before making your choice, swap your home for a vacation and receive instant personalised offers as you walk past particular shops in a tourist destination.

Key Questions

What impact will these emerging trends have on our business plans for the year?

What are the other key trends that we expect to influence demand?

How should we respond?

5   Drivers of Change over the Next Decade

As we look beyond the immediate trends for the year ahead, we need to step back and think about the longer term drivers of change that will shape the world and hence the travel and tourism sector over the next two decades. Below I have summarised ten key patterns of change[3] or 'megatrends' which are likely to shape our economies and hence influence the behaviour of our customers, suppliers, partners, competitors and regulators.

---

[3]   The ten patterns of change were developed on a project commissioned by the American Society of Association Executives and the Center for Association Leadership. The resulting book – Designing your Future – Key Trends, Challenges and Choices for Association and Nonprofit Leaders was published in August 2008 www.asaecenter.org.

5.1   Demographic Shifts

Analysing demographic shifts is critical to determining which customer segments to target and understanding their specific travel and tourism requirements.

The two critical demographic stories for the first half of 21st century will be population growth and ageing, and both will present challenges for the sector. The UN predicts the global population will reach 9.1 billion by 2050[4]. Based on these projections, population growth in Asia to 2050 could outstrip the populations of Europe and North America combined. Indeed, large chunks of Europe as well as Japan and a number of other countries will actually see their population decline amidst the global boom[5]. The UN also projects that up to two million people will migrate from poor to rich countries every year until 2050 with around 1.6 million coming to Europe.

The ageing of the global population will bring with it tremendous financial liabilities for governments, business and families as well as providing a stern test for pension and healthcare systems. The IMF estimates the impact could be ten times that of the current financial crisis[6]. Between 2005 and 2050, the working-age population of emerging economies will increase by 1.7 billion[7], compared with a decline of 9 million in the developed economies. Allied to the regional variation is a general pattern of aging; there will be almost 2 billion (22% of the overall global population) people over 60 by 2050, whereas this cohort currently accounts for only 10% of the global population[8]. In addition, life expectancy continues to rise across the world – in the developed economies estimates are being revised upwards by up to five months every year. Indeed some actuaries now suggest there is a 90% chance that those currently aged under fifty could live to one hundred years of age.

Key Questions

Given the changing ethnic make-up of our economies – what are the implications for how we serve customers – e.g. signage, language skills, catering facilities?

As the over-65's are a growing proportion of society and represent 65-75% of all the wealth in many economies, could this poorly served group in society be increasingly likely to travel and be a larger proportion of the travelling public?

---

[4] U.N http://www.un.org/apps/news/story.asp?NewsID=30159&Cr=family+planning&Cr1=.

[5] U.N http://www.un.org/apps/news/story.asp?NewsID=30159&Cr=family+planning&Cr1=.

[6] The Economist, cited in http://international-financial-affairs.suite101.com/article.cfm/government_deficits_growing_rapidly.

[7] BusinessWeek
http://www.businessweek.com/managing/content/sep2008/ca20080919_403840.htm.

[8] U.N http://www.un.org/News/Press/docs/2009/pop970.doc.htm.

How well do we cater for the needs of elderly travellers?

What specific propositions can we develop that will make our airport, airline or hotel a preferred supplier for older travellers?

How can we encourage positive word of mouth and build the reputation of being elder-friendly – without explicitly marketing to this group on the basis of them being old?

Where is our global radar focused? Do we understand these demographic trends well enough, how are they being incorporated into our plans – what changes are required?

How well do we understand what customers around the world consider to be world class service – who do they think provides it?

What are the implications of an increasingly ethnically diverse population for how we manage our businesses?

Are our staff financially and emotionally prepared to live to 100?

5.2   Economic Turbulence

An understanding of the changing economic landscape helps us identify where future opportunities and competitive threats could come from.

Even without the downturn, economic power was already shifting around the planet. As a result, organizations must rethink assumptions about the balance of global opportunities and risks. The rise of the G20 in relative importance to the G7/8 indicates the growing economic influence of developing economies. Indeed, rising government and personal indebtedness within developed western economies threatens to limit their economic potential with much talk of a lost decade and rich country debt rising above 100% of GDP[9]. At the same time, internal power struggles are evident as governments seek to increase their share of the economic pie in many developed free market economies.

China and India contributed 58% of all global growth in 2007 and it is estimated that BRIC economies could be delivering 40% of all global growth by 2018[10]. Current forecasts from the OECD (Chinese Economic Performance in the Long Run, 2008) suggest that China's GDP could overtake that of the US as early as 2015[11].

---

[9]   IMF cited by the Economist http://www.economist.com/research/articlesBySubject/displaystory.cfm?subjectid=7933596&story_id=13253151.

[10] Ernst & Young, cited by IBEFhttp://www.ibef.org/artdisplay.aspx?tdy=1&cat_id=60&art_id=21193.

[11] OECD
http://www.oecd.org/document/11/0,3343,en_2649_33731_40277515_1_1_1_1,00.html.

A growing emphasis has placed by governments globally on green initiatives as part of their economic stimulus packages – this could create an interesting funding opportunity for travel industry players to accelerate their path to environmentally sustainable operations.

Under these circumstances, leaders must rethink assumptions about global opportunities and risks in the face of a changing economic landscape, new sources of competition, and challenges to waning economic and political leaderships. The emerging economic powers are increasingly shaping the global regulatory landscape, exerting political influence over trade policies, competing for global R&D investments, and increasing domestic consumption. The Middle East's investment to diversify away from oil and gas is also becoming increasingly important – attracting the best talent and ideas and increasingly competing with European cities as global airport hubs and tourism centres. Our estimates suggest that up to US$4 trillion worth of projects have been announced to develop travel, tourism and supporting infrastructure across the Middle East.

Key Questions

How are we and our partners evaluating global opportunities and threats?

What are our contingency plans for a 10, 20, 30 or 40% cut in traditional revenue streams?

How can we position to attract business from the emerging growth centres?

We know that growth will be unevenly distributed, so how can we protect ourselves against further turbulence in Europe – how can we leverage our expertise into growth markets – selling our know how – but not necessarily running other facilities?

Many locations will develop new world class travel and tourism facilities – how can we both compete with them and participate in their growth?

Can we benefit from the growth of new destinations by leveraging our expertise – e.g. Provision of education, training, services, outsourcing of key technology applications?

The Middle East's new economic cities could become innovation centres and the sources of new ideas and competition – is there an innovation opportunity to fund / partner with travel and tourism focused research and development in the region?

5.3   Politics Gets Complex

The tourism industry understands the importance of building strong political support for the role the sector plays in economic and social development. To build effective political relationships we have to understand the issues shaping the thinking and priorities of our political leaders.

The political agenda has become increasingly crowded and complex as increasingly diverse issues, interest groups and challenges compete for governments' attention. The global finance crisis has led to even further complexity inside nations, between nations, and between developing and developed countries.

The G20 economic consensus offers more hope for collaborative approaches to handling future crises. At the same time, the internet and social media are changing the nature of political dialogue and citizen activism. Complexity increasingly manifests itself as risk – 35 countries were on the highest risk 'alert' status in the 2008 Fund for Peace failed states index – a four year high, with 127 countries in 2008 at Alert or Warning status compared to 76 in 2005[12]. An increasing number of individual countries are now considered at higher risk of political instability including Greece and Malaysia – placing greater emphasis on importance of rigorous country due diligence for market expansion plans. While finance remains a key global topic, other concerns over health, education, security and environment will arise. Against this backdrop, there is a rising public apathy – according to a 2009 GfK poll, only 14% of Europeans trust politicians[13].

Key Questions

How does our government view the role of the travel and tourism sector?

Do we have a clear sense of the industry related issues which will be on the political and regulatory agenda for the next few years?

How can we use our industry associations and trade bodies to build a positive dialogue with government on these matters?

5.4   Business 3.0 – An Expanding Corporate Agenda

As well as developing our service proposition, we also have to think about the factors and developments that could influence the way we run our businesses.

Long held assumptions about how to compete and recipes for success are being overturned. The rapid rise of emerging countries has created a wealth of opportunities for business but also a more complex set of challenges. Enhanced global competition, ever widening technological options, a quickening pace of innovation, and the pressure to create new business models have created a great deal of market turbulence. The rise of the internet has opened up new possibilities for communications, collaboration and customer engagement and given rise to a wave

---

[12]   Aon http://aon.mediaroom.com/index.php?s=43&item=1451.

[13]   GfK http://www.gfk.com/imperia/md/content/significant/press/pd_trust_index_august_08_efin.pdf.

of new business models. Across industry sectors there is rising adoption of open innovation and open sourcing for new product and process development.

Expectations concerning Corporate Social Responsibility (CSR) and work-life balance amongst employees are increasing with a growing focus on ethical sourcing. According to Richard Edelman, chief executive of Edelman PR, "Business leaders need to think differently about what it means to be a public company. No longer can their sole objective be to maximise profits." He argues that a new strategy of "public engagement" is needed to restore the public's trust in business. Indeed Edelman's 2009 Trust Barometer found that 77% of Americans and 62% globally trust corporations less than they did a year ago[14]. In contrast, trust in business is rising in China and Brazil.

Against this backdrop, the business landscape is evolving rapidly. Increased levels of women owned business, social ventures and entrepreneurship generally are accompanied by CSR concepts becoming embedded within organizations – becoming critical to recruitment and retention. In a survey of 7200 privately held businesses in 36 countries (Grant Thornton, 2008) 65 percent of the respondents cited that recruitment and retention of staff was the most important factor for doing CSR. Saving the planet came fifth[15].

Key Questions

How are we monitoring customer trust – what are we doing to build it?

What is our strategy for driving innovation in the business – are we embracing open innovation approaches?

What is our view on how the organisation structure will need to evolve over the coming years to stay relevant and competitive?

5.5   Science and Technology Go Mainstream

As science and technology developments move from the laboratory to the marketplace, we can see a range of applications at every level of the sector from the food preparation techniques we use to reducing our environmental footprint.

Nations and businesses alike are now recognizing and seeking to compete on the 'innovation advantage' that comes from leadership and investment in science and technology. Several national recovery packages feature heavy R&D spending – in Germany EUR 965m, France EUR 731M and large portions of China's 10Tn

---

[14] Edelman http://www.edelman.com/trust/2009/docs/Trust_Barometer_Executive_Summary _FINAL.pdf.

[15] Grant Thornton http://www.grantthornton.com/staticfiles/GTCom/files/services/International/IBR%202008%20-%20CSR%20report.pdf.

Yuan are also dedicated to R&D[16] [17]. Technology is increasingly embedded at the heart of business and is becoming a critical part of everyday life for the young middle classes. Technology is also offering an ever-increasing array of options for connectivity and personalization of both products and services.

The Public awareness of the importance of science is also rising, as recognition grows of its contribution in fields as diverse as health, new materials, and environmental protection. The increase in R&D spending accompanies a rapidly evolving personal 'technological ecosystem' that will see the consolidation of multiple electronic gadgets into one mobile device. There is also an increasing blurring of the boundaries between virtual and real worlds – for example using internet connected cameras to provide digital overlays of information on physical real world objects. Indeed, 55% of internet experts in the US believe that by 2020 many lives will be touched by the use of augmented reality or be spent interacting in artificial spaces[18].

Key Questions

How can we tap into the major R&D commitments in government stimulus packages?

How well does the innovation focus in our businesses support our stated strategies?

What is our strategy to stay at the forefront of science and technology innovation that could affect the way firms in our sector operate?

How well do we understand the technologies that could be introduced into our sector e.g. via mobile phones?

5.6   Generational Crossroads

As society ages, important questions arise about how to serve a multigenerational customer base and how to manage a multigenerational workforce.

There is an increasing prospect of intergenerational conflict as values and expectations differ. Each major group – Aging Baby Boomers (born 1946-1964), Generation X (born 1964-1980), the 'Millennial' Generation (born 1980-1994) and emerging Generation Z (1994 – Present) – brings widely differing attitudes to working practices, communications preferences, the use of technology and work-life balance. The challenge for employers will be to create an environment where

---

[16] University World News
http://www.universityworldnews.com/article.php?story=20090320094558110.

[17] HSBC Report, cited by the Economist http://www.economist.com/research/articlesBy-Subject/displaystory.cfm?subjectid=7933596&story_id=13432051.

[18] Pew Survey, cited in http://www.canada.com/Technology/Mobile+phone+main+tool+2020+survey/1078449/story.html.

each group can feel valued and be effective. Indeed, a Randstad USA survey found that 51% of baby boomers and 66% of the generation that preceded them reported having little to no interaction with colleagues from Generation Y[19]. The European Commission's April 2009 Ageing Report warns the economic downturn 'could make the challenges created by ageing more acute,' and lead to intergenerational conflict[20].' With house prices lower and thus individuals' net worth reduced, retirement is becoming less of an option for some baby boomers, further increasing generational tension associated with the workplace.

Key Questions

Should we be targeting all customer age groups or focusing on particular segments?

What are the implications of serving a multigenerational customer base?

How are we addressing the challenges of working with a multigenerational workforce?

5.7   Rethinking Talent, Education and Training

In an increasingly competitive marketplace, the quality and training of staff could be the only true differentiator. This has direct implications for the way we recruit, train, and motivate our people.

The constantly evolving nature of the business environment, the work undertaken and the technologies we use are driving the demand to update our existing skills and learn new ones. Rising life expectancy also implies that our working lives will increase and add further impetus to the need for lifelong learning. The so-called 'demographic time-bomb', describing the pending retirement wave of aging workers, is creating an impending skills crisis for employers – a 31% worldwide talent shortage was identified in a 2009 Manpower study[21]. The talent shortage appeared to be least problematic in India (12 per cent), the United Kingdom (12 per cent), Ireland (14 per cent), China (15 per cent) and the Netherlands (15 per cent).

The constantly evolving nature of the business environment, the work undertaken and the technologies used are driving the demand to update our existing skills and learn new ones. Rising life expectancy also implies that our working lives will increase and add further impetus to the need for lifelong learning. To this end, both schools and higher education institutes are embracing virtual learning.

---

[19]   Randstad http://www.computerworld.com/action/article.do?command=viewArticleBasic &articleId=336575.

[20]   EU Observer http://euobserver.com/9/28033.

[21]   ManPower, cited by Zawya
www.zawya.com/printstory.cfm?storyid=ZAWYA20090408035942&l=035900090408.

Other education issues revolve around employer concerns over graduate literacy, numeracy, employability and the cost of remedial education. A 2008 UK CBI survey found 23% of employers felt graduates struggled with literacy, and 20% complained about poor numeracy. A quarter said they were unhappy with graduates' employability skills. Employers also perceive a growing demand for graduate-level skills – more than three quarters (78 per cent) said there would be increased demand for high-level leadership and management, and two-thirds (66 per cent) said they needed graduates with technical skills[22].

There is growing interest in accelerating learning and improving the quality of training by using virtual worlds such as Second Life to run simulation based education programmes – an approach that has become very popular in sectors such as healthcare. For example, 18 different uses of virtual worlds in UK higher and further education have been identified. Medical sciences, mathematics and art & design feature prominently. Simulations, the visualisation of complex structures and safety roles are also stated as the most popular specific uses of this technology to date[23]. For the travel sector this could be a powerful vehicle for training staff to deal with different customer cultures. By 2019, nearly half of all public high school courses (in the U.S) will be taught online, according to Clayton Christensen, a Harvard Business School professor, and Michael Horn[24]. Nationwide in the US, 700,000 children attended virtual schools as of January 2008[25].

Key Questions

Have we explored the use of online and electronic learning to accelerate and cut the costs of training and development?

What are our industry associations doing to provide such solutions?

Is there potential to share the cost of development of new courses with competitors – using our trade association as a facilitator?

---

[22] CBI Report, cited by the Times
http://www.timeshighereducation.co.uk/story.asp?storyCode=403506&sectioncode=26.

[23] The Spring 2009 Snapshot of Virtual World Use in UK Higher and Further Education, by Eduserv. Retrieved at http://www.scribd.com/doc/12459921/The-Spring-2009-Snapshot-of-Virtual-World-Use-in-UK-Higher-and-Further-Education.

[24] By Cynthia Boyd, reporting in the Minnesota Post http://www.minnpost.com/stories/2008/06/02/2047/the_rise_of_virtual_schools_divides_education_world.

[25] Insight School Wisconsin http://www.insightwi.net/press_detail.aspx?id=17.

5.8   Global Expansion of Electronic Media – More Global Users, More Connected, More Mobile with More Functionality

The industry is beginning to recognise the importance of the internet and social media in raising brand awareness and driving bookings. Even more important now is the need to understand how to derive real intelligence from the data available to us and to use those insights to respond in real time to emerging opportunities. E.g. Imagine a new article or TV programme discusses a particular destination. Airlines and hotels need to be able respond with instant travel offers to those who start discussing the destination on Twitter.

The internet is increasingly becoming a core tool for business and the individual in Western societies, with the developing world catching up fast. Global internet usage grew 265.6% from 2000 to 2007[26]. China has overtaken the US in terms of number of internet users and estimates put the total global web population at 1.6 billion and rising[27]. Social web tools such as blogs, wikis, social networks, virtual worlds and portable computing devices are becoming mainstream – evolving into essential tools for marketing, communications and engagement. At the same time a major rise in both media spending and user-generated content is anticipated. On the downside, increases in cyber crime, cyber war, are also forecast.

Sectors such as mobile internet have significant growth potential – Nokia forecasts the total number of mobile subscribers will rise from 4 billion in 2009 to 5 billion by 2015 and expects extraordinary growth in mobile data traffic – rising 300-fold from 2009 to 2015. Active users of social media (MySpace, Facebook, YouTube, LinkedIn, Flickr) are expected to rise from around 700 million at the start of 2009 to over 1 billion by 2012, representing 75% of all broadband users[28]. By the end of 2008, ecommerce sales to British buyers totalled £40 billion ($82 billion), according to the price comparison site uSwitch.com[29]. Online shoppers in the UK are expected to spend £162 billion ($336 billion) per year on products via the internet by 2020.[30]

The internet can become a platform for sourcing ideas and building sector knowledge exchanges in each country – establishing the central repository of information on developments across the industry. Social networks also provide a powerful tool for understanding customer needs and reaching out with information

---

[26] Internet World Stats http://www.ovrdrv.com/stats/2008/02/internet-usage-growth.asp.

[27] Economist
http://www.economist.com/daily/news/displaystory.cfm?story_id=13007996&fsrc=nwl.

[28] Strategy Analytics http://software.tekrati.com/research/9775/.

[29] Uswitch, cited at LinkingMatters.com http://www.linkingmatters.com/uk-ecommerce-to-total-336bn-by-2020.

[30] Uswitch, cited at LinkingMatters.com http://www.linkingmatters.com/uk-ecommerce-to-total-336bn-by-2020.

and offers. The figures from Personalize Media[31] below give a sense of the true scale of the growth of social media:

- 20 hours of video are uploaded every minute onto YouTube (source You-Tube blog August 09)

- Facebook claims it is adding 600,000 new members per day, and 700 million photos and 4 million videos per month (source Inside Facebook February 09)

- Twitter has added 18 million new users in the last year, with 4 million 'tweets' sent daily (source TechCrunch April 09)

- 900,000 blogs posts are put up every day (source Technorati State of the Blogosphere 2008)

- YouTube claims 1 billion videos are watched every day (Source SMH 2009)

- In Second Life, US$250,000 worth of 'virtual goods' are traded daily (source Linden Lab release Sep 09)

- 1250 text messages are sent per second

- An estimated US$5.5 billion is spent annually on virtual goods (source Viximo Aug 09)

- Facebook gift purchases have reached US$70 million annually (source Viximo Aug 09)

- Flickr has 73 million visitors a month who upload 700 million photos (source Yahoo Mar 09)

- There were 92.5 million mobile social network subscribers at the end of 2008. This is forecast to rise to between 641.6-873.1 million by the end of 2013 (source Informa PDF)

- Over 2.3 trillion SMS messages were sent across major markets worldwide in 2008 (source Everysingleoneofus sms statistics).

Key Questions

What do our staff think are the best ways of using social media to drive the business forward?

How are other firms of a similar size in our sector deploying social media solutions?

What lessons can be learned from how other business sectors are using the internet and social media?

---

[31] Personalize Media, October 19th 2009 http://www.personalizemedia.com/garys-social-media-count/.

5.9   A Society in Transition

Attitudinal shifts can have a rapid impact on demand for different types of travel and tourism – the social media described above can be a powerful amplifier and accelerator for both positive and negative societal sentiments.

Many countries are experiencing an increasingly diverse, multi-generational and multi-ethnic society with changing family structures and evolving views concerning values and standards of behaviour. Higher ethical standards and a sense of the greater good are two of these evolving trends. Increasing expectations are a function of a decline of trust in key institutions. Edelman's 2009 Trust Barometer[32] found trust down from 2008 for most types of news outlet and organisational spokesperson. Corporate or product advertising was the least trusted – down from 20% to 13% in 2009. In the US, trust in information from a company's top leader is at a six-year low at 17%. Outside experts at 59% remain the most trusted purveyors of information about a company. Only 29% and 27% view information as credible when coming from a CEO or government official respectively, declining from 36% and 32% in 2008.

Over half of the Fortune 100 companies now issue corporate social responsibility (CSR) reports.Greater CSR, more transparency, and higher standards in public life are being demanded. These are being driven by growing public awareness of the scale of social challenges, environmental pressures, changing consumer values and a rise in 'ethical consumption'. These will rise in prominence through the communications accelerator effect provided by social media and more widespread adoption of reporting and accountability standards. At the same time, volunteer rates are beginning to decline at a time when budget cuts for many public services mean the need has never been higher.

Key Questions

What is our CSR policy – how clear is it to our staff, customers and key partners?

How can we build an ethical approach into everything we do?

5.10   Natural Resource Challenges

The pressure on the travel and tourism sector to reduce its environmental footprint is expected to be even higher than for other sectors because of the discretionary nature of leisure tourism.

For the last two decades, there have been many voices warning about unsustainable natural resource demands and rising pressures on the natural environment.

---

[32]   Edelman http://www.edelman.com/trust/2009/docs/Trust_Barometer_Executive_Summary _FINAL.pdf.

Forecasts suggest these voices will increase. The International Energy Agency (IEA) estimates that achieving emissions targets could cost over US$11Tn by 2030 whilst energy demand is forecast to increase over 50% by 2030[33]. University College London[34] says climate change poses the biggest 21st century threat to human health, while MIT's May 2009 climate study[35] suggests the threats posed by climate change could be twice as severe as previously projected.

Key Questions

How do we rate against our peers, what practices can we share?

Do we know global best practice environmental standards for our sector across the world?

Can we use industry associations to attract ideas and facilitate experience sharing that can help drive our environmental footprint to zero?

Can we use environmental gains as a lever to strengthen our global standing and competitive positioning?

6   The World in 2030

So what might be the impact be of these change drivers – what could the world look like in 2030? Clearly the trends could combine in different and unexpected ways to create a variety of scenarios. For the purposes of triggering the reader's thinking, and assisting those who are framing 20-30 year strategies, I would suggest starting with the following 'plausible' baseline scenario assumptions and then developing on them to define alternative scenarios.

6.1   Economic Assumptions

- Further economic turbulence and potential downturns are likely between 2010 – 2020, followed by a more stable period to 2030 as excessive risks are removed from the financial markets and most economies repair their finances

- Sustainable growth will still be the dominant driver for most economies

- China could be the biggest global economy and India the fourth largest

---

[33] IEA http://www.iea.org/textbase/press/pressdetail.asp?PRESS_REL_ID=239.

[34] http://www.timesonline.co.uk/tol/news/uk/health/article6283681.ece

[35] http://en.cop15.dk/news/view+news?newsid=1341

- Public sector debt will be a major issue until at least 2020 – for developed economies in particular
- Globalisation and interconnectivity between companies and value chains will continue to increase
- Major new industry sectors will emerge as a result of advances in science and technology

6.2   Political Assumptions

- No major new multi-nation global conflicts will arise
- National geographic boundaries of the current G20 economies will be largely similar to today
- Global institutions such as the UN, IMF and World Bank will still carry influence – although other strong institutions will exist on a regional basis in Asia, Africa, the Middle East and Latin America
- Security, environment and sustainability challenges will remain prominent concerns

6.3   Socio-demographic Assumptions

- The global population could rise to 8.3 billion, with 723 million in Europe[36]
- Global social challenges will remain around poverty, hunger, health and education

6.4   Environmental Assumptions

- Alternative (non-nuclear) energy sources will be common in vehicles, homes and businesses – supplying 20-40% of all demand in most developed economies
- Demand for food and energy are expected to jump 50% compared with 2009 levels[37]
- Fresh water demand could rise 30% on 2009 levels[38]

---

[36] UN Population Division Medium variant http://esa.un.org/unpp/p2k0data.asp.
[37] Professor John Beddington – March 2009
      http://www.thirdeyeconcept.com/news/index.php?page=389.
[38] Professor John Beddington – March 2009
      http://www.thirdeyeconcept.com/news/index.php?page=389.

- Without adaptation to the impacts of climate change, Southern Africa could see declines in production of 15% for wheat and 27% for maize[39]

6.5   Science and Technology Assumptions

- Advances in flight technology will have shortened travel times
- Scientific progress and new technological advances will continue to accelerate (e.g. biotechnology, nanotechnology, next generation computers).
- Advances in experiential technologies will lead to widespread use of developments such as virtual worlds, holograms, 3D projection, 3D television, virtual reality and interactive surfaces.

7   Technology and Tomorrow's Customer

If we now come back to a shorter timeframe and think about the next five to ten years, what are the kinds of customer expectations and resulting technology developments we can expect? Here I list ten developments that I think we can expect to see falling to in place in the period from 2015 to 2020 – and in some cases much sooner:

7.1   Experiential Insight

My cell phone will display 3D holographic imagery and augmented reality overlays that will be used to 'bring to life' a resort and its facilities.

7.2   Efficiency

I will expect that across the entire travel value chain you will capture my details once only and never ask me for the same information again.

7.3   Memory

I will expect hotels and airlines to capture every aspect of my experience as a customer and remember it, use it and build on it to personalise my future trips (e.g. know what pillows I like) and bring me tailored offers.

---

[39] http://www.grida.no/publications/rr/food-crisis/page/3567.aspx

7.4   Eliminate Check-in

A range of technologies such as my mobile phone, passport chip and face recognition could be used at the airport and hotel entrance to eliminate any form of data entry – just hand me my key as I arrive.

7.5   Customised Bargains

Holidays sold entirely through e-bay style auctions.

7.6   Dynamic Pricing

In return for my loyalty, whatever price I was quoted at time of purchase, I would end up paying the lowest price of anyone on the same flight / at the hotel at the same time / on the same tour.

7.7   Multitasking

Software agents will scan the web and search out the best experience for me, construct the holiday and negotiate the price.

7.8   Hear Me

Firms will encourage and incentivise customers to provide testimonials online.

7.9   Loyalty

Go way beyond the loyalty programme – staying or flying with you should bring me a flow of real benefits and special offers – use the power of your database to leverage value for me.

7.10   Single Transaction Trips

On arrival at the airport I would be handed a credit card which I'd use to make purchases anywhere in my destination throughout my stay. At the end I would receive a single bill and make a single payment to a supplier I already trust.

8   Travel in 2015 – What Does the Market Think?

In order to test the market response to the ideas, trends and possible developments discussed in the sections above, we ran a global electronic survey on the Future of Travel to 2015. The survey ran between January and June 2009 and the invitation was issued to our global network and circulated widely via the social networks. A total of 617 responses were received from 58 countries, with the largest respondent groups coming from the USA (29%), the UK (24%), UAE (5%), India (5%), the Netherlands (4%), Germany and Canada (3% each). Of these, 55% came from the travel and meetings sector.

8.1   Survey Themes

The survey looked at a number of issues around the future of the travel sector – focussing on 11 travel related themes:

- Addressing the Economic Downturn
- The Air Transport Industry in 2015
- The Visitor Experience in 2015
- New Revenue Sources in 2015
- Travel Technology in 2015
- Experience Technology in 2015
- Air Travel Volumes and Intentions in 2015
- Environmental Considerations for Travel in 2015
- Travel Budgets in 2015
- Hotel Technology in 2015
- Tourism Investment in 2015.

These are explored in more detail below.

8.2   Addressing the Economic Downturn

Respondents were asked to assess various scenarios for how the downturn may play out, describe their response strategies and answer two multiple choice questions on survival tactics and priorities. Table 1 below shows the five different possible scenarios presented and the percentage of respondents ranking each as likely or very likely. The most common expectation is that the downturn will end in 2010 (60%).

We asked those working in the travel and meetings industry to select all the actions they were currently taking to address the downturn from a long list of possible options. The most common answers were:

- Cost cutting 61%
- Improving customer service 46%
- Emphasis on innovation 47%

Table 1. Recovery scenarios

Parameter	Very likely or likely
The global downturn will end in late 2009 / early 2010, growth will return to 2008 levels by 2012 and the global economy will be booming by 2015. Business revenues will fall on average by up to 20% during the downturn	43%
The global downturn will end in mid to late 2010, growth will return to 2008 levels by 2013 and the global economy will be booming by 2015. Business revenues will fall on average by up to 30% during the downturn	60%
The global downturn will not end until 2011. Growth will only return to 2008 levels by 2014. Growth will continue at those levels through to 2015. Business revenues will fall on average by up to 40% during the downturn	39%
The global downturn will run until at least 2013, growth will only return to 2008 levels by 2015. Business revenues will fall on average up to 50% in the downturn	20%
A temporary upturn in global economies will start in mid to late 2009. However, further shocks in the financial system will drive the world into a much deeper downturn towards the end of 2010. The resulting depression will last through to 2015. Business revenues fall by more than 50% during the depression	25%

- Increasing use of partnerships 44%
- Changing organisational structure 37%

Perhaps the most surprising responses were that just 22% were undertaking staff motivation activities and only 35% were making greater use of the online channel. Not everyone was being affected equally, and so, while 33% were reducing headcounts, 5% were actually increasing staffing and 8% were increasing training expenditure.

When asked "What do you consider to be the three most important priorities for surviving in a downturn?" the top responses selected were:

- Clear direction and strategy 61%
- Customer relationships 51%
- Cash flow management 37%
- Innovation 31%
- Decisive leadership 29%

Again staff motivation was not considered a priority – with only 18% ranking it in their top three and only 9% prioritised greater use of the internet.

8.3   The Air Transport Industry in 2015

The airline sector is facing one of the most challenging periods in its history with 121 airline failures in 2008 and 2009, a rising impact from the downturn, high levels of debt, route closures and mounting losses. In the face of these challenges, respondents were asked to evaluate a series of propositions about how the sector could develop in the period to 2015 – these are presented in Table 2 below. Notably, Asia is expected to become the largest aviation market by 74% of respondents.

Despite the current dire warnings about the fate of smaller airports, only a minority expect to see large scale closures of US (38%) and European (39%) airports by 2015. While the majority (64%) expect that less than half the current low cost carriers will still be around in 2015, there is a strong expectation of renewal in the sector. 62% believe a new era in air transport will open up, with new business models that enable current airlines to survive and a number of new airlines to start up. Rail is expected to see strong growth in Europe with two thirds of respondents (66%) believing that travellers in Europe will favour rail over flying as compared to only 18% for the US – a reflection of the relatively under-developed US rail infrastructure.

Table 2. Air transport scenarios for 2015

Parameter	Very likely or likely
Airline consolidation and route closure will mean less than 100 US airports will be offering scheduled daily flights	38%
In Europe, only major cities will be able to maintain a commercially viable airport	39%
Asia will be the largest aviation market	74%
Airline consolidations and failures will result in only one or two major international carriers on each continent	45%
Middle East airlines will have bought up many of the most well known airlines in Europe, North America and Asia	30%
A new era in air transport opens up with new business models that enable current airlines to survive and a number of new airlines to start up	62%
Less than half the current low cost carriers will still be operating around the globe	64%
There will be a massive growth in low cost carriers	49%
Business class only airlines will have at least 10% of the premium market on every continent	48%
Travellers in Europe will favour rail over flying	66%
Travellers in the US will favour rail over flying	18%

8.4   The Visitor Experience in 2015

Prior to the downturn, there was growing emphasis on the nature of the visitor experience and the importance of understanding how consumer attitudes were changing around the purpose, duration and preferred destination for their vacations. To assess the relative future importance of these factors, respondents were asked to assess a number of statements about the visitor experience in 2015.

While 47% think it is likely or very likely that they will be taking more vacations, 49% expect them to be shorter, but only 25% expect to follow the current growing trend of taking more one night breaks even to long haul destinations (e.g. 4-6 hours away). Economic pressures are clearly influencing respondents – only 21% expect to purchase more luxury travel as compared to 70% who say they will increasingly purchase low cost breaks. In line with the low cost focus, the trend towards online research and purchasing of travel is expected to continue. 75% say they are likely to use social networks to research trips and seek out deals and 96% say they will use the internet to book the bulk of their travel.

Despite recent forecasts of the growth of hub hotels, only 24% say they will be attracted to stay in integrated facilities that combine an airport, hotel and leisure facilities. While 82% expect relaxation to be a primary driver of their vacation, 76% say the cultural experience will be an important influence on their decision. 61% expect sustainability to be an important influencing factor. The reaction against over-development of destinations is clear – with 80% saying they will increasingly seek out less popular, more unusual and less commercialized destinations.

8.5   New Revenue Sources in 2015

Respondents were asked to assess the likelihood of six strategies which the travel sector might adopt to generate new revenues in the face of growing pressure on price and margins. 81% think that product vendors will be willing to pay to present to the 'high net worth' individuals who are 'captive' in an airport, flight or hotel room on a holiday. Fully 84% expect that vendors will test new products in flight or in customers' rooms and survey their opinions via the seatback TV / room TV. Given the increasing amount of time passengers spend waiting in airports, 67% think it likely that we will see 'experience lounges' in airports that pay high net worth individuals and business customers to test out new products.

As marketing strategies become ever more targeted and consumer profiling techniques are refined, 54% think product manufacturers and marketers will take proven high spenders on free product testing conventions or holidays. As travel agents come under increasing pressure from direct booking, 67% of respondents think agents will try to monetise their customer base by charging companies to survey their network of customers and then share the rewards with customers. 48% think airports will run short business and personal development seminars for customers waiting to travel – for which a fee would be payable.

8.6   Travel Technology in 2015

The only area where the majority of respondents expect major technology advances is in security. So for example, 90% expect the security clearance will be based on biometrics e.g. fingerprint-based IDs, 3-D face digitization, and iris scans. Furthermore, there is a growing sense that airports will use technology to speed up the flow of passengers – with 71% believing that airports will increasingly drive check-in and security clearance offsite to car parks, rail stations and inner city check-ins to improve terminal throughput.

Despite the regular headlines and reports of new travel technology developments, expectations of progress by 2015 are relatively low. In their comments, most expect the downturn to dramatically curtail research and development in new transport technology. For example only 49% think a prototype hypersonic commercial jet will have been tested successfully and just 49% expect a dramatic increase in air taxi services carrying up to 20 passengers at a time, flying in personal jets from private airports. A mere 10% believe flying cars will be legalised for local flights.

Commercial space travel is still seen as a distant dream for most of us. Just 29% consider it likely that commercial space flight will be available for less than US$20,000 per flight by 2015 and just 17% expect the first space hotels to be accepting guests for overnight stays. Slightly closer to home, 29% think we might see the arrival of helium-filled airship hotels that would allow tourists to visit multiple locations by day, sleep in the airship by night and provide low-altitude photo-opportunities.

8.7   Experience Technology in 2015

While the rates of development and take-up of experience technologies such as virtual reality are increasing, there are mixed expectations over how quickly such technologies will be adopted in the tourism sector. The desire for physical experience appears to have been a strong influence in shaping respondent expectations – with a clear preference for those developments which enhance rather than replace a travel experience. For example, 75% believe visitors will have a single payment card for use at all shops, restaurants and leisure facilities at a destination – with all charges appearing on a single hotel bill. However, only 44% expect the introduction of dynamic pricing applications that guarantee a traveller pays no more than anyone else in their cabin on the flight or in an equivalent room in the hotel while they are staying there.

Enhancement rather the replacement seems to be the most commonly expected role for augmented reality technologies. 69% think augmented reality headsets will be used to provide overlays for almost all tourist attractions, showing extra information and allowing visitors to see how the attraction would look at different times of day and under different weather conditions. However, only 35% believe that due to large increases in tourism and growing environmental concerns, many places will be forced to restrict access, with most people only able to visit replica sites or view them in Virtual Reality and that only the rich and important will be able to visit the real sites. Even less – just 23% – subscribe to the idea that you will be able to download virtual experiences direct to your brain via the internet so you can have the memory of visiting a destination without ever leaving home.

8.8   Air Travel Volumes and Intentions in 2015

Respondents were asked to forecast what would happen to a range of key indicators by 2015, these are listed in Table 3 below. As can be seen from these initial findings, there are significantly higher expectations for growth than decline in the cost of domestic and international flight, in the volume of low cost flights on inter and intra-continental routes and in the volume of international airline passengers.

Table 3. Air travel volumes and intentions in 2015

Parameter	% expecting a rise	% expecting a fall
Cost of domestic flights	62	27
Cost of international flights	63	31
Number of domestic flights you will take personally	28	30
Number of international flights you will take personally	41	24
Volume of flights handled by low cost carriers within each continent	65	25
Volume of inter-continental flights handled by low cost carriers	57	24
Volume of domestic airline passengers	46	38
Volume of international airline passengers	56	32

8.9   Environmental Considerations for Travel in 2015

The issue of environmental impact is an ever present topic in any discussion about the future of the industry. 77% expect that offsetting of emissions will be mandatory for all airlines. However, only 24% expect that regulation and / or consumer attitudes will have hardened so much that hotels and venues that do not have a zero environmental footprint (waste, energy use, emissions) will be out of business.

There is a growing expectation that offsetting costs for meetings and conventions will need to be borne by either the event organiser (63%), the sponsors (62%) or the local convention and visitor bureaus (49%) rather than directly by the individual event attendee or exhibitor.

Only 26% think passengers will face personal carbon limits that dramatically restrict the number of flights they can take. Furthermore, just 19% believe that business people will need to apply for permits to fly, proving the business benefit outweighs environmental impact. Should personal restrictions be introduced, 36% think human rights laws will be used to ensure people can fly as much as they want to see their families. 52% expect that carbon emission limits will force severe restrictions on the cruise industry as shipping emissions start being included in national CO_2 limits and 47% expect that a prototype zero emissions jet will have been tested successfully by 2015.

8.10 Travel Budgets in 2015

A key concern across the sector is the impact of the downturn on longer term spending plans and budgets– with many suggesting that the shift to teleconferencing and virtual events could place a big dent in both travel volumes and the budgets for individual travellers. Table 4 below shows the forecasted impact on key travel parameters by 2015. As can be seen, across most parameters more respondents have an expectation of higher rather than lower activity and of rising prices and budgets for travel and hotel stays.

Table 4. Travel budgets in 2015

Parameter	% expecting a rise	% expecting a fall
Number of nights you'll spend in a hotel domestically	30	25
Number of nights you'll spend in a hotel internationally	44	21
Price of a 5 star hotel room	56	28
Price of a 3 star hotel room	43	34
Number of conferences and meetings you'll attend	29	34
Your budget for travel	46	32
Your budget for hotel attendance	41	31
Your budget for conference / meeting attendance	36	36

8.11 Hotel Technology in 2015

Internet connectivity is no longer perceived as a differentiator and 96% think that business hotels will all offer free wireless broadband as part of the standard offering. Integration of customer data across the value chain is expected to improve with 84% expecting customer information to be shared between travel agent, airline and hotel to completely personalise the visitor experience.

Despite the advances made in robotic technology, their use in hotels is considered some way off. So, while 55% think that by 2015, guests will be able to conduct an entire hotel stay without contact with human staff, only 25% think robotic in-room butlers will be common in 5 star hotels. In the room, only 42% believe visors and large wall-hanging polymer displays will be used to make rooms seem just like the home or the office at the flick of a switch. Only 43% think In-room mirrors will show you how your outfit will look in different settings e.g. meeting room, daylight, bar or nightclub.

8.12   Tourism Investment in 2015

The final set of questions looked at future directions for tourism investment. Given the scale of the sector, more and more destinations are now looking at travel and tourism as a key pillar of their economic development strategy. 78% of respondents believe a clear tourism investment strategy will be key to a destination's survival.

In terms of funding, 68% think public-private partnerships will be the main way to advance tourism investment in their country. 66% believe tourism investment will increasingly be driven by the private sector in their country while 44% suggest it will increasingly be driven by the public sector. The prime focal areas for tourism investment in respondent countries are expected to be leisure (59%), hotels and resorts (54%), local infrastructure (56%) and airlines and airports (41%).

8.13   Survey Conclusions

The study provides some very strong messages on how both customers and the industry see the travel and tourism landscape evolving. Clearly the majority are expecting the recovery to take place in 2010. The long term impact is expected to be more far reaching, with a reshaping of the aviation sector to create new profitable business models and serve the growing demand from Asia. The nature of travel is also expected to change with a large number (70%) expecting to take lower cost trips and a significant number anticipating the same or higher amounts of travel and spending per trip. At the same time relaxation and cultural pursuits will be stronger influences on vacation choices than sustainability concerns. The vast majority express a desire to move away from mass market offerings to discover more unique and unspoilt destinations.

As the industry struggles to come to terms with the full impact of the downturn, there is strong expectation of innovation in business models that will generate new revenue streams to help offset falling prices and reduced margins. Technology advances are expected to progress relatively slowly in the means of travel, hotel facilities and leisure experiences. Most believe that environmental concerns will result in mandatory carbon offsets for airlines. However, hotels and individual travellers are expected to be left to take responsibility for their own environmental footprints.

Finally, tourism investment is expected to be driven by the private sector rather more than the public sector with public-private partnerships expected to be the most common model. 78% believe a clear tourism investment strategy will be key to a destination's survival.

The findings suggest that there is still huge cause for optimism and that the industry can emerge from the downturn well prepared to cope with the changes expected in the coming years. To ensure survival, the critical challenge will be to ensure current decisions are informed by well thought our views of the future and deep insight into the trends, attitudes and values that will shape the purchasing behaviours of future customers.

Key Questions

Views on what tomorrow's tourist will expect and value will change constantly – how are we tracking these customer insights and benchmarking ourselves against those needs?

How much time do we devote to understanding a reflecting on the trends, forces and developments that could shape demand over the next five years or more?

9   Building a Future Ready Organisation – Practical Actions

So our heads are now full of ideas, trends, new concepts, emerging opportunities and possible challenges. What next – how can we respond, how can we break thinking about the future down into more 'bite sized' tasks that we can work with? In this section I have outlined a range of practical actions that you can start working on immediately to future proof your organisation. This is a menu not a step by step guide – you do not have to follow every action and you don't have to do them in the order listed. The idea is to offer a range of approaches that will suit different types, size and style of organisation. I hope you find them useful.

- **Make Time for the Future** – What can you STOP doing in order to create time to work on your future? Allocate yourself some dedicated time each week to read and think about what's coming up

- **Identify Critical Trends and Assess Their Impact** – Review this chapter. Pick out what struck a chord and those trends that will have the biggest potential impact on your environment and your organisation and share them with colleagues. Discuss what the biggest opportunities and threats might be as a result of these trends – how do your current strengths and capabilities stack up against them?

- **Ask the Customer** – Ask key customers what the 5-10 top issues are on their business priority list. What are the big trends they see coming towards them. Brainstorm how you can help address those issues.

- **Encourage Continuous 'Horizon Scanning'** – Have a prominently placed 'future wall' for staff to put up articles and ideas that could be of relevance – use it to facilitate discussion.

- **Focus on the Vital Few** – pick 1 or 2 key areas that you want to focus your efforts on first e.g. reducing environmental footprint / costs, using new technology, developing customer insight, etc. Allocate some dedicated time to the investigation – don't rush to action – focus on understanding the issues first – consider a range of alternatives.

- **Developing Customer Insight** – How can you identify the 'unarticulated needs' people do not express? Don't rely on market research.

- **Customer Focus** – Put the customer at the heart of your organisation. Involve them in the design of your next new service development.

- **Challenge Your Assumptions and Practices** – Do a 'what if' session – e.g. What would we do if our local airport closed? What if we had to run the organisation at half the current cost, producing half the waste, and consuming half the energy? Force yourselves to look for 'out of the box' solutions.

- **Thinking Laterally** – Do you have solutions that could be perfect for potential partners to test out in new markets – or that could help them launch new products?

- **Encourage 'Outside in' Thinking** – Involve people from outside the sector when you're designing your next offering – invite students from art and design colleges to come up with ideas on how they might design service changes.

- **Creating Markets of 1** – People want more personalisation from their suppliers. How can you build this into your offerings for every customer?

- **Responsiveness** – If people enjoy more spontaneity how can you build it into your offer? How quickly can you react to individuals needs?

- **Identify Technology Best Practices** – Do some research using the internet to find examples of how others in the sector are using the technology to serve customers – look at the potential of social networks, blogs, virtual reality, podcasts, webcasts.

- **Integrating the Technology** – If people want to lead increasingly mobile life styles, how will that impact your offer? Can you integrate their laptops, PDA's, iPod's and Blackberry's into your service proposition?

- **Sign Up to Social Networks** – join forums www.LinkedIn.com and start learning how they are being used across a range of industries – join in the discussions – ask participants who they think are the best in your sector and why?

- **Look for Environmental Savings** – Investigate how you can reduce costs for you and your customers by reducing waste, energy and carbon emissions. Look for sector initiatives already underway.

- **Adapting to Changing Lifestyles** – If people are living longer and there are increasing numbers of older people in society, what special needs might they have? How can you accommodate them? E.g.: large lettering. People are getting larger, how can you accommodate these people?

10 Conclusion – Facing Up to Critical Questions

The patterns of change, key trends, ideas and future developments discussed in this chapter highlight the scale of the issues and immense opportunities facing the travel and tourism sector. The number of airline closures over 2008 and 2009 highlight that these are very challenging times for the industry and many will undoubtedly fail. To survive and thrive the industry will have to think the unthinkable, open up to innovative new ideas, respond quickly when opportunities do emerge and prepare for a range of different possible futures. The turbulence in our environment raises critical questions for players across the industry – success will depend on how we answer them:

- How good is our 'future radar' – how much time do we devote to thinking about 'what happens next'?

- What if bookings or revenues fell 20%, 50% or 90% – how would we respond?

- What strategies would we adopt under each of the four scenarios outlined above?

- Are we maximising the opportunities to reduce our environmental footprint?

- If we are in an area with increasing risk of adverse weather, what are the criteria for determining whether we carry on, sell up if we can or just close down?

- What are we doing to keep staff motivated, develop new skills and maintain or extend service levels?

- How 'magnetic' is our business – how open are we to ideas from the outside?

- What benefits and opportunities could emerge if we consider partnering with those with whom we traditionally compete?

- How can we develop a 'culture of foresight' and make thinking about the future part of everyone's job?

The Future of Mobility – Scenarios for the Year 2025[1]

Irene Feige

1 Why Are We Looking into the Future of Mobility?

Mobility is part of our life – not just today, but also in future. Whether on the way to work, when travelling on business or going on holiday, in leisure-time traffic or goods transport: All these manifestations of mobility set the foundation for our society and characterise our lifestyle. Mobility opens up free spaces, it creates new margins. However, it also causes burdens and obstructions for both the individual and for society as a whole. This entails the ongoing and consistent challenge to create forms of mobility offering mankind appropriate benefits while keeping disadvantages and inconveniences to a minimum.

The question is how can we perceive mobility in the future, and what must be done in the process of this development? The purpose of the present study[2] is to provide a clearly oriented focus on long-term mobility issues. The study is based primarily on scenarios developed by some 80 experts in science, business, federations and associations, describing what passenger (and goods transport)[3] might be like in the year 2025.

2 Looking into the Future: The Scenario Technique

While many visions of the future that are prepared for planning or research purposes are in fact conceivable, they cannot always be followed in terms of the logic of their design and their development. Scenarios, by contrast, are systematically

---

[1] Summary of the ifmo-study, see also www.ifmo.de.

[2] The initiators of the study are the BMW Group, Deutsche Bahn AG and Deutsche Lufthansa AG. MAN Nutzfahrzeuge AG was a further contributor to the project in the context of preparing the first freight transportation scenarios. The Bundesministerium für Bildung und Forschung (Federal Ministry for Education and Research) has financially sponsored this project. ifmo was responsible for the overall project management.

[3] Not included in the present text.

R. Conrady and M. Buck (eds.), *Trends and Issues in Global Tourism 2010*,
Trends and Issues in Global Tourism, DOI 10.1007/978-3-642-10829-7_27,
© Springer-Verlag Berlin Heidelberg 2010

extracted from the present situation. They are visions of the future that are logical and consistent. A scenario includes both the description of a possible future situation and the developments which lead to this situation. Of course there is not only one imaginable and plausible path that will lead into the future, rather many different routes can be conceived and underpinned with reasoning. In this way, alternative scenarios can be constructed.

As a matter of principle in preparing a scenario, the basic assumption is proceeded from the perception that any given topic will be very strongly influenced by outside forces. If, then, the intent is to understand what development such a topic may take, one has to assess first how the relevant factors influencing the topic will develop themselves. On the basis of this prediction, therefore, visions of the future can be worked out that for the most part will be consistent.

These perspectives are enhanced by a further important element of the scenario technique: the inclusion and analysis of what is termed "events breaking with trends".

These refer to events whose occurrence initially is not discernible in the trend analysis. They occur suddenly and unexpectedly and may direct the development process of the scenarios into an entirely different direction. Such events could include technological innovations, unexpected political or economic developments, natural disasters, terrorist attacks or wars.

The advantage of the scenario technique is that the individual scenarios are not investigated in isolation from one another, as is normally done in prognoses.

Rather, the various links and reciprocal dependencies and the ways in which they impact mobility are presented, as is the effect they have on the actions taken by the various stakeholders. Along with the general economic and political framework conditions, technical innovations and societal developments are considered.

3   What Will Our World Look Like in the Year 2025?

Mobility depends on numerous underlying conditions and parameters. It is influenced by factors such as incomes, the division of labour, preferences in consumption, as well as the price of energy. That is why this project initially analyzed how all of those factors might develop that could have a particularly significant impact on mobility.

In the present study the following driving forces were identified as main catalysts for the development of passenger traffic in the coming twenty years:

- Development of the population in terms of geographical criteria and regional structures,

- Gross domestic product in Germany,

- Framework conditions in terms of regulatory policy for road traffic,

- Significance of traffic policy within general policy,

- Total investments made into the traffic infrastructure system,

- Framework conditions in terms of regulatory policy for rail traffic.

In the following the scenario "Mobility Calls for Action" will be described in more detail. Thereby we take a retrospective look from the year 2025. What has happened between 2005, the base year for our projections, and 2025?

4 Scenario "Mobility Calls for Action" – A Look Back from the Year 2025

Average Growth of German Industry at 1.8 per Cent a Year

Significant efforts were required in the years from 2005 to 2025 in order to promote economic development and keep the standard of living in Germany on roughly the same level as in 2005. During this period the fast growth of foreign trade particularly with China and India had a very positive effect on the German economy.

Comprehensive, far-reaching reforms were required to at least more or less set off adverse developments in previous years in educational policy and social security. Under the pressure of high unemployment in the early years of the century, the labour market was deregulated step-by-step, weekly working hours being increased in nearly all sectors of industry, and minimum wages lowered. The retirement age was increased in the same process, with options for taking early retirement being cut back. As a result of these changes, the cost of production in terms of wages per item manufactured decreased significantly. But even so, GDP growth of more than 2 per cent was achieved only in exceptional cases, the average rate of GDP growth in the last 20 years amounting to approximately 1.8 per cent.

Income Spread Continuing to Grow

With the overall development of the economy being weak, the disposable share in household incomes increased only slightly over the level in 2005. A further point is that this growth was not spread over all income classes, the income gap between poor and rich becoming larger and the middle class among the population as a whole growing smaller.

While the relatively small group of high-income citizens has grown, the number of economically weak citizens has increased far more significantly.

Personal Spending Habits Changing

Despite the slight increase in disposable household income, expenditure on consumption has largely stagnated. By contrast, expenditure on private old-age and health provisions has increased significantly. But there has also been a change in expenditure on consumption and in spending habits: The shares of expenditure have shifted away from classic consumer products such as clothes, shoes, furniture and household appliances towards telecommunication and mobility products.

Significant Increase in Mobility Expenditure

Expenditure on mobility has increased in both relative and absolute terms over the 2005 figure. This is attributable, first, to the increase in prices for using transport services and participating in traffic, and, second, to the fact that mobility still has high priority in the everyday life of the population.

The unequal development of incomes has had a polarising effect on the demand for transport: While, on the one hand, there is growing demand for low-cost (mass) transport and no-frill offers, people are also willing to pay larger amounts of money for expensive, comfort- and lifestyle-oriented mobility (expensive cars, first class flights, etc). In other words, certain segments of the population can no longer afford many kinds of mobility, while a small group of approximately 15 per cent is highly mobile and accounts for nearly half of all long-distance passenger transport (including long-distance commuters).

In all, passenger transport is up by only 10 per cent – a very small increase compared with former periods. This means that the volume of passenger transport has continued to grow apart from the development of the economy as a whole, a trend already appearing around the turn of the century.

Service Sector Gaining Increasing Significance

The services sector has shown particularly large growth rates in the last 15-20 years. Ever since the turn of the century, high-income groups among the population have shown growing private demand in particular for personal, leisure-time and consumption-oriented services. The options available in this sector have been consistently expanded and varied to an increasing extent. People with the funds required also use the services of private caterers as well as style and fitness advisers.

Compared with GDP growth, sales of company-related services have also increased over-proportionally, albeit at a slightly lower rate than at the beginning of the millennium. Apart from demand for logistics services, demand has increased in particular for knowledge-intensive services of the type rendered, say, by research institutes, development offices and marketing agencies.

Relating all this to transport, we see that these developments mean an increase in particular in short-distance travel (rendered for example by a service provider to the customer or vice versa) and an increase in mileage covered in business and commercial transport.

Demand for Gainfully Employment Still Covered

In absolute terms, demand for labour has remained largely unchanged versus 2005. This is attributable to various developments pointing in opposite directions: First, streamlining of job operations and the migration of many companies moving abroad has destroyed numerous jobs in Germany. The second point, however, is that far-reaching reforms in the labour market in recent decades have served to create new jobs even with the GDP showing only relatively minor growth. As a result of these reforms, demand for labour has increased on all levels of qualification. So far, up to the year 2025, and presumably in the years to come, this demand has been met largely by the growing share of female employees, by a longer working life (entering employment at an earlier point in time and retiring later), and by the growing number of immigrants. However, the average age of persons in gainful employment has increased significantly.

Most likely, however, the demand for employees and, therefore, an appropriate workforce, will no longer be covered after the year 2030.

Population Remaining Constant Only Due to Immigrants

At approximately 82 million, the population of Germany in 2025 has remained roughly the same as in 2005. However, this is only attributable to political intervention leading to a (net) balance of 200,000 immigrants per annum.

German Population Growing Older

The German population has continued to grow older in the course of the last 20 years: While in 2003 20.5 per cent of the population were under 20 years of age, the share of this group in 2025 has dropped to just 17 per cent. In absolute terms, this represents a decrease from 16.9 to 14.3 million. By contrast, the share of 60- to 80-year-olds has increased in the years from 2003 to 2025 from 20.4 per cent (= 16.9 million) to 25 per cent (= 20.6 million). The age group of over 80-year-olds has grown by 80 per cent, up from 3.4 million to 6 million (from 4.1 to 7.3 per cent of the total population).

The number of single-person households has increased at the same rate as the number of over 60-year-olds: While in 2003 14.4 million citizens lived alone, this figure has now increased to 19.4 million. By contrast, the number of multi-person households is down from 24.5 to 23.1 million.

Demand for Transport Changing in Quantitative and Qualitative Terms

Demographic developments in the last 20 years have affected the demand for passenger transport in both quantitative and qualitative terms. Although the population has remained at the same level – with the number of traffic users also remaining unchanged versus 2005 – the increase in single-person households has resulted in an increase in travel and more complex travel chains due to unabated demand for social contacts.

Looking at the individual groups of traffic users, we see that the use of transport by school-children, in many cases the very backbone of public short haul passenger transport, has significantly lost its potential.

By contrast, the use of transport services by senior citizens has increased significantly, leading to different demands made of transport providers: First, there is the group of affluent "young and active senior citizens" who enjoy travelling and look for high-quality means of transport; second, there are those senior citizens who have to live on a smaller budget and require inexpensive mobility options.

Since a growing number of transport users are however limited in their mobility for reasons of age alone, appropriate means of transport suitable for senior citizens are essential for transportation purposes.

The group of immigrants also shows two levels of behaviour in the use of transport: While economically weak immigrants mostly live in densely populated areas and use short haul passenger transport, immigrants with a higher income show a demand both in everyday transport and when travelling on vacation to attractive holiday regions and to their home countries for fast and high-quality transport options.

With the number of persons gainfully employed and, accordingly, the age groups of highly mobile citizens remaining unchanged due to longer working lives and earlier entry into professional life than in 2005, the quantitative figures alone do not show any change in travel behaviour. A decrease in transport mileage and capacity is not to be expected until after 2030, reflecting the anticipated decrease in the number of persons gainfully employed.

Social Relationship Networks Growing Larger

The geographical spread of the population also has repercussions on social relationships and, accordingly, on the distances people cover in their everyday lives: An increasing number of people are prepared to travel longer distances between their place of residence and employment and to pursue their social contacts. Some of the most important reasons for this trend are:

- Husband and wife both being gainfully employed.

- More frequent change of employers and place of employment while maintaining the same place of residence.

- Growing number of weekend commuters due to significant regional differences in the cost of living.

- Changing forms of human relations such as living together/living apart or "patchwork" families.

- Focus on infrastructure and transport options as the foundation for mobility.

Balance of Employment Orientation and Active Leisure Time

People seek to conduct a performance-oriented professional life as well as live and enjoy an active lifestyle in their leisure time. These parallel worlds of dedicated work and active leisure time are promoted and fostered by innovative employment contracts and regulations introduced in the interest of flexible company operations and the wishes of employees to personalise their working hours. Flexible features in professional life such as sabbaticals, annual or lifetime working time accounts as well as various models of part-time employment have in the meantime become the rule in job and employment relations.

This development has almost inevitably led to a further increase in leisure time traffic, in terms of both short trips and cross-border tourism, where in recent years transport capacity and mileage have increased once again.

The extension of weekly and lifetime working hours, on the other hand, has slowed down the general pace of growth: With people now working more hours a week than in the past, and with ongoing work and employment now also being quite natural for the plus-60 age group, growth rates in leisure time transport have dwindled in the last twenty years and are lower than, say, in the 1990s.

Flexible working hours have served to slightly spread out the peak loads previously experienced in job-related commuter traffic.

Daily Schedules Becoming More Complicated

With an increasing number of women entering gainful employment, the daily routine of many families has become significantly more complex. Most people are therefore required to carefully plan their routine and ensure a high standard of efficient time management. People tend to handle several errands at the same time, using in particular their car for such complex travel requirements. So despite very customer-oriented options are now available, public short haul passenger transport still suffers from inherent drawbacks in this respect.

Traffic Behaviour Becoming More Flexible –
With the Automobile Remaining Highly Important

With working hours and concepts becoming more flexible timewise and in terms of work locations, and with traditional family and household structures increasingly dissolving, not to mention the increasing complexity of everyday life, the share of regular trips (people travelling at the same time to the same place) has decreased. This means that choosing the appropriate means of transport has become less of a routine.

This has two effects on the behaviour of people choosing the most appropriate form of transport: First, the automobile has become even more significant, since it may be used flexibly at any time for virtually every purpose. Second, this development, together with the higher cost of mobility, a greater focus by many on the cost of transport and prices in general, as well as fundamental changes in mobility behaviour, has significantly fuelled demand for individualised mobility.

This trend has opened up good opportunities in the market for innovative providers of mobility services such as mobility advisors, as long as they are able to offer information on travel connections and transport options in the form of clear, readily available inter- and intra-modal transport chains. Demand has indeed increased as a function of the differences in services offered and fares charged for various types of transport, making alternative options more attractive.

New Market Potentials for Providers of Automotive Mobility

The main winners of a new pragmatic attitude towards the automobile are specialist companies providing mobility services for the motorist. Whether it is car rental, car sharing or short-term leasing, with your mobile card or mobile phone you are able to book a car within a matter of minutes. Then the user is able to pick up his car near to his place of residence or current location, maybe with the car even being driven to his doorstep.

In other words, an increasing number of people use such automobile services when and where they require them, without tying down their property and funds. Accounts are then settled conveniently via intelligent systems. Electronic detection systems within the car, in turn, are able to adjust specific features such as the seats, mirrors and radio, even extending all the way to the car's interior design and layout, to the personal wishes and requirements of the respective driver.

The Customer Is the Winner

The customer benefits most significantly from this inter- and intra-modal competition. Highly convenient comfort features such as electronic information and communication systems, a higher standard of travel comfort and – at least in part – outstanding service on board are now just as natural to the customer as punctuality, reliability as well as fares tailored to specific target groups and levels of capacity.

Rail Transportation – Rail Transport Increasing on Main Routes

The position of railbound transport in inter-modal competition against road and air transport has been significantly strengthened. The capacity of railbound passenger transport on major routes has increased over-proportionally to the overall volume of transport, inter alia on account of

- longer commuter distances (in particular weekend commuters) and the more widespread distribution of social networks,
- concentration of the population within just a few densely populated areas,
- an increase in business travel,
- an increase in (short) vacations.
- and attractive offers in the competition among various means of transport.

In all, the shift in the modal split of transport systems away from road transport and domestic flights has however not been that great since 2005 due to people moving away from sparsely populated areas formerly served by the railway system.

Air Transportation – Rapid Deregulation of Air Transport

With the air transport market already being largely deregulated in 2005, developments in this area have continued at a rapid pace. Following an initiative by the European Union, the EU/USA Open Sky Agreement was concluded in 2010, allowing complete deregulation of the European and American air transport markets. Restrictions in and between the major markets in America, Europe, and Asia have also been cut back increasingly. Provided slots are available, all airlines are now able to offer regular services between any airport of their choice.

The process of concentration in the airline market has continued. Only a few of the small traditional carriers have survived, most of the small companies being bought up by the large airline groups. Some have concentrated on lucrative niche markets and have therefore been able to survive over the years.

EU-Wide Harmonisation of Air Traffic Control Completed

Air traffic control, which for years was a bottleneck in Europe, has also improved significantly. Making substantial political efforts, governments and authorities have succeeded in harmonising air traffic control throughout Europe, with positive effects in terms of punctuality, safety, and burdens on the environment.

Flying Has Become More Efficient

By increasing the capacity of airline hubs and harmonising air traffic control, there has also been another positive effect: The many delays in domestic German air travel at the beginning of the millennium giving rise to growing criticism have largely become a thing of the past – just like other problems previously irritating many people such as long trips to the airport sometimes in congested traffic and tedious security and handling processes which almost wasted the time saved by flying on short distances. Today the time required for flight security has become much shorter on account of biometric testing procedures and the acknowledgement of frequent flyers as trusted passengers.

Air transport is not only punctual in most cases, but also time-saving even on shorter distances. And although the objectives for checking in on short flights (15 minutes) and long flights (30 minutes) have not yet been reached, the use of new technologies and organisational concepts has expedited most procedures quite substantially and overcome security problems. A final point is that many newly built inter-modal connections to public short haul passenger transport or regional transport make travel to and from the airport more efficient and smoother than in the past.

Air Mileage Up Over-Proportionally to Overall Transport Mileage

Air transport, benefiting from the improvements and developments experienced, has become far more efficient in recent years. Despite the over-proportional increase in air transport compared with transport as a whole, delays are now more the exception than the rule. Apart from the strongly segmented range of flight options, the growth of international tourism and an increasing volume of business travel are the main factors responsible for the increase in air transport as a whole.

5   What Does All This Mean to Our Mobility? – How Mobile Are We in the Year 2025?

The Scenario "Mobility Calls for Action" sets out a clear path into a mobile future in the year 2025 based on most fundamental and consistent decisions: Substantial re-allocation of budget funds, use of new financing tools and much greater direct participation of users are just some examples. All transport providers will concentrate increasingly on their strengths. Indeed, all these changes are necessary in order to remain "only" as mobile at the end of this period as we already are in the year 2005. A considerably larger volume of goods will reach its destinations more or less just as fast and with the same punctuality as today. And passenger transport will also flow at the same rate as it does in today's world.

A further point is that the use of mobility will be more pragmatic. The choice of means of transport will be less of a routine than in the past. There will be more multi-optional users choosing the railways, the car or the aircraft, depending on their individual requirements. But this fundamental flexibility will be set off by financial restrictions in many cases due to limited household budgets. The result will be a large market of low-cost offers, with today's no-frill flights marking only the beginning of a development in which we will see extremely inexpensive long-distance bus services and a growing number of low-priced cars in the market.

The scenario describes a consistent, conceivable picture of mobility in the future. But to make it reality, substantial challenges have to be overcome and major policies must be put into place by politicians. And at the end of the day all these steps will only prevent the situation on the road, with our railways, in the air and on water from becoming worse. Considering the anticipated increase in traffic volume, this is actually quite a satisfactory result. But how the situation might also develop if the decisions required are either not taken at all or not in time, will be briefly described in an alternative vision of the future.

Future of Global Aviation

Candan Karlıtekin

Consumer preferences change constantly in line with technological developments. The new and unique set of products and services of today's world embodies air travel, for a wider spectrum of people relative to the recent past. Especially for emerging markets and developing economies, civil aviation has been demonstrating a remarkable growth stemming from overall economic development and shifting demand between different modes of transportation.

The introduction of the Low Cost Low Fare Model (LCLF) created a new segment of air travellers while attracting part of the existing passengers along. As legacy carriers struggled to adjust to this new business model, they also increased capacity, started to reduce cost and enhanced their products. The ease of finding finance has enabled both LCLF and legacy carriers to lease new aircrafts in large numbers leading to an excess capacity. This development, coupled with the intensive competition and falling prices, stimulated demand both in low cost and legacy segments in line with the increased seat capacity.

The ease of global finance supported all sorts of investments, mergers and acquisitions in many sectors including the air transportation. Prices of commodities and energy started to increase, bringing them up to a point where economic realities can no longer support. Global economic performance which once laid the ground for a widespread and remarkable air travel experience, now has been demonstrating a contraction following an unprecedented financial meltdown and excerting its immediate effect on airlines with few exceptions.

We have reached a new state of the industry and new developments are incipient with respect to the new global financial climate, falling demand, capacity adjustments, predatory competition and acute environmental concerns.

1. **Protectionism**: In difficult times, the lack of and/or the difficulty of a worldwide coordinated response leads to counterproductive reactions. The heat of rising unemployment on politicians is attempted to be cured by protectionist measures. Experience suggests that these measures are far from being capable of creating jobs even in the short run because shrinking global trade and cross-border activities increase unemployment and incomes. In spite of this well established reality, protectionism may be an immediate response. At least this would impede the pace of further liberalization through

tight Air Service Agreements (ASAs), simply because there will be less passengers and cargo to carry and fewer entries of carriers to the market. Thus, economic protectionism in general (not restrictions in aviation) dampens the drive and the need for further liberalization in aviation. This makes air travel more expensive which in turn discourages demand.

2. **Economic Slowdown and Finance**: Many investors who have chosen airline business as a well collateralised field to earn plausible return to their funds may face defaulting airlines and the difficulty to replace their assets i.e. aircrafts with other carriers. Many carriers with suboptimal capacities, improper operational scope and scales as well as unbalanced business models may go out of business as the ease of finance disappears and economic slowdown lingers. It is not going to be surprising to observe bankruptcies, mergers, acquisitions and re-scalings in line with sound business models. This can be seen as an opportunity for healthier companies to cease others unable to adjust. Thus, economic slowdown and competitive financial markets will put pressure on airliners to come to the right size to be viable. This drive translates into a **higher concentration** in airline business but not necessarily to a lesser competition.

3. **Foreign Ownership of Airlines:** The potential impact of foreign investment in airlines seems to continue to be a concern in terms of national security, employment, domestic and international competition regardless of their genuinity. However, the robust standing of established domestic parties will continue to be a barrier to cross-border acquisitions and/or the recapitalization of troubled airlines. Naturally, protection of airlines through highly restricted ASAs is going to continue to be detrimental for consumers. This practice also impedes the optimal use of resources as it outrules optimal global networks to be built under a coordinated management. Once more, the company scale, the network scope, and the route frequency of any carrier or group of carriers will matter unless designed and operated optimally beyond a critical threshold.

4. **Competition:** Competition will continue to be tough and predatory at times between Alliance Blocks. Competition will also keep its strength within alliances. Coupled with the effect of non-alliance majors and LCLF carriers, travellers will continue to benefit from falling prices. This will be possible due to higher concentrations and optimal resource allocations in civil aviation as depicted above. Although in economic downturn new entries to the sector will be limited, this will not adversely affect effective competition.

5. **Selection of Network Models (Point-to-Point vs. Hub-n-Spoke):** P-P requires more resources to be employed to serve a given volume of air travel relative to the H-S model. Although congested skies around major hubs pose a bottleneck which also leads to scarcity of slots, this can be overcome with high capacity and low cost per seat aircrafts. P-P models will deliver

the same service of course with more convenience to customers but at a higher cost due to low capacity and high cost per seat aircrafts. While legacy carriers will stick to H-S models, the P-P model will be more meaningful for LCLF carriers with high density seat configurations. This would mean that LCLF carriers may find niches to validate their models while easing off congestions in major hubs. In sum, the induced selection of network models will lead to lesser confrontation between legacy carriers and LCLF carriers. This also means that these models address different needs and are going to coexist.

6. **Market Segmentation and Product Differentiation**: Following from the previous point, market segmentation is a tool which needs to be employed in order to assemble different products for different customer segments. It is also a mechanism by which airlines stimulate demand by bringing cost in line with price that one is willing to pay for a highly differentiated product. This is not limited to lower-end customers implying that in the future a "comfort class in long haul", which is between tourist class and business class, will create a new market and/or ease off impediments to corporal travel demand. Airlines may select from a spectrum of different hybrid business models to serve different markets. A particular business model can accommodate different products in the same cabin and/or in the same fleet via sub-fleets. According to textbook terminology of economics this is nothing but leaving the least possible room for consumer surplus that you create income as close as to the willingness to pay. Thus, small scale companies alongside with bigger ones can identify a niche with the proper choice of equipment and proper design of product.

7. **Saturation of Air Travel Markets**: This concept is not necessarily closely correlated with congestions in major hubs of North Atlantic, Europe and other megacities. It rather has a strong connotation to loss of dynamism and economic saturation one can attribute to the level of economic development and socio-demographic background. Even though global economic recovery makes its way, emerging markets and other developing economies will demonstrate double digit growth figures for several reasons. Among them, one can mention an unlimited growth of the per capita income, uncongested skies, less environmental sensitivity due to pressing growth needs, shifting industrial production away from the developed world, continuous shift from other modes of transportation, rising living standards and smaller base from which growth figures are calculated.

8. **Taxes, Levies and Charges**: For politicians and bureaucrats it is tempting, administrable, convenient and popular (in the eyes of masses) to tax air travel for reasons of environmentalist concerns. Without bothering to compare to surface travel, the first thing seems plausible to discourage air travel indirectly by making travellers pay excessive sums for the damages caused by CO_2 emissions, noise and other externalities. Let alone the waste and misuse of funds collected for this purpose, it puts another pressure on the

airlines in addition to the competitive and highly regulatory aviation framework. Since capacity constraints are being removed gradually by freer skies, the need to replace engine efficient aircrafts with obsolete ones continues to be the practice in face of increasing fuel prices and vanishing world petroleum deposits. Civil Aviation itself has to be considered as an infrastructure for a better world to achieve development through a considerate growth and deserves due attention of politicians and bureaucrats.

9. **Changing Nature of Demand**: Climate change is a new phenomenon affecting air travel by generating new travel needs stemming from new patterns of demographic mobility. Many new destinations will substitute others as climate change warrants. Shorter and more frequent travels will be on the rise. Leisure travel abroad will change patterns depending on origin countries and age distribution of travellers in a way yet to be determined. Medical tourism will gain momentum as the developed world will have to cut back from mounting health expenses of the aging population unless they find a miraculous solution to their social security problems.

10. **Security**: Political tensions, globalization of local problems, rising living standards and corresponding needs for energy sources, barriers to labor mobility, growing intolerance and many other issues tend to put air travel into a unique target which provides highest level of public attention and propaganda in the eyes of terrorist circles. Since leading politicians tend to ignore root causes and insist on fighting consequences by expensive, useless and exaggerated measures, the cost of all security mania will continue to bother airlines and air travellers.

11. **Infrastructure Bottlenecks**: Air Traffic Control systems and airports need to be well maintained, developed and expanded to cope up with changing patterns. Measures have to be taken to eradicate the negative effects of airports being the natural monopoly and sustain a proper level of capital expenditure. Unfortunately, regulators tend to be less enthusiastic in playing a facilitative role in overcoming bottlenecks in infrastructure. Seeing airports as a source of income, rather than a facility by which people are enabled for a better life and regarding spending money for ATC and other safety related fields as just another public expenditure may not change in the future unless a visionary perspective is obtained by politicians.

Competition, innovation, efficiency, viability, safety, security, infrastructure development and emissions trading are few words airlines are going to be surrounded with all the time. The future of civil aviation is challenging, demanding and driver for innovations and technological advancements. This is and will continue to be a sector in which a lack of or slow adjustment to the changing circumstances will be punished immediately. Airlines will turn into companies which produce air travel and air cargo service for all without country and boundary based regulations just like perfumes, banking services, hamburgers and other globally managed goods, services and brands.

Commercial Jetliners – History and Forecast

Richard Aboulafia

1 Market Overview

1.1 Introduction

Our Commercial Jet Overview covers all Airbus and Boeing jets, and Bombardier's CSeries. It excludes the former Soviet jetliners which hold well under 1% of the market, so this analysis provides a picture of almost all of the world market for civil jetliners larger than 108 seats. Large regional jets, especially Embraer's ERJ 190/195, provide some competition at the bottom end of this market, but these are covered in our Regional Aircraft overview.

We start with a summary of findings. Then we have a section devoted to the general health of the civil aviation business. This is followed by an essay on the two manufacturers, and where they stand. We conclude with our forecast of the next ten years, in terms of units, dollars, and market share, accompanied by some comments about scenario variables.

1.2 The Big Picture

You can save time by simply scanning the tables and charts and remembering the following points:

- This is the last major sector of the economy to be unaffected by a serious and prolonged recession so far. The airline industry is in very bad shape, and despite the backlog and government finance this pain will start to affect manufacturers within the next year. The current high production rates can be extended through the first half of 2010, with a relatively mild downturn after that. The market will peak this year at 964 planes worth $61.3 billion.

- We forecast production of 8,919 jetliners worth $624.3 billion over the next ten years (2009-2018). This includes 6,490 single aisle planes worth $298.6 billion, and 2,429 twin aisle planes worth $325.7 billion (all of these numbers are in 2009 dollars).

R. Conrady and M. Buck (eds.), *Trends and Issues in Global Tourism 2010*,
Trends and Issues in Global Tourism, DOI 10.1007/978-3-642-10829-7_29,
© Springer-Verlag Berlin Heidelberg 2010

- Compare these numbers with the last ten years (1999-2008), when 7,685 aircraft worth $502.5 billion (also in 2009 dollars) were delivered. Despite today's airline industry troubles, this remains a long-term growth market.

- The 787 is the biggest single question mark hanging over this market. Like everyone else, all we can do is watch and wait. Our forecast assumes a first flight in 2010 and an EIS in the first half of 2011. We also assumes that the plane can achieve performance close to its promised specifications, at least after the first 40-150 production models are built.

- Airbus's response to the 777 and 787, the A350 XWB, looks less ambitious than the 787, but if the 787 doesn't perform as planned, the A350XWB could look great due to its more conservative design approach. In any even it should perform well against the 777. Given constraints on Airbus's new product development spending (largely because of the investment needed by the much less relevant A380), the A350XWB looks like a smart strategy. Our forecast calls for Boeing's 777-X, a new or derivative response to the A350XWB, to arrive in 2017.

- We think Bombardier's CSeries will enter enter service in 2015. Its appeal is uncertain, but if it performs well and attracts solid orders it could precipitate new or updated narrowbody product introductions from Airbus and Boeing. But our forecast doesn't call for A320/737 replacements to arrive before the end of our ten year horizon.

- There's no way to tell how the USAF refueling tanker contract will play out. We have a generic, independent KC-X forecast line bolted on to our commercial jet numbers (adding 58 twin aisle planes worth $10.2 billion to our forecast).

- 2004 was the first year Airbus enjoyed a higher market share than Boeing (in deliveries revenue). But in 2006 Boeing surged ahead in value of orders, backlog, and deliveries, the first time it won in all three metrics since 2000. It continued its lead in all three in 2007, but the situation reversed again in 2008 with Airbus pulling ahead in orders and deliveries. Boeing 's share will jump to 60% when the 787 arrives, but the A350 will restore Airbus's share to 45% after 2014.

- Our forecast calls for a 55%-44% market share split in Boeing's favor over the next ten years (with just 1% going to Bombardier). But there are two enormous variables: 787 program execution and aircraft performance, and Airbus's ability to bring a competitive A350 XWB to market.

1.3   Jetliners Wait for Hard Times to Hit ... Finally

By any market health indicator, jetliner production is well overdue for a significant fall. Looking at the broader economy, airline traffic, airline profits, or used aircraft prices and availability, this is a market that simply does not need new aircraft.

In fact, capacity reductions among most major airlines indicate a need for accelerated retirements, not a continuation of record level jet production.

Yet both Airbus and Boeing continue to insist that demand justifies these high rates. The likely reason for this insistence has to do with broader economic uncertainty. It's easy to find possible signs of a recovery, even as all meaningful indicators stay bad. It's also easy for manufacturers to take solace in record backlogs, despite their lack of firmness.

1.3.1 Signs of Hope, or Not

Any discussion of air travel demand, and therefore jetliner demand, starts with consideration of the fact that we are dealing with the worst economic situation since the jet age began. There is no disguising the magnitude of the world economic downturn. Until April, the International Monetary Fund had tentatively forecasted that the world would grow at a 0.5% pace in 2009. But that has since been revised, with expectations of −1.4% shrinkage. This means that 2009 will be the first year without world economic growth since World War Two.

One thing that is becoming clear is that the cause of this downturn – a devastating near-collapse of credit markets and financial liquidity – was a discrete event. There might be additional similar shocks ahead, but the crisis that led the world's economy to its current condition ended sometime in the first quarter of this year. But the timing of a recovery, let alone a return to economic growth, remains quite uncertain.

It's quite possible that the world faces a prolonged period of structural readjustment, with much lower levels of growth for the next five years or longer. Several prominent economists and commentators have stated the risk of this development at about 20%. But nobody believes that a depression of this magnitude is a baseline scenario. Rather, what we are dealing with is an unusually difficult cyclical downturn.

On the positive side, it is possible that the economy is doing better than it appears, and that we will enjoy a faster than expected recovery. The last two recessions were relatively brief – both the 1992 and 2001 downturns lasted a mere eight months each. But the difference this time goes beyond the mere severity of the numbers. The previous two downturns were classic business cycle downturns, with consumer and corporate demand placed on hold and inventories built down. This time, in addition to a massive inventory build-down (evidenced by record air cargo shipment reductions) we also have a serious process of de-leveraging. The amount of money available for investment has been severely curtailed. Government stimulus programs, in the US and other countries, are nowhere near enough to compensate for the falloff in private sector investment cash.

As a result, this downturn has already become the longest since the Great Depression of the 1930s. So far (starting in early 2008 and through the first quarter of 2009) the net worth of US citizens has fallen by over $12 trillion almost 20%.

One characteristic of this business cycle will likely be high volatility and numerous "false start" recoveries. Stock markets, especially in the US, have made considerable gains since the precipitous drops of late 2008 and early 2009. Also importantly, corporate profits have made a slight recovery. However, the composition of these profits tells a different story. The only profits increase has come from a recovery in the financial sector. Some of that increase is related to the arrival of government funds, such as the Troubled Asset Relief Program (TARP). Some of the recovery is also likely due to the sector's recovery from a wave of bankruptcies in the previous quarter.

Yet most By contrast, the manufacturing sector, what some term the "Main Street" economy, is still under heavy pressure, and manufacturing profits are still falling. Since the recession began US industrial production has fallen by 17.3%, the sharpest drop since the Great Depression. Slack demand is still translating into lower sales. Unemployment is still rising, pushing 10% in the US. There's talk of another stimulus package, but in many sectors there's still overcapacity and it's difficult to identify any particular growth drivers in sight.

Government intervention is also prompting growth elsewhere, with uncertain sustainability. In July, China said that its economy grew by 7.9% in the second quarter of this year. But much of this was due to a $585 billion stimulus spending package.

Another reason to suspect that a recovery might be premature concerns inventory build-downs. According to the International Air Transport Association (IATA), year-over-year air cargo demand, as measured in Freight Ton Kilometers, fell by over 20% starting in each month from December through April. In May, it declined a mere 17%. Also in May, orders for durable goods rose 1.8% from April, a welcome affirmation of slightly greater demand. However, it's important to note that after an unprecedented de-stocking of inventories, there needed to be at least a small recovery after warehouses were completely emptied out. It's quite possible that the only good news story here involves a slight easing of credit, helping to facilitate orders for goods.

Another problem that will likely hobble the recovery is stagflation – slack demand coupled with high costs for commodities and other key goods. The best example of this is oil, the price of which has been growing at rates that are completely disconnected from world economic numbers. The price of oil, of course, is the most important variable cost for the airline industry. Compounding its relatively high price is market volatility, the severity of which has helped to inhibit effective price hedging.

Assuming a baseline scenario of a longer than usual recession, we can expect world economic growth to remain negative or weak through 2008, 2009, and much of 2010. This means travel demand will remain anemic, with no hope for 2009 and only sluggish growth in 2010.

1.3.2 Unpleasant Numbers

Airline losses can best be described as grievous. In 2008 the industry lost $10.4 billion, and it's on course to lose about the same amount this year. While some of those losses are due to bankruptcies and other isolated problems, it's also quite clear that almost nobody is making money in this business.

While passenger travel demand hasn't fallen as fast as the awful cargo numbers mentioned above, it has been hit hard. For the past five months of 2009 demand has declined about 7.7% year-over-year. There are no signs of improvement – May demand fell 9.3% year-over-year. The type of traffic that has fallen off is also quite concerning. Business and premium travel numbers are off by about 15-20% in passenger traffic volume and well over 20% in value (the greater value drop is attributable to ticket discounting, another unpleasant development). Typically, economy class travel is more sensitive to a downturn and premium numbers hold up better. Since premium traffic is the source of most airline profit, this aberration from the norm is having a terrible impact on the industry.

It's also noteworthy that unlike in the last downturn, this time there are no identifiable safe havens. Even the fast-growth Mideast carriers have seen some recent market softness, with an unprecedented traffic numbers, with a –2.8% decline in September. Russia, India, and China are no longer beacons of hope. And this time, low-cost carriers are not serving as new traffic stimulants, as they did in 2001-2003.

With a market environment like this, airlines have only been able to avoid a financial catastrophe by mercilessly cutting capacity. Through May, IATA member airline capacity had been reduced 3.9% relative to the same period in 2008. These cuts haven't been deep enough to avoid the terrible losses cited above, so clearly additional capacity needs to be eliminated.

Asset values and lease rates have fallen, particularly for slightly older equipment. And, of course, orders have completely collapsed. In 2005-2008, Airbus and Boeing booked a total of 8,099 firm orders. As of halfway through this year, Boeing had scored a single order, net of cancellations. Airbus's total was 68.

In short, there isn't a single industry indicator that can be viewed as positive. If there are indeed "green shoots" in the broader economy, they have not translated into air travel demand. Jetliners are the ultimate lagging indicator of world economic health.

With capacity shrinking and the airline industry losing money, and with limited prospects of resurgent economic growth producing air travel demand anytime soon, all hope for sustaining deliveries lies with getting rid of the existing fleet. Last year, over 1,100 jets were parked. As of mid June, there were over 2,400 parked jets. This includes 837 relatively new and competitive models, up from 266 just 18 months ago. Yet the industry will soon run out of obsolete jets to retire. Indeed, many airlines are starting to park relatively new equipment, such as 737 Classics or 15 year old A320s. This too is contributing to declining asset values and lease rates.

However, it's possible that this process of driving out used planes with new models stays intact for artificial reasons. US and European governments, through their Export Credit Agencies (ECAs) are increasing their support for jetliner finance to an unprecedented extent, providing funding when airlines, private banks, lessors, and manufacturers balk. ECAs on both sides of the Atlantic have announced that they are prepared to double the support they provided in 2008. As long as US and European Government credit ratings stay intact, it's quite possible that government money becomes the cash source for as much as half the transactions in the business. This would broadly mirror the "cash for clunkers" subsidies provided to the automobile industry. Except, in this case, many of the aircraft being replaced are far from clunkers.

In short, it's quite possible that government money will contribute to industry overcapacity and premature obsolescence of existing equipment. This will hurt the leasing companies that own those older jets. Thus, ironically, government money will be used in ways that hurt some of the financial institutions that have needed government money for bailouts.

Bizarrely, many executives and commentators have blamed inadequate financing for the industry's woes, implying that they would be bringing on new planes despite the awful market environment Yet even with this financial distortion, much of the airline industry is talking of orders deferrals, even when there's a financial penalty involved with not taking delivery of a jet.

Yet deliveries continue at a record pace. Due to the 2008 Boeing jet strike, deliveries this year will increase relative to 2008 even if rates stay the same. While a few minor adjustments have been made to production schedules, they primarily affect 2010 deliveries. Therefore, output this year will easily exceed 950 jets for the two primes.

To a certain extent, Airbus and Boeing are actually being rational by maintaining high production rates. Inadequate supply chain capacity can suppress jet production in good times, and if the two companies think the world economy will make a strong return to growth in 2010, it makes sense to stay the course. They don't want suppliers to cut capacity.

Yet at the July 2009 Paris Air Show, many suppliers were quite wary, and several implied that they were expecting significant production cuts starting in 2010. They too are quite rational. If they see little hope of that fast recovery, then there's much to be lost from having inventory, workforce, and plant that's suddenly idle.

1.3.3 No Help from the Backlog

On certainty is that sustaining production rates depend on an economic and travel demand recovery, and have no relation to the much touted backlog of unfilled orders. The two big primes alone have over 7,000 jets – seven years of production at current rates – on firm order. Airbus CEO Tom Enders said at the Paris show that even if 1,000 jet orders were cancelled, Airbus would still have years of production at current rates. Both manufacturers have spoken of overbooked backlogs, at the least in the near term, implying that they could easily compensate for demand softness among some customers.

Yet in practical terms, this means little. The backlog, like the market, tends to behave as a surprisingly cohesive entity. At the last market peak (January 2001) there were 3,200 jets on backlog. At the bottom of the last market trough (January 2003) there were 2,700 jets on backlog. That modest reduction was more than accounted for by deliveries. Only 80 cancellations were recorded in 2002/2003, so the core backlog remained intact. Yet production rates fell by 30%. Airlines deferred *en masse*, and the backlog did nothing to protect the industry from the impact of the recession. It's a simple and timeless equation. When airlines make money, they order planes. If airlines keep making money, they take delivery of those planes.

Assuming, therefore, that this backlog has no bearing on keeping production rates up in an economic downturn, and also assuming that there is no recovery imminent, it's a safe bet that 2009 will be the peak of the market. Sometime later this year, the manufacturers will announce production rate drops in 2010. Our forecast calls for narrowbody production rates to drop by about 30%, with a trough year in 2012. The twin aisle products, however, will likely stay intact, because international traffic will likely recover faster than domestic markets. Twin aisle numbers will also be boosted by the technological stimulant of new product developments, particularly Boeing's 787 and Airbus's A350 XWB.

Of course, paying for these new jets, and the associated engines and other components, is also a drain on Airbus, Boeing, and supplier company resources. The need to keep revenue high to fund these products is arguably the biggest single factor that could keep jetliner production rates at a higher level than justified by market demand.

1.4 Airbus and Boeing: Beyond Head-to-Head

As recently as 18 months ago Boeing looked set to achieve the unthinkable: a major strategic victory over Airbus. The strength of the 787 program, a superior product line strategy, and serious product and company structural weaknesses at Airbus looked set to guarantee Boeing a two-thirds market share for a decade or more.

Yet today, the picture is far more complicated. Due to 787 problems Boeing has lost much of its lead, and its long-term product line advantage is far from certain. The collapsed market for jet orders also means far less emphasis on market share. Each company faces major market and technical challenges. The great jetliner game has become much less of a head-to-head story.

1.4.1 The Dream Stumbles

When Boeing launched the 787 Dreamliner program in 2004, the company went from product development laggard to leader. After a damaging 13-year new product development hiatus, Boeing appeared to find a killer product for the best part of the market. While Airbus stumbled with its A380 super jumbo, a highly problematic program fraught with delays and cost overruns yet offering no more than marginal commmercial relevance, Boeing had created the best selling jet yet launched. There were 56 orders in 2004, 232 in 2005, 160 in 2006, and 369 in 2007.

Meanwile, 737 and 777 program ramped up to meet strong demand, and the latter plane completely vanquished the competing Airbus A340. Boeing's defense revenues showed strong growth too as the company profited from the best simultaneous civil and military market upturn in decades. As Airbus struggled to launch its next-generation A350, a long-range response to the 787, it suffered a series of management scandals and crises. Christian Streiff, who resigned as Airbus CEO in October 2006 after three months, said it would take Airbus a decade to catch up with Boeing.

Yet one year later the competitive picture began to change. In September 2007 Boeing announced a 787 first flight slip from September to either November or December. However, the May 2008 in-service date was retained, calling for a new aggressive 5-6 month flight test schedule. Inevitably, the news in October was worse. The company announced a significant program restructuring, with service entry delayed until November or December 2008.

In December 2007 another announcement shifted the 787's first flight until the end of the second quarter of 2008. Certification and first deliveries were shifted to early 2009. In March 2008 Boeing also announced that additional design work was necessary to strengthen the composite center wing box.

This too was not enough. In April 2008 Boeing announced another six month delay, with first deliveries scheduled for the third quarter of 2009. Boeing officials said this schedule was relatively conservative, and reduced anticipated 2009 deliveries to 25 aircraft. Yet in December 2008 there was a fifth delay. First flight was scheduled for the second quarter of 2009, with first deliveries in mid 2010. The program seemed to be spiralling downward, rivaling the A380 for sheer programmatic dysfunction.

Much worse was to come. In March 2009, Boeing reiterated its current plan for 787 production. Yet about one week away from its intended first flight in June, Boeing announced another delay due to wing-to-body join cracks. A new schedule will not be provided until the third quarter of the year.

But even if the schedule starts to stabilize, there are major concerns about the Dreamliner's technical virtues, at least for the first few years of production. In late 2008 International Lease Finance Corp. chief Stephen Udvar-Hazy indicated that 787 weight gains would reduce the aircraft's range. Also in late 2008/early 2009, several carriers did what was previously unthinkable: cancelling their 787 orders. While the first 31 cancellations were from relatively unimportant customers with traffic and profitability concerns, they punctured the notion that the 787 was an unbeatable product, and that a delivery position was a cherished and valuable asset. Even if the first batch of 787s offered a fuel burn improvement over current equipment, drastically cheaper fuel prices removed some of the 787's appeal relative to keeping older depreciated aircraft, particularly since an imploded cargo market reduced the resale value of those older aircraft. And the 787 delays gave some carriers the right to cancel with little or no penalty.

By March there were indications that Delta would cancel the 787 orders it had acquired in its merger with Northwest. The same month Shanghai Airlines directly criticized the 787, with Chairman Zhou Chi staing that 787s "don't fully meet the quality that Boeing touted earlier."

There are few doubts that Boeing will be able to improve the 787's performance during the first few years of production. But that still means an additional delay until Boeing has a competitive product that can threaten Airbus's position in the mid-market niche. In the meantime, Boeing might find it needs to incentivize customers to take early production 787s, hurting the company's margins and reducing its ability to quickly follow the initial 787 models with new product developments.

1.4.2 Airbus Benefits

These 787 problems have basically been a windfall for Airbus. They've resulted in badly needed revenue and breathing room needed to create a competitive response.

Since the 787 delays were first announced Airbus has enjoyed record A330 demand. A total of 142 net orders were recorded in 2008, on top of 198 in 2007. The latter represent the highest order level yet achieved by any Airbus twin aisle jet. Many of these A330s have gone to leasing customers, who are enjoying relatively high A330 lease rates compared with a weak broader market. It's very likely that some of Boeing's penalty payments related to 787 delays are going directly to A330 leases, indirectly benefitting Airbus.

The most direct benefit to Airbus of the 787 delay has been time to get the A350 response right. After the resounding failure of the first four A350 proposals, including a "firm" launch of the third version that went nowhere, Airbus seems to have found a strong product with the A350 XWB. With nearly 500 sales, the new Airbus plane will revitalize Airbus's mid market twin aisle product line, taking over from the A330 after the latter plane is eclipsed by the 787.

It's also worth noting that 787 technical problems might put the A350XWB in a good position. The 787's monolithic composite fuselage design is a high risk approach. It promises a revolution in aircraft manufacture, but if it does not work out as planned (i.e., if its design goals are compromised by the need for additional structural reinforcement) the A350XWB's more conservative skeleton/panel fuselage could look like a smart alternative.

Of course, it won't be easy for Airbus to bring the A350 XWB to market. A comparison of the two companies' independent research and development spending records tells two very different stories. Boeing took a product development holiday, but after the 787 launch the company has ramped up very fast. It is now spending billions of dollars and a relatively high percentage of sales on the 787, plus the 747-8 and 777 Freighter. All of these have gone over budget, but there are few doubts that the company can find the necessary resources.

By contrast, Airbus has spent the past eight years spending a very healthy level of resources on product development. However, almost all of this has gone into the largely irrelevant A380. The challenge is to keep this level of expenditure equally high in order to bring the A350 XWB to market by the target date of 2013. Jetliner deliveries will ramp down after 2009 due to a very weak air travel market, so to maintain the current level of spending Airbus might have to spend 12% or more of sales on new product development. Since Airbus parent EADS is heavily dependent on key stakeholders providing the cash, there are legitimate reasons to question the availability of resources to make the A350 XWB schedule happen on time. EADS also has the severe distraction of the disastrous A400M military transport program.

Yet here too there has been a key change over the past year. Government aid to industry has suddenly become acceptable again. Airbus needs this support more than Boeing does.

In October 2004 the US filed a World Trade Organization (WTO) complaint against European subsidies to Airbus, and whether it succeeded or failed, it clearly put Europe on notice that large aid packages would no longer be tolerated. With tens of billions of dollars going to the US automotive industry, and hundreds of billions of dollars going to the US banking industry, it is very difficult to imagine that the international rules covering state support to industry will not be transformed, if not obliterated. Even if the US wins the Boeing WTO case, any effort at enforcement would be rendered problematic by the threat of European cases in other sectors of the economy.

It is also worth noting that from a government standpoint aerospace suddenly looks like a relatively inexpensive and safe way to generate jobs and help the economy. By comparison, as of March 2009 US aid to General Motors and Chrysler has exceeded $17 billion in loans, with billions more requested. This dwarfs any aid Airbus might need to make the A350 XWB happen.

In January 2009, the French Government took the first step, announcing a plan to provide up to 5 billion euros (about $7 billion) to support Airbus plane sales. The French Government plans to inject the money into banks which will then finance the aircraft sales. "The French state is not giving money to Airbus," French trade minister Anne-Marie Idrac told Reuters. "It's not a subsidy, which would distort competition, it's a question of fluidity in the financing of Airbus clients where it is needed, and this in coordination with other countries who are stakeholders of Airbus." This aid will make a difference. In the 2002 downturn, Airbus avoided any serious production rate ramp down because it was nicely exposed to the markets that were safe havens – low cost carriers, India, China, and the Mideast. This time, there are no safe havens.

Predictably enough, the US Government has not mentioned legal action. Instead, as noted in our first section, the US Export-Import bank has announced plans to increase its support of Boeing jetliner sales.

In short, the erosion of international agreement on aid to industry will benefit Airbus's ability to withstand the market downturn and to bring the A350 XWB to market.

1.4.3 Much in Common

Boeing retains some key advantages, including the 777, a better corporate financial structure, strong access to the US defense market, and of course the postponed promise of the 787. Yet it is clearly no longer the likely winner in the great game with Airbus. Assuming the A350 XWB arrives by early 2015 (a good forecast given the big resource questions, and recent aircraft program execution precedent), Airbus will be able to recover and maintain a solid 40-50% of the market. But from the standpoint of 2009, it's quite possible that this game has ceased to matter. The two companies are likely to spend the next few years not caring much about each other.

For one, with over 7,000 orders on backlog, market share has suddenly become a non-issue. These orders are roughly evenly split between the two. Both sides are scrambling to rearrange orders and line up financing needed to keep deliveries at their current rates (450-500 planes for each company). Battling for new orders is irrelevant and, given the wretched state of travel demand, impossible. Even much of the vaunted 787-A350 XWB market has been decided, with only a small number of notable (and delayed) competitions remaining.

Also, there are fewer questions concerning product strategy. Boeing will need to focus on 787 program execution. The -8 and -9 will need to be followed by a -10. Airbus, of course, will spend at least the next eight years introducing the three major A350 XWB variants, the -800, -900, and -1000 (it will also need to resolve the A400M). If the A350 XWB-1000 does particularly well, Boeing will need to think about a 777 replacement or upgrade, but a 777-X launch before 2012 looks unlikely, at best.

Meanwhile, on the single aisle front, Airbus and Boeing both agree that with inexpensive fuel the development of new narrowbodies can and should be delayed until 2020. The only question concerns Bombardier's CSeries. If it succeeds, Airbus and Boeing might each need to come up with a competitive response. But without that third party factor, both companies would just keep building A320s and 737s through the next decade.

Clearly, the great Airbus-Boeing game is changing. As the industry enters a potentially severe downturn, this is much less a head to head competition. Instead, the two companies will face common challenges. The great game is now about backlog management, program execution, and arranging finance for hard times.

1.5   How the Future Looks Today: Market Share History and Forecast

A few notable points in our chart:

- 1977-1996: Airbus gradually obliterates McDonnell Douglas and Lockheed. Boeing looks on, largely secure with its 60% market share.
- 1997-1999: Boeing, seeing that the competition is now head-to-head, fights a market share war. It wins. And loses. While Boeing's share of the market grows, low pricing and production snafus destroy profitability.
- 1999-2004: Boeing lies quietly horizontal. Low levels of spending on new product development, and an emphasis on profitability above market share, result in serious market share erosion. Emboldened, Airbus launches the

A380, which would have worked great if Boeing didn't come back to life and counterattack with the 787 in 2004.

- 2006-2014: Despite serious stumbles, Boeing gradually increases its share, largely on the strength of the 777 and 787.

- Beyond 2014: The A350 XWB helps Airbus return to a 45% market share.

The last two bullets are merely forecasts, highly dependent upon several of the key variables, discussed below.

1.6   Our Baseline Scenario, and Scenario Variables

Our forecast below makes myriad assumptions. We can't forecast the key exogenous matters – oil prices and world economic growth – but we can look at the issues within the industry. Here are the key hinge issues that could affect the future.

- **The 787.** Big questions: operating economics, performance goals, production development costs, and of course schedule. **Our forecast calls for it to arrive in 2Q 2011, with a product improvement plan that makes it perform close to the promised level within two years of service entry.** But as this is written nobody can forecast with any confidence what will happen next.

- **Manufacturer Behavior.** Airbus and Boeing say they're holding the line at current production rates (aside from the 787, of course). That might be possible with greater government financing and/or a faster than expected market turnaround, but the traffic airline profit numbers tell a very different story. **Our forecast assumes that narrowbody rates come down by about 30%, with a trough year in 2012.** Twin aisle rates generally stay at an even level, however, since we'll probably see a faster recovery in international traffic.

- **Bombardier's CSeries.** A promising plane, with a remarkably feeble launch, and an even worse production plan. So far,it's basically the sound of one airline clapping. But with additional customers, and maybe even an ILFC endorsement. Airbus and Boeing would then need to consider a new or re-engined A320-X/737-X with either PurePower, or CFM's new Leap-X, also introduced at Farnborough. After all, losing much of the A319/737-700 market, and perhaps some of the A320/737-800 market, is not a palatable outcome for the two majors. Alternatively, in two or three years Bombardier could be left with Lufthansa and a few bit players. If that's the case, Airbus and Boeing can relax and resume stamping out today's A320/737. **We assume a modest level of success – not enough to influence anyone's product launch decisions.** Closely related to the next topic:

- **Narrowbody Rejuvenation. Our forecast says both sides put off narrowbody replacement launches until the end of our forecast.** We merely assume modest and incremental product improvement efforts. But as noted above the CSeries bears watching. Airbus and Boeing might need to update their narrowbodies with PurePower or Leap-X. And if those new engines won't fit under the current wings, one or both companies might need to launch new planes. In addition to the CSeries, the big driver here is fuel prices.

- **Airbus Restructuring and the A350 XWB.** We think Airbus is finally on the right path in terms of management and subcontract arrangements, although there is considerable risk ahead. **As for the A350, our forecast says this time they got it right, and that it arrives in early 2015.** But as noted in our A350 section above, this will be a major challenge. There could be further delays.

- **Tankers.** A very big issue indeed. With the Democrats in charge, Northrop/EADS stands little chance of winning a sole-source contract. Given the inevitability of protests, Boeing's chance of keeping a sole-source contract is only modestly better. A dual buy might be the only way forward. Or, the requirement might be pushed out, yet again. **We have a generic KC-X line that does not call for a winner** (and therefore the numbers do not go towards company totals). See the forecast section of this report, or Teal's Special Mission Aircraft overview for more thoughts.

- **The 747-8.** Looks good as a cargo plane. But the cargo market has been hit hard. Also, beyond Lufthansa, will it find favor as a passenger version? In favor: strong performance numbers, a respectable niche, and a few likely customers that haven't bought any A380s (Cathay, JAL, ANA). Mitigating against: Airbus's aggressive A380 sales efforts. **Our forecast assumes a fewmodest passenger orders, and just under two per month rates.** There's slightly more upside than downside for Boeing.

- **777-X.** When (before or after 737-X)? What (all-new or major derivative)? **We think it arrives as a new plane in late 2017.** That makes it the next all-new large jet to be launched. But much depends on the A350-900/1000. If the new Airbus jets start attracting blue chip orders (outside the Mideast), Boeing could counter with a more aggressive 777 replacement plan. If the A350 stumbles along, Boeing might keep the current 777 through the end of the next decade with minor improvements.

But all of this tends to change, fast. When using this report, you can obtain the very latest spreadsheet covering the numbers below from Teal Group's subscriber website (or your WMCAB analyst).

2 Market Statistics

Units Produced	2009	2010	2011	2012	2013	2014	2015	2016	2017	2018	Total
Airbus A318-321	386	335	280	255	270	290	320	370	370	370	3,246
Airbus A330	74	70	62	56	48	40	14	10	8	—	382
Airbus KC-30/45	—	2	4	5	6	6	6	6	4	4	43
Airbus A340-500/600	10	6	—	—	—	—	—	—	—	—	16
Airbus A350XWB	—	—	—	—	—	—	50	75	90	90	305
Airbus A380	14	18	20	20	22	22	20	20	18	18	192
Boeing 737	376	310	240	220	245	265	290	360	360	360	3,026
Boeing 747-400	8	—	—	—	—	—	—	—	—	—	8
Boeing 747-8	—	4	14	18	20	20	20	20	20	20	156
Boeing 767	14	12	12	12	9	—	—	—	—	—	59
Boeing 777	82	66	56	52	52	54	46	44	25	6	483
Boeing 777-X	—	—	—	—	—	—	—	—	8	60	68
Boeing 787	—	—	30	60	85	110	120	120	130	130	785
Bombardier CSeries	—	—	—	—	—	—	20	34	48	48	150
Total Units	**964**	**823**	**718**	**698**	**757**	**807**	**906**	**1,059**	**1,081**	**1,106**	**8,919**
KC-X	—	—	—	—	2	2	8	14	16	16	58
Total with KC-X	**964**	**823**	**718**	**698**	**759**	**809**	**914**	**1,073**	**1,097**	**1,122**	**8,977**
Total Airbus	**484**	**431**	**366**	**336**	**346**	**358**	**410**	**481**	**490**	**482**	**4,184**
Total Boeing	**480**	**392**	**352**	**362**	**411**	**449**	**476**	**544**	**543**	**576**	**4,585**
Bombardier	**—**	**—**	**—**	**—**	**—**	**—**	**20**	**34**	**48**	**48**	**150**

Dollar Value ('09$ Bns)	2009	2010	2011	2012	2013	2014	2015	2016	2017	2018	Total
Airbus A318-321	17.56	15.24	12.74	11.60	12.29	13.20	14.56	16.84	16.84	16.84	147.69
Airbus A330	7.99	7.56	6.70	6.05	5.18	4.32	1.51	1.08	0.86	—	41.26
Airbus KC-30/45	—	0.24	0.47	0.59	0.71	0.71	0.71	0.71	0.47	0.47	5.07
Airbus A340-500/600	1.25	0.75	—	—	—	—	—	—	—	—	2.00
Airbus A350XWB	—	—	—	—	—	—	7.00	10.50	12.60	12.60	42.70
Airbus A380	2.66	3.42	3.80	3.80	4.18	4.18	3.80	3.80	3.42	3.42	36.48
Boeing 737	16.73	13.80	10.68	9.79	10.90	11.79	12.91	16.02	16.02	16.02	134.66
Boeing 747-400	1.38	—	—	—	—	—	—	—	—	—	1.38
Boeing 747-8	—	0.72	2.52	3.24	3.60	3.60	3.60	3.60	3.60	3.60	28.08
Boeing 767	1.43	1.22	1.22	1.22	0.92	—	—	—	—	—	6.02
Boeing 777	12.30	9.90	8.40	7.80	7.80	8.10	6.90	6.60	3.75	0.90	72.45
Boeing 777-X	—	—	—	—	—	—	—	—	1.30	9.72	11.02
Boeing 787	—	—	3.45	6.90	9.78	12.65	13.80	13.80	14.95	14.95	90.28
Bombardier CSeries	—	—	—	—	—	—	0.70	1.19	1.68	1.68	5.25
Total Units	**61.30**	**52.85**	**49.98**	**50.99**	**55.35**	**58.55**	**65.49**	**74.13**	**75.49**	**80.20**	**624.33**
KC-X	—	—	—	—	0.35	0.35	1.40	2.45	2.80	2.80	10.15
Total with KC-X	**61.30**	**52.85**	**49.98**	**50.99**	**55.70**	**58.90**	**66.89**	**76.58**	**78.29**	**83.00**	**634.48**
Total Airbus	**29.47**	**27.21**	**23.71**	**22.04**	**22.36**	**22.40**	**27.58**	**32.92**	**34.19**	**33.33**	**275.20**
Total Boeing	**31.84**	**25.64**	**26.27**	**28.95**	**33.00**	**36.14**	**37.21**	**40.02**	**39.62**	**45.19**	**343.87**
Bombardier	**—**	**—**	**—**	**—**	**—**	**—**	**0.70**	**1.19**	**1.68**	**1.68**	**5.25**

Share of Dollar Value	2009	2010	2011	2012	2013	2014	2015	2016	2017	2018	Total
Airbus A318-321	28.65%	28.84%	25.49%	22.75%	22.19%	22.54%	22.23%	22.71%	22.30%	20.99%	23.66%
Airbus A330	13.04%	14.31%	13.40%	11.86%	9.37%	7.38%	2.31%	1.46%	1.14%	—	6.61%
Airbus KC-30/45	—	0.45%	0.94%	1.16%	1.28%	1.21%	1.08%	0.96%	0.63%	0.59%	0.81%
Airbus A340-500/600	2.04%	1.42%	—	—	—	—	—	—	—	—	0.32%
Airbus A350XWB	—	—	—	—	—	—	10.69%	14.16%	16.69%	15.71%	6.84%
Airbus A380	4.34%	6.47%	7.60%	7.45%	7.55%	7.14%	5.80%	5.13%	4.53%	4.26%	5.84%
Boeing 737	27.29%	26.10%	21.37%	19.20%	19.70%	20.14%	19.71%	21.61%	21.22%	19.98%	21.57%
Boeing 747-400	2.24%	—	—	—	—	—	—	—	—	—	0.22%
Boeing 747-8	—	1.36%	5.04%	6.35%	6.50%	6.15%	5.50%	4.86%	4.77%	4.49%	4.50%
Boeing 767	2.33%	2.32%	2.45%	2.40%	1.66%	—	—	—	—	—	0.96%
Boeing 777	20.06%	18.73%	16.81%	15.30%	14.09%	13.84%	10.54%	8.90%	4.97%	1.12%	11.60%
Boeing 777-X	—	—	—	—	—	—	—	—	1.72%	12.12%	1.76%
Boeing 787	—	—	6.90%	13.53%	17.66%	21.61%	21.07%	18.62%	19.80%	18.64%	14.46%
Bombardier Cseries	—	—	—	—	—	—	1.07%	1.61%	2.23%	2.09%	0.84%
Total Airbus	**48.07%**	**51.48%**	**47.43%**	**43.22%**	**40.39%**	**38.27%**	**42.12%**	**44.41%**	**45.29%**	**41.56%**	**44.08%**
Total Boeing	**51.93%**	**48.52%**	**52.57%**	**56.78%**	**59.61%**	**61.73%**	**56.81%**	**53.98%**	**52.48%**	**56.35%**	**55.08%**
Bombardier	—	—	—	—	—	—	**1.07%**	**1.61%**	**2.23%**	**2.09%**	**0.84%**

What's Next for European Online Travel?

Carroll Rheem

Innovation and technology are enormously important for all industries, but they are especially critical for travel and tourism, which, as the world's largest industry, is continually at the forefront of change. The way consumers interact with travel companies is transforming at breakneck speed, and technology will drive as much change in the coming decade as it did in the past one. The phenomenon of social media has shifted power to the consumer – more and more people are being influenced by the opinions, reviews and referrals of fellow travelers than professional editorial content. Searching, shopping and buying – once distinct terms describing different behaviors – are blurring at a furious pace. And as sophisticated mobile devices get into the hands of an ever-increasing number of travelers, a desktop Web strategy will no longer be sufficient. This article will review some of the most important online travel and technology trends shaping the way Europeans will plan and purchase their travel in the years to come.

1 Mobile

This is the year mobile applications will start having a significant impact on the travel industry. Not only are millions of smart devices in the marketplace, but the network speed is increasing quickly and dramatically. In 1995, companies waffled about whether or not they needed Web sites, and today no business could survive without one. In 2009, a robust mobile strategy cannot be an "if" – companies that consider it optional will have to play an expensive game of catch-up.

While early mobile efforts by travel companies are often miniaturized versions of Web sites, consumers are looking for a different experience on their mobile screens than they are on their computer screens. And while consumers are not likely to book lengthy holidays on their mobile devices, they will book, re-book and change travel reservations as plans change. Being able to service consumers through the twists and turns of travel is a powerful proposition. Beyond travel product transactions, a significant bulk of travel expenditure occurs at the destination. Many travel companies have not been able to tap into this opportunity very effectively because consumers do not usually think about destination activities at

R. Conrady and M. Buck (eds.), *Trends and Issues in Global Tourism 2010*,
Trends and Issues in Global Tourism, DOI 10.1007/978-3-642-10829-7_30,
© Springer-Verlag Berlin Heidelberg 2010

Fig. 1. Mobile Applications

the time of purchase. Mobile applications provide an ideal vehicle for travel companies to reach consumers when they are in the destination – just as they are actively thinking about which sightseeing tour they want to take and which restaurant they'd like to try.

Location-Based Services

Advancements in mobile technology (e.g., GPS capability) provide travel companies with myriad possibilities for location-based services. Having a solid mobile strategy is not necessarily about selling airline tickets and hotel rooms – it's about offering customized, locally relevant goods, services and deals. For example, imagine that a traveler lands in Paris and has opted into receiving SMS messages from his hotel. When the system (via GPS) recognizes that the customer is in range, it can send a welcome with directions, transfer recommendations and discounts. Because the company can understand where the consumer is in real time, its offers can be spontaneous and immediately relevant. Because of the timeliness and contextual relevance, consumers are also very likely to be open to receiving these types of messages.

2   Semantic Web

While the semantic Web is still in its early stages, when fully realized, it will entirely redefine search – and therefore, the way travel companies approach and manage search. Ten years ago, Web sites were created just for human eyes. But as technology has improved and search robots have become bigger and more advanced, Web sites have become designed for two different readers: one human, one robot. The semantic Web is already enabling the first iterations of the next generation of Web sites that, instead of simply manipulating words and content,

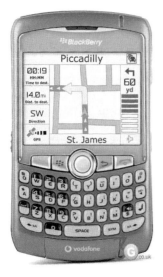 

Fig. 2. Mobile Applications

attach a layer of context and meaning to text. This enables sites to frame content according to the meaning of the content and allow applications to "understand" it, thereby delivering relevant, high-quality information. So, for example, when searching for "apple," the engine will take into account your history and preferences and determine whether you're looking for Apple the computer company or information about the fruit.

In the travel arena, the advent of the semantic Web translates into customers spending less time spent wading through irrelevant information when planning their trips. For example, suppose someone wants to plan a week-long vacation with his spouse and 11-year-old twin boys, and the family can spend up to $2,500.

Fig. 3. Apple vs. Apple

On today's Web, these criteria could lead to hours (if not days) of searching, filtering, sorting and comparing multiple selections for flights, accommodations, car rentals and user reviews, and many of these options will preclude or oppose the others.

The next generation of search, however, would respond to the same query by delivering a neatly crafted and highly relevant package, as if it were constructed by an experienced and trusted travel agent who has known the client for years. Both the input and the output of the search experience will become more intuitive. Unlike today, when the term "summer vacation with the kids" returns Web content with that specific text, the future of search will yield relevant results based not on the text, but on its meaning for the user. Based on existing knowledge and user preferences, the engine would "understand" that the user was looking for a trip for one week in July with two adults, two children, two adjoining rooms in a 3-star hotel with a pool, a large rental car and an outdoor activity-rich destination no farther than four hours via plane.

Early Semantic Search Efforts

Some of the earliest forays into semantic search in travel have been geared as tools for businesses to use rather than consumers. Condensing and categorizing thousands of traveler reviews and other user-generated content is a well-suited task for semantic technology, and is very useful for companies eager to track and make sense of the volumes of content written about their products. Consumers are already interacting with some semantic elements integrated into general search engines like Bing and Google, though many are likely unaware of behind-the-scenes enhancements to the search experience. To the user, further integration of semantic capabilities will simply equal better, more relevant search results, and new travel-related search engines that utilize semantic search technologies are on the horizon.

3   Customization

For the vast majority of travel companies, the content displayed is the same for every traveler who visits their Web sites. But some companies, especially full-service online travel agencies (OTAs), are investing in technology to change this by using information collected about the user to customize his or her experience. By looking at a mix of observed behavior like searches and product click-throughs (e.g., viewing 4-star hotels), as well as gathered information like trip motivation (e.g., relaxation, adventure), these OTAs strive to make tailored recommendations rather than just displaying the same products for every user. Most customization efforts are more focused on merchandising/advertising than search results, particularly for air products, where the lowest fare still reigns supreme. Not surprisingly, air-specialist OTAs are not as focused on customization, often preferring to keep their products as simple as possible.

Fig. 4. Amazon.com

One major challenge to customization is building the right logic to make relevant recommendations based on more than just price. For example, a consumer looking for a quick getaway would be better served by a display of weekend deals in Paris, even if the rates are not exceptional, rather than huge holiday discounts in Sharm-el-Sheikh. Accordingly, OTAs are largely more focused on crafting display algorithms that drive consumer relevancy rather than yield. The Amazon model of additional product recommendations is often looked to as inspiration.

Behavioral Targeting

Advertisers have long idealized the concept of 1:1 marketing. While this concept is still far from reality, it is commonplace today for advertising to be customized to a consumer's Internet behaviors – Web sites visited, searches conducted – and for these advertisements to be placed on sites outside of the observed behavior. Advertising networks have long used observed Internet behaviors to serve targeted ads to consumers, and now travel companies like Expedia are building their own advertising networks to make use of the information they gather about consumers on their sites.

4   Media Versus Transaction Models

For a long time, the travel industry has earned its living on transactions. Suppliers still make most of their money this way, as does much of today's travel distribution ecosystem. But given the host of available new technology and media, such as metasearch, intermediaries are now starting to drive revenue via advertising – mainly PPC (pay per click) and PPA (pay per action). Fewer and fewer startup companies dare to enter the transaction arena, knowing the stiff competition they'll face from heavyweight OTAs and suppliers. Instead, they choose to build business models that drive consumer relevance and traffic with the goal of selling advertising and referrals to distributors and suppliers rather than flights or rooms to consumers.

The line between marketing and distribution costs is all but disappearing – revenue managers are becoming experts in online merchandising, and marketers are becoming ever more focused on performance-based advertising (particularly in mature online markets). A holistic understanding of the cost of sale will be critical as paid search costs hit a ceiling of inefficiency and suppliers face a situation where even performance-based ads can become more expensive than commission or merchant margin on a per-transaction basis.

5   Differentiation Beyond Price

When travelers were asked why they prefer their usual purchase channel in *PhoCusWright's European Consumer Travel Trends Survey*, price was the most common response at 40%. Broadness of selection came in next at 24%. Brand trust and customer service both reached 13%, and while these motivations fall significantly behind price and selection, they are considered the most important factors by sizable groups of consumers. While price is undoubtedly a vitally important element of the consumer proposition, as better and wider distribution networks develop, prices will become more consistent across channels. A consumer proposition that touts just price and selection has a limited lifespan, particularly if all the players are claiming to have the best prices. As online markets mature, companies must look to enhance their brands with something more – a means of differentiation. For some it might be simplicity, for others it might be high service levels, while still others might choose environmental friendliness. Whatever the positioning, it will become increasingly important to strike a relevant chord with consumers at a level beyond price.

6   Travel Company Media Offerings/Monetizing Downstream Traffic

Travel companies are often resistant to moving away from a "walled garden" approach that keeps visitors confined to their Web sites, as they don't believe the benefits of a media model enabling consumers to click out of their Web sites will outweigh the costs. There are many opportunities, however, to monetize traffic that do not involve sending consumers to competitor sites. Travelers represent an attractive demographic for advertisers, and selling advertising space to complementary non-travel products (i.e., cameras, luggage) can offer new revenue streams.

Many European OTAs are in the midst of testing these media products. Working with advertising networks presents an efficient alternative for smaller OTAs that may not have the resources to manage ad space directly. The challenge is, of course, to sell downstream traffic without eroding conversion. Some OTAs may even consider a hybrid OTA/metasearch model that attempts to capture the best of both worlds. While much uncertainty remains about the viability of various media programs, the industry will witness a great deal of testing and experimentation with different business models in the next few years as companies try to better monetize their traffic and devise creative solutions that fit their market positioning.

The incorporation of a media offering to drive new advertising revenue has met with mixed success in the U.S. In 2008, Orbitz experimented with displaying third-party sponsored links in its booking path, only to pull them off the site after the testing period was over. The economics were simply not found to work in Orbitz's favor. Travelocity has been displaying ads for its IgoUgo brand continually for quite some time, but IgoUgo is a referral site rather than a booking site and is a sister brand. While the ads are directing consumers outside of Travelocity's domain, they still remain under the larger company umbrella until the user clicks off the site. They are also displaying a controlled set of sponsored links (as opposed to a third-party sponsored link display that might show direct competitors). Expedia's approach has become more focused on creating its own advertising network with its PassportAds product, which serves behaviorally targeted ads to consumers on other Web sites.

Fig. 5. Travelocity.com

7   Social Media

7.1   User-Generated Content (UGC)

User-generated reviews, as one of the earliest forms of social media, have become ubiquitous among brands that offer hotel products. Smaller companies that do not have the user base to effectively build their own cache of reviews often work with third parties like TripAdvisor to ensure they have enough coverage. In the U.S., OTA user reviews have become the most widely influential Web site feature in the travel planning process — beating out professional reviews and even photography – and user reviews are continuing to gain significant influence among European travelers. A number of hotel companies have crossed the hurdle of posting UGC on their Web sites, though in more of a "guest book" format rather than a review. Photography, video, and concierge-like recommendations about destination activities will likely become the next frontier of traveler-generated content.

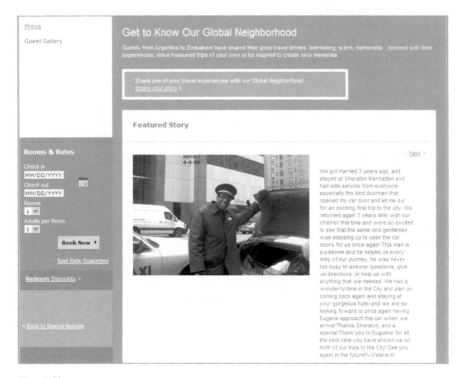

Fig. 6. Sheraton.com

7.2   Social Networks

Social networks and the overwhelming buzz that accompanies them are being received with mixed enthusiasm by travel companies. Many are actively managing their brand presence on social networking sites like Facebook and micro-blogs like Twitter, dedicating staff to monitor and engage with consumers on behalf of their brands. Unlike email messages that require deletion and therefore some degree of effort, Twitter messages ("tweets") are not as intrusive – the feed format does not necessitate interaction with every message even for those who are "following" a company. Many companies are using Twitter as a customer service tool as well as a promotional vehicle to run contests and extend their brand interaction with travelers even when they are not actively planning a trip.

The most advanced travel companies are building applications on existing social network platforms to enable consumers to share their travel plans and facilitate group planning and input. Some, however, remain somewhat skeptical about social media's importance and ultimate impact on business, viewing it as something to watch rather than something important to actively engage with. Some of even Europe's largest brands have yet to build their presence on social networks and micro-blogs.

Fig. 7. Twitter.com

7.3   Driving Engagement Through Social Networks

While some travel companies may remain skeptical about the ability to use social media to drive transaction revenues, maintaining and monitoring a brand presence wherever consumers choose to discuss travel has important value. Word of mouth has tremendous power in consumer travel decisions and social media applications like Twitter allow companies to essentially "eavesdrop" on conversations and interact with consumers directly. The value of social networks for public relations and customer service is, at the very least, reason enough to build a branded presence in popular networks.

Interaction with consumers outside of a Web site adds a new facet to brand identity so that companies become more than just a URL, driving new touchpoints and higher levels of engagement. Many startup companies are focused on developing applications that help consumers plan and share their travel experiences both inside and outside of existing social networks. Travel industry incumbents are not all standing idly by, and some are widening their focus beyond the transaction to build their own branded applications.

Of the top 10 most trafficked Web sites in the world – regardless of ranking site – five or six are comprised entirely of user-generated content, including MySpace, Wikipedia and Facebook. UGC is highly influential among travelers, especially younger ones, and is therefore critically important for travel companies to recognize and manage. Many companies have created outlets for their customers to connect, and the acquisition of professional services to monitor social media and represent brands in the blogosphere may be one of the best investments travel companies can make in the near term.

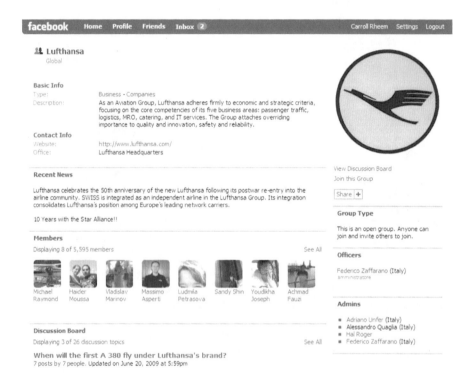

Fig. 8. Facebook.com

8   Metasearch (Travel Search Engines)

The theoretical proposition of metasearch is extremely well suited for European markets. The ability to consolidate comprehensive product selection and booking channels solves a problem for travelers who may not even be aware of all the options available in the fragmented travel marketplace. Metasearch represents both competition and partner value for transaction-driven OTAs and supplier Web sites. On the one hand, they compete for consumer attention, but they also represent an important source of referrals. While it was once presumed that supplier branded Web sites would receive the vast majority of referrals, metasearch brands in the U.S. have found that this is not the case and OTAs receive a sizable portion of their traffic. While metasearch is still in the early phases of European consumer adoption, a number of brands such as Travelsupermarket and Skyscanner are gaining traction, particularly in mature online markets. Domination is still very much up for grabs, and with the flurry of new entrants into the metasearch arena in the U.S. this year, European markets are likely to see a mix of local and global entrants vying for the consumer.

* * *

It may be tempting for travel companies to retreat into "safe mode" during times of low demand, but recessionary forces act as catalysts for change. Reliance on what has worked in the past is no guarantee of future success as industry players strive to deliver better products to edge out the competition and consumers open up to trying new things in the hopes of finding the best value for their money. The trends described in this article are not happening at some unknown future time – they are transforming the way consumers research, shop for, purchase and interact with travel today. Companies that wait until market conditions improve to invest in their future will find that the rising tide will not lift all ships equally.